THUNDER'S GRACE

To James:
Thank You for
coming back "Remember
You are very Special!
God Bless You.
Love
Thunders

Thunder with Grandma Grace in 1985

THUNDER'S GRACE

WALKING THE ROAD OF VISIONS WITH MY LAKOTA GRANDMOTHER

MARY ELIZABETH THUNDER

EDITED BY AUGUSTA OGDEN

Station Hill Press

Cover painting by Catherine White Swan.
Back cover photo by David Vaughn.
Art and photographic credits appear on p. 260.
Published by Station Hill Press, Inc., Barrytown, New York 12507.

Distributed by the Talman Company, 131 Spring Street, Suite 201
E-N, New York, New York 10012.

Cover design by Susan Quasha, assisted by Vicki Hickman.
Text design by Susan Quasha and Vicki Hickman.

Library of Congress Cataloging-in-Publication Data
Thunder, Mary Elizabeth, 1944-
    Thunder's grace : walking the road of visions with my
Lakota grandmother / Mary Elizabeth Thunder : edited by
Augusta Ogden.
        p.   cm.
    ISBN 0-88268-166-4 : $14.95
    1. Thunder, Mary Elizabeth, 1944- 2. Lakota women—
Biography. 3. Lakota Indians—Religion. 4. Sun dance. 5. Lakota
philosophy.
I. Ogden, Augusta. II. Title.
    E99.D1T533 1995
    978'.004975—dc20   95-1202
                                                         CIP

Manufactured in the United States of America

CONTENTS

Richard, Beth & Johnny as children with their dog Harry

DEDICATION

In the Native American way as I have lived it and learned from it, I see all living beings as our relations. Teachings of Honor, Respect, Patience, and Gratefulness are primary. First honored are the Elders, the Old Ones, and the Children, the Young Ones. The Old Ones are preparing to make their journey back to the Spirit World and the Young Ones have just come from there, so it is in this way of honoring the Old and the Young that we recognize that they are smarter than we are!

The Lakota People say: *Mi Takaye Oyacin!* . . . Amen to all of my relations . . . (I always add to this in my thinking) — and everything with life!

This book is dedicated to, written for, and made possible because of Grace Spotted Eagle. Here it is, Grandma. I love you and miss you. I hope you feel it is what you wanted said. So, this book is dedicated to the memory of Grace Spotted Eagle, who passed into Spirit, October 10, 1987.

Grandma Grace was born July of 1921 on the Pine Ridge Reservation, South Dakota. She spent most of her adult life in Denver, Colorado. During the 1960s, she traveled extensively throughout the United States speaking for Indian Rights. She spoke for the White Roots of Peace back in the 60s and 70s. She was instrumental in rallying support and participating in Wounded Knee II in 1973, and she was involved with the American Indian Movement during its formative years. She was the half-side of Wallace Black Elk. Grandpa Wallace and Grandma Grace helped so many people with their talks and lodges. Grace lost a child early in life, but had many adopted children. She inspired all that heard her, whether in a crowd of thousands or in the dark of the Sacred Sweat Lodge. Grandma Grace wanted us people of the human race to return to the Spiritual Way of Life — in touch with nature, in touch with each other, to avoid self-destruction. I remember well traveling with her and Grandpa for many, many years.

My eternal gratefulness goes to the following Elders: Wallace Black Elk, Leonard Crow Dog, Dennis Banks, William Baker, Grandfather Fools Crow, Buddy Red Bow, Luciano & Cheryl Perez, Grandmother Twylah Nitsch, Grandmother Kitty, Oowanaha Chasing Bear, Martin High Bear, Rolling Thunder, The Chipps Family — Victoria, Charles, and Godfrey, Buck and Vicki Ghost Horse and The Elders of the Wolf Song Peace Elder Councils. To all the Elders now with us and those who are in the Spirit World who have taken the time to share, I thank you.

To my mom/stepmom, Harriette Alice Crickmore, "Mumsey," the woman who raised me, loved me like her own. I thank you and love you.

I dedicate this book to my children: Richard Earl Grimes, wife Starr Davee, and grandsons Nathaniel Ellis, Nico Ezra, Caleb Ezekial, Little Richard; Beth Evelyn Grimes, fiancée Rick Marshall, and grandchildren Joshua Elliott Bowman, Heather Emory Bowman, and Marissa Sierra Er'rin Marshall; John Eric Grimes III, wife Susan, and granddaughters Nicole Elizabeth and Brittany. I hope this book will add some insight, to why I went on the road and, per their view only, dropped out of their world in 1982. Perhaps this story might help them understand why I had to journey at that time. I love them so. They have been my true teachers, and I thank them for being my children in this life and for all the love we have shared. I also dedicate this book to Aaron Gene Brocker, my nephew, who at age eight gifted me with the name for this book, *Thunder's Grace*. This book is for my children, my grandchildren, and all children to remember Grandmother Grace Spotted Eagle.

To my precious husband Jeffrey "White Horse" Hubbell, who brought love, joy, and friendship into my world. I love and thank you for helping me write this book, for joining me on path, and for supporting me so well in my life and work. To Sally Plummer, Horse's mom, and to me the best mother-in-law in the world. To Horse's family, who have been so supportive and loving.

To the father of my children and the man who was my partner and fellow adventurer for some twenty-three years of marriage, whom I shall call, for this Book's purposes, Wonder. I shall always honor, love, and be grateful for all we shared and taught each other.

For all who helped with this book:

Tsultrim Allione, for being such a wonderful example of Teachership / Sisterhood and for modeling support for other women by obtaining the publisher for this book; Cyndi Cross, for being my present secretary and bringing the last pieces together; Augusta Ogden, Roadie, for the hours of editing that gave birth to this book; Susan Ray, for her sensitive and expert editing of the final manuscript; Carolyn Ball, for adding the skills of a published author and for being my secretary so long; Pat Cross, who transcribed Grandma's UN speech and who says doing it changed her life; Carl and Merinda Bennett, who gave us our first printer; Vicki Redd Ghost Horse, for transcribing hours and hours of tapes; Hillary Hammond, who read the whole book to all the group one cold, rainy day in December; Michael Hull for being there; Nancy Moore, for giving us a home for over two years in which to write this book; Lynne and Glenn Perrine; Pat Ross, for putting a computer together piece by piece so I'd have the tools to write with, and for being my secretary for thirteen months while we kicked out wonderful stories and pictures for the world; Jimmy Schulman for helping edit and bring pieces together; David Vaughn for all the pictures and video work; Michael Herring for his helpful review; Lynne Terrazzas, for filing all those pieces; Jude Tolley, artist; White Swan, the artist that sat beside me as I talked and drew the pictures of my memories; Chira Morgan, Elizabeth Gaines, Sparky Shooting Star, Kim McSherry, for being there for so long and helping me on this journey, and who also loved Grandma so much.

To all the people who have called me Teacher, from whom I have learned so very much, and to all the people who gave me a home on the Road.

To my Warriors, who have traveled on the Road and experienced all of this with me: Jeffrey "White Horse" Hubbell, my oldest son Richard, who were my ultimate warriors; Wade Batterton, Bonnie Biggs, David Corrado, Tina Emerson, Butch "Buffalo Horse" Hennigan, Chris Johnson, Augusta Ogden, Martin "Gentle Bear" Rastall, Jerry Rushing, and Jim "Wolf" Yoxall.

To the present Ranch Staff (better known as "Ranchies"): Suzanne Day, Caroll Weaver, Elyssa "Bird Song" Moseley, Ryan Micah "Spirit Hawk" Moseley, and daughter, Beth Grimes, son-in-law, Rick Marshall, grandaughters, Heather Emory "Wamblee Gleska" Bowman and Marissa Sierra Erin Marshall.

To past "Ranchies": Carolyn Ball, Bonnie Biggs, Paolo Belettati, Charlie Bowman, Libby Cheramie, Jo Don Chipps, Cyndi Cross, David Carrado, Lynne Lambert, Randall Notgrass, Wade Batterton, Dana Sireno, John and Susan Grimes, Richard and Starr Grimes, Annie Hart, Sparky Shooting Star, Christopher Johnson, Martin "Gentle Bear" Rastall, Patricia Ross, Jimmy Schulman, and Tom Tirotta. Somehow we have done it together!

A special Thank You to the following, for providing a support base to my work as I wrote this book: Rose Alisandre, Donna Barros, Cheryl Breeze, Debbie Bonniwell, Dr. Tony Breuer, Sherilyn Edwards, Michele Feray, Jacqueline Gelzer, David & Sarah Karnes, Kayron LaLonde, Becki Martinez, Monia Marcantel, Bart & Linda Melton, Judy and Dennis Muhn, Penelope Newcomb, Marisabel Olivares, Carre Otis, Jackie Partin, Dr. Arlette Pharo, J.R. Phipps, Stephen & Mary Rudowski, Catherine Sanders, Walt & Joanne Thompson, Diane Webb, Dona Werner, Cora Winkler, Vicara, and to everyone who has helped Thunder-Horse Ranch make it through the "night!" Thank You!

And last, yet always first, to the Great Mystery for giving me life, a second chance at life, and the opportunity to meet Grandma. I am so very grateful! *Mi Takaye Oyacin!*

✸ ✧ ✸

AUTHOR'S PREFACE

The reason I'm writing this book is to shut up Grandma Grace Spotted Eagle. She just keeps talking to me from the Spirit world, on and on and on. It's just like it was when she was here on this planet in the physical body. When she was alive, she never hesitated to tell me what to do, then how to do it, and then how I'd done it wrong. For years, I thought my name was Shut Up. Often her teachings would be accentuated by the beat of a drumstick pounding away on the top my head. She would set up the most outrageous, impossible situation you can imagine, then fling me in at the deep end and order me to fix it. And somehow, once I got past total panic, confusion, embarrassment, or fear for my life, I would then hear Spirit or find the golden lesson buried in each circumstance. For, above all other things, Grandma was a teacher of how to live and how to love. She would bring me to my limits and then, with humor, love, and sometimes the drumstick, show me that there were no true limits.

Grandma was a traditional Lakota Elder, deeply alive with the spiritual heritage of her people, always walking at the side, and in the shadow, of her half-side, Wallace Black Elk.

For some reason that is a mystery to me to this day, she chose me to be one of her many adopted daughters, to learn from her and to help her out. Grandma used to say that having so many adopted children would always keep her words and teachings "alive". I think she realized that if I did not learn how to live, I would die. For many of the half-breed and Native American people, it is not learning how to die that is difficult; it is learning how to live.

So Grandmother Grace Spotted Eagle, my adopted spiritual mother and guide, came into my life, and nothing has been the same since. Grandma passed into Spirit World several years ago, but before she left, she asked me to write this book, especially for other women, to share that there is hope for change in our lives. I personally pray that all people, men and women alike, receive this message in a good way.

For me, Grandma Grace was like a keyhole through which a woman who was angry and dissatisfied with life (me) could receive glimpses of beauty and grace. She helped me to access the cellular memory that could bring me to a state of Knowing. This Knowing, or remembrance, of *"what a woman is"* helped me rejoin the Dance of Life. Grandma provided a way, through Spirit, that helped me to let go of rage and despair, shame and anger, and begin to walk the path of *"gratefulness and beauty of life."* "You know," she would always say to me, although, of course, I did not *know* then, "it is your job this time around to be a Goddess." These were heavy words coming from this "little yappy woman" as many called her. I would look at her and feel she would probably be considered the furthest thing from a Goddess imaginable in the minds of most modern-day woman. But to me she *was* a Goddess/Medicine Woman/Mother, even as I smiled to myself and said, "Boy, is she off on this one!" She said that this time around, in living my life for all people, especially in learning and teaching women things, I might be able to complete the journey of my soul. That was quite a thought for a woman who often hated herself and who many times made the statement, "I just can't work with women. I like men better." When I was young, I remember wishing I had been born a man, for then life would be much better. Now, of course, I have completely changed those thoughts and wish sometimes that I had never thought them or said them. But they had a place in my life; if nothing else, they served as a gauge to measure my growth by. Today, I love being a woman, a wife, mother, grandmother, and sister in all ways.

In recent years I have been close to many examples of the Goddess: Tsultrim Allione, Grandmother Twylah Nitsch, and Grandmother Kitty. However, Grandmother Grace Spotted Eagle was always the one leading me on, with her drum stick and her curt words, in my quest towards the realization of being a woman, of freely expressing nurturing and gratefulness, and living fully in tune with the creation principles of beauty on this planet.

As I write these words, I find that I am crying, crying because I miss Grandma so much. She was quite a woman. Some saw her as scary, but I always saw her as a spiritual master hidden in a physical body. At times, she was unreasonable and explosive, but these blowups were always well-timed to illustrate or catalyze a Universal lesson or truth. To me, she was warm and funny, real, cagey, and shrewd.

At a Sundance in Oregon, in 1987, Grandma told me she was going to die. Then she went on to discuss the particulars of her passing. Through my tears and with my heart breaking, Grandma spoke to me and made me vow many things. It would not be long before I was to discover that the process of fulfilling those vows would change my life. That was always the way it was when she was alive, so why would it be different when she was gone?

In the honoring ceremony, during the four days right after her passing, I was given specific things to do. I was to help Grandpa Wallace Black Elk, her beloved half-side, with several tasks, one being to clean out all of her possessions from the home they had shared together. "What ever you do, daughter, don't let anyone see my old clothes," she said. Grandma always wore the simplest clothes, usually those that were given to her, and I always thought she was beautiful in whatever clothes she wore, but she was ashamed for anyone to see them. Another vow was to write this book about her. And she wanted me to Sundance for her the following year to help her spirit make its transition.

During that same Sundance where Grandma and I had our last talk together, I also sat in a tepee with Grandpa Wallace, talking through the night until the appearance of the Morning Star. As Chief of the Sundance, watching out as only a loving parent would for all the Dancers, he told me that Spirit had said I should write down the words of my Sundance journey and my experiences with Grandma Grace. I remember looking at him — I loved him so — and through tears I said, "Sure, Grandpa." So in the same year and during the same dance, both Grandma and Grandpa told me to write this book. Coincidence? I don't think so!

There are several reasons it has taken a long time to do what they asked. First, the book had to be written when the time was right, for I did not want to write less than the best for Grandma. Also, it felt strange writing about Grandma Grace so much, with Grandpa Wallace in the background, even though I knew this book was meant to be about her and not so much about Grandpa, as wonderful and power-ful a being as he is in himself. Finally, it has been painful to write this book. Sometimes it felt as if its words were being pulled from my heart, and as if I might lose all that I had left of Grandma, these memories. But one of her best teachings was to walk through my fears. So here I am, walking my talk and talking my walk. I love and honor both Grandma and Grandpa, and this book is a grateful recognition of my loving vows of honor to both of these beautiful ones.

What is a Sundancer?

Sundancer. This word echoes in me like the voices of my ancestors, like old memories of other times and other loves, like the heartbeat of my Mother the Earth, the Great Drum, like the smell of sage and cedar, and like a morning prayer before sunrise, when I can see the dew and smell the freshness of the world in its pristine perfection, and I am so very grateful.

A Sundancer Is:

A Native person who has a prayer or vision to Sundance and who, according to tradition, must be accepted by a Council of Native Peers / Elders to be allowed to Dance to the Sun for four days without food and water, praying continually for the People so that the people might live.

I was instructed by several Elders to pledge to Sundance because I had had a "Death Experience," and needed to thank the Creator, The Great Mystery, for life!

A Sundancer is what I am. I had to die to be able to write those words. Leonard Crow Dog once introduced me to some of his friends by saying, "This is my niece and she is a Sundancer." The words flipped back and forth in my mind. I had Sundanced many times, but I had never really considered myself a Sundancer until that moment.

It has been a strange and miraculous journey that I want to share with you along with my memories of the Dance and the other side of the Dance.

This journey has taken me through experiences in the physical, mental, emotional, and spiritual realms of life. I have learned how one can live simultaneously in all those worlds. My journey has been my search to be in tune with the heart and mind of the Universe.

My journey started when I was disillusioned and very unhappy with myself and the world around me. Life had not measured up to my expectations. I felt alone and put down. I had eaten until I was almost 300 pounds, trying to find some nourishment in life. I just wanted to die. I found myself a servant to everyone — husband, children, family, jobs, life.

I loved passionately, but felt I could not be loved in return. There was not much for me to be grateful for in my world, I thought. That is not such a good way to live, so SOMETHING had to happen.

It did. I had a heart attack. Louise Hays says in her book, *You Can Heal Your Life*, a heart attack represents squeezing all the joy out of the heart, hardening the heart.

With the heart attack, everything changed.

It was as if I had died of the old to be reborn anew. Everything changed — my way of thinking, of being, and of becoming. The new way was the way of living and walking a spiritual path, becoming a Sundancer.

I have learned of the many obstacles that come up when you decide to embark on a spiritual journey. The Universe seems not to provide a safe, warm environment for the growth of our spirituality, nor does it groom us carefully to become spiritual masters. In fact, we don't seem always to know that that is what's happening. I don't think that being on a spiritual path was ever a real, conscious decision for me. I don't remember waking up on a Thursday and saying, "Today I will be spiritual."

Instead, somehow I found the space some twenty-five years ago to start learning a life of prayer while raising three children, working every day, cooking, cleaning the house, going to PTA meetings, Girl Scouts, Cub Scouts, political groups, and doing all the other things that fill the life of a working mother. The Creator leads you into the space for a spiritual opening in the right time.

For most of the past decade, I have lived on the road, traveling continually across the United States. I have lived in my car or van and carried with me only those ceremonial items and personal possessions that I needed. I have traveled alone, with my first husband and kids, with my Elders, and later with students. I have walked in service to the Creator, always letting Spirit direct my steps and choose where I next needed to be. I have always loved God/Spirit/Great Mystery.

The Sacred Pipe

My Lakota Elders told me to go out on the road and follow the Sacred Pipe. What is the Pipe? The Pipe is a wonderful instrument of peace that one can hold and pray with to the Creator. Its bowl is made from red stone and comes from and represents Mother Earth. The stem is made of wood from a tall tree that touched and represents Father Sky. When these two pieces come together, all life finds a Universal balance — stone and wood, male and female, heart and mind, body and Spirit — a Oneness, a Union, together and inseparable, that which we humans are striving to find with all.

The *Cannupa Wakan* [Sacred Pipe] is my life. When I pray with the Pipe, I stand at the center of the four directions, the Center of All Things. Then the Spirit carries my thoughts and prayers to the Great Mystery through the vehicle of smoke. The Elders say that we were once like this smoke, without body, without form, and able to pass freely back and forth from this physical body/Center of the Universe to the Creator. When I hold the Pipe, I become part of the divine order of Creation. We pray for all things that have life.

At the Sundance, we gift to the Spirit the only things that we have to give, our bodies and our Pipes in Sacred Prayer for All. As Grandma would say, "Just saying you are a Sundancer does not make you one! You have to live your prayers, become your prayers, remember your prayers, and most of all, don't walk on your prayers. Some people pray prayers, then forget those prayers the very next day. That is what I call walking on your prayers!"

Believe me when I say that being with my Elders saved my life. After being with them for years, I was told I had the ability to see the Other World with all my senses, senses like hearing, seeing, smelling, tasting, feeling, and more. The Elders told me that there were more senses available to each one of us than the ones we use. They would call people that only used five senses a five-sensory person, and say that a five-sensory person is crippled in the Today World, for they cannot see or sense Spirit.

They said I was *Iyeska*, an old Lakota word for Spirit Speaker. *Iyeska* also means half-breed. When I first heard them call me that, I thought they meant I was a fat, half-breed, white woman.

Having all those senses was exactly what made me think of myself as crazy. While working for a mental institution as a visiting psychological researcher, I often found myself talking to the patients, one-on-one, on a purely philosophical basis. I've often wondered if those people were really "crazy," or if they just were touching another level of consciousness or even genius. Many of the Old Ones later told me that people perceived as crazy people were sometimes in touch with another realm or could see or hear things that other people could not.

It has been quite a journey in itself, unraveling the mystery of the Spirit talk I'd hear, seeing things, hearing strange sounds in my ears, or smelling horrid odors in clean environments and then discovering these smells were some form of negative entity looking for a new home. Since childhood, I've had an ability not only to "see" the spirits, but also to see the colors of the field around a person's body, the aura. I also was gifted the ability that I call Vision. I have had many dreams that have come true. Many times in my life I have gone into what people describe as an altered state, or trance. Sometimes I have been rendered helpless or unable to drive or talk during this experience. I realized early on that not a lot of people around me had similar experiences, so many times I would never share what I saw. Yet, I knew that my experiences were special, and I also knew that I should act on the guidance I received in some concrete way. Sometimes my "visions" were only strong or strange images or intuitions, yet many times my own life or that of another was saved, or at least spared unnecessary grief, because I acted upon the information given to me in these "visions."

I've been told that all people are born with full psychic ability. It's the culture that quickly shapes what is acceptable and what is not acceptable, and most of us just fit into the acceptable cultural mold.

I learned that the Indian way of life is a heart-centered way of life, where the seen and the unseen work closely together. A lot of Indian people are raised with the utmost respect for spiritual things and the belief that Spirits or "helpers" are a part of our everyday lives. My solace and salvation has been to learn a way to live in which all the worlds are recognized in my everyday life.

The way I share these stories may show the way the Elders taught me, that of relating an event or experience to illustrate a lesson. It is a circular rather than a linear approach, free of the "illusion of time." As is typical of the spiritual path, my lessons came through experience, and sometimes they became clear only five or ten years down the road.

I want to share with you some of my capers with Grandmother Grace. I want to tell you about some of the Elders who became my teachers, about some of the obstacles to perception that I had to overcome, and about the events in my life that led me to the Sundance, most of which Grandma had a big hand in.

I will share some of the Visions I received from the Spirit world and my growing awareness of all the psychological benefits of the Indian ceremonies, as well as the experiences of everyday life that lie on the other side of the ceremonies.

I will tell you of some of the ceremonies I've experienced, people I've met, and the things that helped me to shift and move through my emotions.

I offer not only the shamanistic and visionary side of my walk with Grace Spotted Eagle and as a Sundancer, but also the personal side, that of a human being just doing the best I can, walking through these amazing events.

On this Sundance walk, guided by a Sundance vision, I learned the lessons of the Five Directions — East, South, West, North, and in the fifth year, the "within space," or the center of all those directions and lessons. Each year I walked the way of one of the four winds, although not in the traditional E/S/W/N order, for the very first year the Sundance Chief had said that he knew from information the spirits had shared with him that I would start working on lessons of the West.

I walked to the West and learned about going inside myself to learn from the teacher within: the West is the place of contemplation.

The walk of the East brought me to many Eastern and Tibetan masters, and I learned of enlightenment.

The path of the South taught me of pureness of thought, trust, and relationships.

The last way was to the North, where I found lessons in the wisdom of the Elders and the children.

I walk from one year of Sundance Season to the next. The calendar year for me has changed to one based on the ceremonies and the seasons. Life for me has become a ceremonial way of living twenty four hours a day.

Life as a ceremony. A ceremony should be filled with Joy, Celebration, and Gratefulness. Why does it seem that we are not so happy to be alive? Perhaps the world is no bigger than the Sundance arbor or maybe not even as big as that. I know when I walk into that Great Mystery Circle of the Sundance, the prayers that all the Sundancers make seem to affect the whole world — my world and the world of others.

The other day, Charles Chipps, Sundance Chief and brother friend, said, "Thunder, what if everyone just lived the word *Mi Takaye Oyacin* every second, every minute, every hour? What a wonderful world this would be!" I agree. *MI TAKAYE OYACIN!* Grandma Grace used to say in Lakota, *"CIKSUYA CANNA `SNA CANTEMAWA`STE YELO,"* which means, "Whenever I remember you, my heart is happy!"

Grandma Grace was very wise. She set me the task of writing this book at a most crucial time for the planet. We two-leggeds of this Earth, we Earth people must give up our "stuff" now so the planet can heal, or else Mother Earth may have to get rid of the people.

Some twenty-five years ago my Elders shared an ancient prophecy with me, a prophecy that I feel strongly at work on the planet today. In February 1987, as per my Elders' words, there was the Day of Two Suns, The Supernova, a sign of the consummation of the love between Mother Earth and Father Sky. From their union, seeds of life, neutrinos, began to rain down on—and through—our planet, begetting changes in the consciousness of the people. I believe that Mother Earth is now pregnant. When a woman is pregnant, she quickly learns that she must now take care of herself in a gentle, loving way. She must learn to love herself and pamper herself because she is responsible for new life. The only time I ever treated myself as if I really loved myself was when I knew I was carrying new life. Sometimes a woman wonders, "What am I bringing this child into?" Really, isn't that what we all are feeling right now?

Some Elders say that as of 1993 we have nineteen years left to elevate our consciousness so our Mother Earth can bring the child of a new way of being to full term. If we don't change, then she might — no, they said *will* — abort. We can't waste time any longer. We must take full and total responsibility for our lives and how our lives, prayers, and decisions effect others!

These are some of my reasons for writing these words and "talking the story" to you, dear Reader. My prayer is that the words I write are written and received in a good way, and that nothing written herein will cause hurt or harm to anyone or anything living. I pray that in these words my Elders will feel my heartfelt honor for them and our way of life and religion. I have truthfully represented the lessons without revealing sacred secrets of rituals, except where I have gained permission to do so. I feel no one can duplicate Spirit on paper. I am only writing my own experience of Spirit.

Mi Takaye Oyacin! Amen to all my relations and all things with life.

Wallace Black Elk and Grace Spotted Eagle with Mary Thunder and Bill Lyons (standing left to right), Horse, Sparky, Butch and Nancy Moore (sitting left to right)

EDITOR'S PREFACE

In the fall of 1986, I left my job as Editorial Coordinator of *Glamour Magazine* with the vague dream of writing a book. Through a rather remarkable stream of events, I found myself less than a year later leaving New York in an aging Chevy van with Mary Thunder, Jeff White Horse and Butch Hennigan. I stayed with them for the better part of a year-and-a-half, crossing the United States several times and meeting literally hundreds of people from all walks of life. I was privileged to meet some of Thunder's Elders from the Lakota and other Native American tribes, and was able to attend and participate in many ancient traditional ceremonies.

Among many other things, Mary Thunder is a master storyteller. Probably the greatest challenge in editing this book was to translate to paper the resonance of the spoken word. I had to learn about a different way of thinking — away from the linear intellectual mode I'd always used in my working life to a more *circular* mode, based on the intelligence of the heart and spirit as well as the mind.

Thunder could not have written this book from a strictly chronological point of view. The stories connect and resonate in a circular timeless pattern. It is the *truth* of the events that matter here, and sometimes the truth can only be discovered on reflection, through later experience. The pattern — the essential connectedness — of all things becomes all important.

Thunder taught me that one of the gates that opens the mind and heart to illumination is laughter. Many of her stories are extremely funny and, at the same time, have deep lessons that can create transformation in one's life.

Being on the road with Thunder, I saw in action how she allows her life to be guided by Spirit. In the habit of trying to control my world, the concept of the "flow" was not always easy for me to understand.

Her way of teaching is experiential, not theoretical. Her teachings are indivisible from her life. I learned on our travels that everything that happens has meaning and is part of a wider pattern of truth. Thunder taught me about a different level of sensitivity and awareness that can reveal the lessons to be found in the events surrounding us.

When Thunder began writing the book, I was surprised at the preparations she made. I was concerned with notebooks and typewriters; Thunder was more concerned that our office be clean and orderly so that our thoughts would have clarity. She created a special altar on which she placed certain items connected to the memories or events we planned to discuss. Over and over again, strange things happened. Thunder would tell a story involving someone she hadn't seen in years, and that night they would call on the phone out of nowhere. If the stories were particularly emotional, sometimes the computer screen would just go blank. The repairman could find nothing wrong with it. After a few hours' break, the computer would suddenly work again and the story could be finished, perhaps with some of the painful emotions diminished. Eight-hour candles burned down in two while we worked on the Sundance stories.

Thunder's way of telling a story weaves together many threads of events or trains of thought, and just when you begin to wonder what it all means, all the threads tie together in a beautiful pattern that illustrates an essential truth or lesson. Her stories echo from past to present to future and back again, because it is not the sequence of events that matters so much, it is the *pattern* of energy that is revealed. There are stories within stories within stories and, when we lose the need for linear time, we find ourselves in a place beyond time, where universal truth lives and speaks. It is my hope that the reader will be able to feel and sense the pattern that flows through these stories and receive the healing energy that is available here.

Mary Thunder is a truly remarkable woman who has actualized in her life, in this time, an almost mythic journey. She showed me that there is a way of life alive and well in this country, a road of spiritual thought that I thought could only be found in legends or dreams. Some of the greatest lessons I received were in the unlikeliest places — who ever expected life transformation at K-Mart or McDonald's!

As is typical of Thunder's way of teaching, writing this book became an experiential adventure rather than an intellectual exercise. Mary

Thunder wrote this book to show people that change — deep, lasting change — is possible in their lives. The process of working with her certainly changed what I thought was possible to me in my life. It is my hope that, for you, reading it will do the same.

I would like to thank my mother, Martha Singleton Williamson, my father, Dr. Herbert Ogden, my stepmother, Jan Ogden, and my sister, Dr. Joan Ogden for their love and support during this time; and above all I would like to thank Mary Elizabeth Thunder, for her love and willingness to share her wisdom with all the people and for asking me to edit her words.

Augusta Ogden

Augusta Ogden, Horse, Grandpa Wallace, Butch "Buffalo Horse" Hennigan, and Tina Emerson on visit to clean Grandma's things from the house, January, 1988

INTRODUCTION

Yehwehnode,
Twylah Nitsch, Seneca

Welcome, old friends and new friends of Mary Elizabeth Thunder. I am grateful she asked me to write an introduction to her book. It gives me the opportunity to tell of a little known gift this roving teacher has and how the Elder, Grace Spotted Eagle, in her wisdom, saw the potential nestled in her protégé.

In every generation of humankind, there are Messengers of Love, Truth, and Peace. These Messengers are linked for life through a Sacred Bond with Motherearth. Notice, we spell Motherearth as one word because she is a "Whole Entity."

Sensitivity to Motherearth identifies one Messenger to the next. These Messengers know of this connection to each other through a feeling of "Wholeness" that they carry in their Vibral Core or Solar Plexus. This awareness happened to me when I first met Mary Elizabeth Thunder several years ago. It happened again when I met Grace Spotted Eagle. Nothing was ever mentioned, though Grace and I both knew Mary Elizabeth Thunder was not aware of her gift. Grace Spotted Eagle took the responsibility of awakening Mary Elizabeth Thunder to her mission as a Messenger. She was grateful her tactics paid off with merit.

Mary Elizabeth Thunder knew something was happening to her but didn't know what. This book is her way of telling the world how Native Elders awaken their people, her way of saying Thank You to Grace Spotted Eagle, who now speaks to her from the Other Side. To us, there's only a thin veil between that prevents us from touching physically; but the Spiritual Touch has no boundaries. The teachers who pass from the physical realm into the spiritual are not bound by a physical time schedule. Sometimes they forget they were once physical.

Grandmother Twylah Nitsch, Seneca, standing by a tree at her home on the Cattaraugus Indian Reservation

Our Elders have said that every woman is a nourisher of truth within and every man is the protector of truth within. It is important to remember that we are both male and female within. This duality is not separate. It assures our wholeness within. Love Within, Truth Within, Peace Within . . . Within Within, the Within.

The Elders add that every woman is, in her physicality, an extension of Motherearth, and every man carries the Sun in his heart as a spiritual good. This unity within, between Motherearth and the Sun, produces life for Time Eternal.

Threaded throughout this book is Mary Elizabeth Thunder's appreciation of Grace Spotted Eagle's "Gems of Wisdom." Sometimes Elders seem fierce in character to create an awakening, but they get the job done!

Native People have experienced a rapid transition into the dominant culture. But our Elders have said, "A time will come when other people will seek their truths from the mouths of our Ancient Ancestors." Survival is based upon Native Wisdom. The transition is marked by those who seek wholeness because they have walked in Moccasin Tracks before.

Dear Readers, as your eyes see truth within the words of this book, know that the lesson is not hidden, but perceived through your link to Motherearth. A thread of awareness is ever present and reveals its truth when the time and place is appropriate. Love, Truth, and Peace flow along these corridors of Inner Knowing. The key to this Inner Knowing is gratitude. Day after day we find ourselves standing at the Portal of Love, Truth, and Peace, waiting for something to happen.

Mary Elizabeth Thunder has expressed her appreciation and carries on where Grace Spotted Eagle left off. Her readers can find her awakening laced in and between the lines with Native American Wisdom, Prophecy, and Philosophy. In writing this book, Mary Elizabeth Thunder walked through the portal of Love, Truth, and Peace.

Da Naho Nyah Weh Swenio
(It has been said. Thank you, Great Mystery)

Yehwehnode,
Twylah Nitsch, Seneca

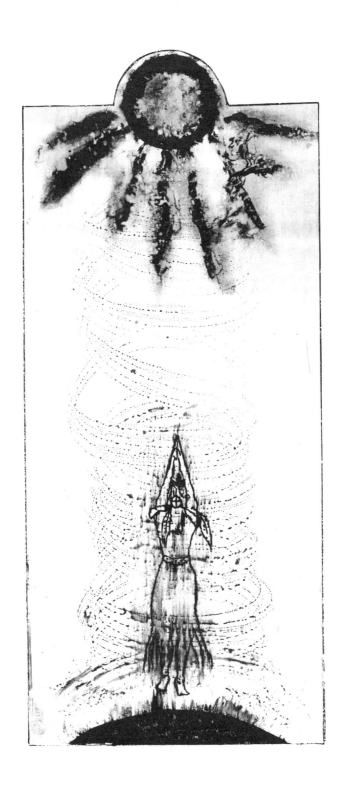

In a vision, a Spirit came and told me that you're sent back to this earth over and over and over and over and over again until you become whole. That's why I Sundance. It's a way for me to come closer to who I am seeking to be — whole, in balance, in touch with the Spirit.

MARY ELIZABETH THUNDER

1

✸ ❂ ✸

WIWANYANK WACIPI
The Sundance
Gazing at the Sun, Dancing

Before I get started with my story, I feel the need to provide you with a framework for understanding the Sundance, for it's at the Sundance that a lot of the experiences that I will be talking about in this book take place. I also must say that I do not claim to be any authority on this subject, just a participant. This is my experience, and only my experience of and belief about this sacred ceremony, as I have learned it from my Elders and my own Sundancing of many years.

Throughout the flow of events that led to the prophesy of my heart attack and what followed, an energy had been building. It was the call of the Sundance, a call which at first I did not hear. It is an old call, like remembering something, like something that comes up from the very depths of your soul and erupts into your life in the most unexpected ways. This memory is old, genetic in nature. It is a way, I have been told, for a soul to elevate itself on this planet Earth through praying for the people and sacrificing the body in honoring and gratefulness to the Great Mystery.

In the old days, I have been told, the Sundance was the center of the Sioux way of life, a kind of communal vision quest. The center pole, as it was called, the Tree of Life, was usually a Sacred Cottonwood Tree that was selected by a young girl. The tree was then cut, but never allowed to hit the ground. Upon cutting, the Warriors would catch it in mid-air and then carry the tree, sometimes a forty-foot tree, many miles, never letting it touch the ground. After much ceremony, a hole was dug in the middle of a prepared arbor, and the tree, almost like a baby being carried in the arms of its loving father (the Warriors), would be planted into the ground to stand tall. Before the tree was put

SUN DANCE

MEDICINE MAN
CHIEF LEONARD CROW DOG

SPONSORED BY
CHIEF LEONARD CROW DOG
ARCHIE LAME DEER
JERRY ROY
CLYDE BELLECOURT
NED MEDCALF
JOHN ROY
ALL SUN DANCERS

IN MEMORY OF

JOSEPH SHIELDS
FRANCIS PRIMO
WHO DEDICATED THEIR LIVES
TO PRESERVING THE INDIAN
WAY OF LIFE, TRADITIONALLY
AND IN THE SPIRITUAL
WAY OF GENERATIONS
BEFORE THEM.

PURIFICATION   JULY 28, 29, 30, & 31
SUN DANCE   AUG. 1, 2, 3, & 4, 1991

LOCATION   **CROW DOGS PARADISE, ROSEBUD
LAKOTA-SIOUX RESERVATION,
ROSEBUD So. DAKOTA.**

TO HAVE THE UNDERSTANDING OF THE KNOWLEDGE OF THE CREATOR
THAT ALL THINGS OF CREATIONS LIVE AS ONE

ABSOLUTELY NO
CAMERAS • ALCOHOL • TAPE RECORDERS • DRUGS • FIREARMS
NOT RESPONSIBLE FOR THEFT OR ACCIDENTS

up, there were two cut-out rawhide figures, a Man and a Buffalo, placed at the top. Beautiful cloth banners in the sacred colors —yellow for the sun, blue for the sky, green for Mother Earth, red for the red people, white for peace and purity, and black for night — were hung from the branches of the tree, along with offerings of tobacco wrapped in cloth. The dancers' pipes were laid in front of a painted buffalo skull that was filled with sage and placed at the head of the Dance ground.

For four days, from sunrise to sundown, the Warriors would dance to the great drums and the songs, blowing the high, piercing notes of their Eagle bone whistles, their heads and ankles wrapped in sacred sage. For four days, the Warriors neither ate nor drank, testing and demonstrating their fortitude and endurance, praying to Wakan Tanka, the Great Mysterious, holding their vow in their hearts. On the third or fourth day, those who had vowed to do it demonstrated their bravery by piercing their flesh with Eagle claws or wooden pegs attached to thongs hanging from the tree or to buffalo skulls, which they dragged behind them as they danced. They demonstrated their generosity, gratitude, courage, and fortitude by offering their flesh, the only thing they could truly call their own, and dancing until they pulled away and their flesh broke open in a sacrifice that might bring the wisdom of a vision. The last round of the Dance ends with the Dancers giving blessings with their Dance fans of Eagle feathers to all the supporters who come and join them at the edge of the Great Mystery Circle. Then a great feast!

The Sundance energy is so powerful that even just deciding to go to offer support at a Sundance can begin to work change in your life. All of your core issues come up in your face for you to see and deal with. Blocks, fears, and old patterns manifest in your outward reality so they can be released before you enter the Sundance camp. If you try to hold onto them and bring them with you, the Universe will fully manifest them right there and then to help you get the lesson.

At my first Dance, the father of my children and my friend Fred were the only people there to support me. In later years, I have had many beautiful people of all races accompany me to the Dance. Before I take anyone into the Sundance camp, I spend time, a lot of time, talking to them about some of the issues that may come up for them in this place of powerful, primal energy. I expect the people in my camp to dress and behave in a way that is respectful and consistent

ORIGINAL WAY OF THE LAKOTA WAY

SUNDANCE

ROSEBUD INDIAN TERRITORY

CROW DOG ANCESTRAL HOME

ORIGINAL DREAM HAS
NEVER GONE AWAY

IKCA WICASA WAY

All Decendants of Chiefs:

HOLLOW HORN BEAR	IRON SHELL	TWO STRIKE	
ONE STAR	BALD EAGLE	SPOTTED TAIL	EAGLE FEATHER

PURIFICATION DAYS

AUGUST 5 - 8

SUNDANCE DAYS

9-12   1984

CROW DOG PARADISE

with the traditions of the Sundance camp and the Native American traditional culture. I tell the people who go with me to move their "stuff" to another area of their awareness before they approach this sacred ancient ceremony. All energies are magnified at the Dance — positive and negative. I warn them not to get lost in their own personal chaos, which would be very easy to do. I have seen people come out of the Sundance and just be real crazy and I never want that to happen to any of my friends who come with me to help out.

I am careful — very careful — about who comes to our camp. I am responsible for anyone who stays in my camp. Once I was publicly slapped in the face by an Elder grandma because one of my female supporters at the Dance had gotten involved with an Indian drummer and created a lot of disturbance and chaos.

These Indian people are dancing and sacrificing for their families and future generations. They don't have the time to be worried about someone breaking a fingernail. If you are lucky enough to be asked to come, then you darn well better be ready to support this ceremony, in their way, on their land.

Again, we come to the question:

What is the Sundance?

If I were talking to a group of Indians, I would not have to say anymore and would not have said as much as I have. Usually, Indians just smile and know. But who knows where the winds of time will scatter the pages of this book, so I will try to define the Sundance.

I have been told that it is the oldest and highest Plains Indians ritual of initiation. In other indigenous cultures, such as the Aztec, Peruvian and even the Egyptian, there were ceremonies related to the Sun as the Source, as an aspect of the Creator.

Native Americans usually refer to the Sun as Grandfather, or Father. The children, or Sundancers, are dancing on the Earth, which is called Grandmother, or Mother. The Dance re-energizes the Earth Mother and makes a connection between the Earth Mother and the Sky Father, balancing male and female energies, whether the dancer is male or female. Usually, at a traditional Sundance, there are more men dancing than women.

For a Native Person, it is a time when people come to dance together, in unison, while maintaining their own personal prayers and visions.

Usually, the Sundance is held once a year in any given place, in the Summer, when the Sun is the highest.

To build a nation requires more than symbols. People's lives, thoughts, and actions must be linked to knowledge that is passed from generation to generation. If everything belongs to the Great Spirit, then the only thing a Dancer has to offer as a prayer is his body. The Sundance teaches this way.

The Dancers dance around a single Cottonwood tree, the Tree of Life, for four days with no food or water. To do this is a vow and a way of life. They seek to live life with the highest integrity, so that when they return to that Sacred Sundance Tree and go into the Sacred Great Mystery Circle, they go into it as pure and as clean as possible, because the Spirits are with them all the time. There in the Great Mystery Circle, the Spirits will talk to them, warn them, and tell them of many things, especially those that they have not done in a good way. The Spirits will hear the Dancers' prayers and help their families or sick friends. During the Dance, the Dancers pray for healing, for help with life's trials, for the peace and benefit of the world; they pray so that the people might live. It is a way to be totally in the Spirit World. When you're in the Dance, that's all there is. It is a complete act of surrender. Your very body and spirit are depending on the Sundance Chief and the rhythm of the drum. There is no food or water or outside thoughts to take your mind off of the dance and your prayers.

Richard Erdoes writes in his book, *Crying for a Dream*:

> *A person would make a vow to dance in order to take away sickness from a friend or relative, or to bring a warrior back alive from a battle. A man might want to suffer so that the tribe would live. Viewed by government agents and missionaries, the Sundance was a savage, bloodthirsty rite which had to be suppressed. And so, in the face of the Constitution's guarantee of religious freedom for all, the Sundance and all other Native American rituals were outlawed in 1881. Even taking a sweatbath became a punishable offense. In his 1882 report, McGillicudy, the agent at Pine Ridge wrote: "The heathenish annual ceremony termed 'the Sundance' will, I trust, soon be a thing of the past." He was wrong.*

The Sundance simply went underground. It was finally permitted again during the administration of Franklin D. Roosevelt, "without self-torture," at the insistence of the missionaries. Many white agents for the government saw the Sundance as self-torture because they did not know the purpose of the ceremony. It is said by many elders that the Sundance is to allow men to share the blood of their bodies with the Earth Mother. It is understood that women already do this through their moontime, or menstrual cycle. Women give of their pain through childbirth; men have the opportunity to make such offerings through the Sundance. Women nurture the seeds of future generations and men commit their lives to the protection of these generations through Sundancing.

Grandpa Fools Crow told me once that he personally crusaded for over forty years to bring this Sacred Ceremony back to the Lakota people. Back in July of 1975 or so, when I first went to Crow Dog's Paradise in Rosebud, South Dakota, the Dance was still illegal. Warriors on horses maintained surveillance while the Dancers danced.

It's hard to know what else to write here. How can you convey with words and paper something as old and as sacred as this Dance?

Why Did I Become a Sundancer?

Because I had had a death experience and was told by Elders that I must Dance and gift my body back to the Creator who had brought me back to life.

The Dance itself is the dance of death, transformation, and rebirth. It is done for the renewal of the Earth at the time of year when the Sun is highest, to ground the energies of Father Sun into Mother Earth. Then life will be better for the people. It brings rebirth and nourishment, so life will be better for the whole planet.

Grandpa Henry Crow Dog, Leonard's father, said, "When the prairie grass is high and the earth green and the choke cherries are ripe for the sacred food, then we gotta dance."

Thomas E. Mails, in his book, *Sundancing at Rosebud and Pine Ridge*, offers an outsider's insight into the importance and meaning of the Sundance to the Lakota:

> *The Sioux announcers repeat over and over again as the pledgers dance: "This is our religion, this is our religion, this is our religion."*
>
> *I confess that when I first heard this chant, I was puzzled. Were the announcers, I wondered, saying that the Sundance alone was their religion? That couldn't be, since the Sioux performs numerous other ceremonies. Finally the meaning dawned on me. The Sundance performance, at one point or another during the four days, includes every aspect of the Sioux religion. Everything spiritual they do on a year-round basis is represented within the single ceremony. That is what makes the Sundance so great and so special. Therefore, if a person goes to a Sundance with this understanding and watches carefully, he will see revealed before his eyes the essence of the Sioux religion as practiced from the time of the White Buffalo Maiden until now. Some things may be emphasized more than others, but nothing is left out.*

At the writing of this book, I have danced in over twenty Sacred Sundances. I started dancing at Mount Hood, Oregon and Crow Dog Paradise in Rose Bud, South Dakota. I have lived to see my husband, Horse, pierced in the chest, hanging from the Tree of Life; my two sons, Richard and John, pierce and break from horses; my son-in-law, father of my grandchildren, pierce and pray for his babies; and many brothers, sisters and friends participate in the Dance. To me, this is a good way of life. I feel very lucky to have lived to see all of these things, for, at one time, I was ready to die and give up life. Now I am seeing my family take vows and make sacrifices to God just to be able to pray for others on this Earth Mother. It was one thing for me to be able to do these things, but I never dreamed or wished for anyone else to take on this pretty difficult way of praying and living life. I am so proud.

Describing the Sundance could be likened to describing the sacred ceremony of the birth of one of my children. Most people experience birth as bloody, painful, and certainly traumatic; but in truth, I could not describe to you the sequence of events or even the pain. I can only remember the joy of hearing my child's first cry. What I remember from Sundance is always the joy of the presence of Spirit and the transformation and the healing. It is an honor to Sundance. Giving birth, dying, and Sundancing are the most sacred and transformative experiences I have ever known.

When the singers sing from the drum at Sundance, they are saying, "Grandfather, pity me. I am suffering. Help me dance. Take my body and my energy so that the people might live."

God has and is a part of every one of us, so every human is sacred. Even the man or woman who behaves in a rude and ugly manner has a spirit, but Grandma used to say that a person with a rude and ugly manner, Spirit would only hurt instead of help.

Dancing in the Sundance, we learn to Walk Our Talk in balance, and to let go of the parts of ourselves that are only interested in the personal "I." I learned to sacrifice my personal "poopoo caca" so that the sacredness and gratefulness of my life could be restored. Self-sacrifice is not denying one's needs; it is choosing to willingly sacrifice one's limitations, through action. When we are in pain and we slow down in the Dance, the Chief sometimes says, "You chose to dance, not me, so stop that self-pity and collapsing into the pain where you might die. Just get up and keep dancing, Sundancer!"

Sundance touches your Soul. It seeks out that which is your greatest block or test, magnifies it a thousand fold, and mirrors it back to you for you to see, know, and deal with. Those whose fears are deeply hidden from themselves are in for a very big shock when facing the Sundance. If you are open to all energies, truly open to healing yourself, the Dance will show you your fears, blocks, limitations, and how to overcome them with the help of faith in a higher consciousness, God, Creator. Yes, you have to be willing to look at yourself and also to see all around you, for whatever is happening is a mirror for what is going on inside of yourself. A lot of people say they want to hear or see the truth, but you better be sure when you are dealing with the Dance. The Dance will show you the whole truth and nothing less.

As you become more aware of how blocks, fears, and limitations are showing up in your life, you become better prepared to release them.

If you resist letting go and hold onto attachments past their time, they can become disruptive and even life-threatening forces in your life.

The only way to break free of a trap is to discover how it is put together. In discovering how the trap is made, a warrior is able to free him- or herself. If you learn how you are put together, you can free yourself from what keeps you from being free and loving to yourself and others.

You Don't Have a Soul; You Are a Soul.

This is what the Spirit told me.

You have a body and you have a mind, but you *are* a soul.

For some, the body and the mind control them. The ultimate state of living as a human being is one in which the being controls the mind and the body. Then nothing is impossible.

One of my teachers taught me that you fast in the Sundance not for God, but to rid yourself of your own disbelief. You fast to move yourself to the faith to believe again that all things are possible with Spirit intervention. In the Dance, I have fallen down, feeling that I cannot go on. Then I finally have begged for mercy from the Creator to help me. I then have been able to get up and dance with renewed strength. Where did this strength come from? Certainly not from me. I have felt the very organs in my body jump from hot sun, no water, and exhaustion; but only after I prayed and surrendered to God, begging for help, would my mouth fill up with water and my strength come back to move my body again. You fast to reach the understanding that it is not the physical body that makes the spiritual commitment in this life, but the Soul.

We Are More Than Flesh.

This understanding establishes you as the master of your own household, your body. You must take care of your body, for that is the vehicle that Spirit works through. When you can accept these principles, the Spirit has told me, then you can be a true friend to others and yourself. In this state, you are one with all life. Until you can control your body, you have not mastered anything.

Our Number One Fear on This Planet Is Death

What happens if you are not afraid to die? Then that fear or block releases into the forward motion of the Universal flow. We were born to learn the lessons of Life and Living, not only of dying. It is up to us to honor our own choice to be here on our Earth Mother and to fulfill our purpose or destiny before we return from whence we came. In a Sundance vision, the Spirit told me that we make a conscious choice to come back to this level of consciousness on Earth. At the time, that was a little hard to believe. I asked the Spirit why my life had been so hard and hurt so much. The Spirit showed me that when I chose to come back to Earth, I made choices — such as having a mother who would leave me, an alcoholic father, etc. — that would give me the maximum opportunity for learning and growth.

Because we are afraid to die, our great pastime is keeping ourselves out of pain. What if we just prayed and moved through whatever pain we were in, instead of covering it with addictions? Then we would learn how to ask the Great Mystery or Higher Source for help. One of the Elders once told me that if we could fully experience all our real feelings and give them full expression, we would not have to keep re-creating them over and over. Would this not be a healthier way? I feel that we take on drugs, alcohol, and other addictions because we fear pain, and addictions cover the pain or hide it away. When I'm feeling a pain, let's say, of the heart, I just breathe and experience it, thank it for coming, analyze it, and see what I can learn from it. I try not to give way to fear or any of the other negative emotions.

I have chosen to dedicate myself to pain for the four days of the Sundance. Doesn't that sound better than pain for three hundred and sixty-five days of the year? During that time, I just live in the now and, in this way, I can even experience some joy and celebration. By Sundancing, I have learned to give up the fear of dying and move into my pain instead of trying to cover it or avoid it.

Also, I have learned the lesson of *Completion*. I have learned that when you complete pieces of your life, it gives you more life energy. Every thought, picture, or memory you carry has life energy to it. Every time you complete something, either old or new, you free up more energy to work for your life, and so there is less to hold you back from your visions or goals. I heard a teacher say that a soul is born with only so many units of life force. This life force is what we live with all our lives. Since I feel that any decision I make effects seven generations backwards and forwards, then my quitting smoking, for instance, may just mean that the seven generations behind me will not have to deal with the addiction of smoking cigarettes. Making this prayer and taking this action may mean that I add to my total amount of life force, and so to the life force of generations that follow.

Thoughts are things. In the Dance, we are always being told to watch how we pray. If thoughts have life, form, substance, and energy, then what you think is what you may become. What you pray for you just might get. I remember a girl who prayed at a pipe ceremony for a man to come into her life. Later this girl called me and bawled me out for "fixing her up with a con man." I asked her what she had prayed for. She said she had prayed for a handsome man with money and dark hair. I asked her what the man now in her life looked like. "Well, he is dark and handsome." "Does he have money?" "Yes," she said, "but he is a burglar!" "Next time," I said to her, "pray for a man with integrity also!"

I have learned to release the old and grow into the new me. This new "me" or "us" will be reborn again and again to bring each of us closer and closer to the cosmic child within.

Dear Readers, I know in my heart that the changes do not have to be hard or violent. It is important to pray for gentleness. I always listen to the inner voice.

One day, an Elder, with dark, dark eyes looking into mine said, "If Mother Earth is pregnant and we are all going to be reborn, Thunder, will yours be a hard birth or an easy one? Or will you choose not to be born at all?"

I believe in the 1990s our great challenge, the challenge upon which our survival depends, will be to learn to become one with all aspects of Life. *Aho Mi Takaye Oyacin!* We must learn to live in harmony with ourselves, each other, the Earth, and the Cosmos. Walking our Talk.

In order to do this, we must become aware of all aspects of the Self within. The Warrior's most perilous journey is to the regions within. Those who need someone else to blame for their predicaments are going to be lost. Those who aren't afraid to face the Truth of the Inner Self and to seek Higher Truths must be dedicated to personal responsibility and personal awareness. By releasing all expectations, hurts, or patterns we have outgrown, we will begin to become more and more of who we truly are in the greater plan. We then will be walking towards wholeness with Respect, Honor, and Gratefulness.

To me, responsibility is the ability to act and act again as a co-creator with the Divine Will of God.

The picture you hold of God
Is What You Are Becoming.

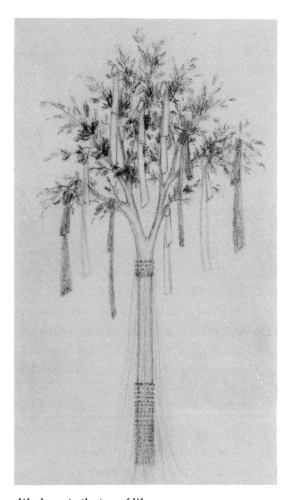

We dance to the tree of life

So many things have happened and so many miles have been traveled on the road over the last ten years that I hardly know where to start.

But as I remember back to that sunset in Oregon at the Sundance where Grandma told me to write this book, I see her giving me a list of chapters. She said, "Okay, write this down!" Her eyes twinkled as she saw me jump to get paper and pen in the middle of the woods in the dark. "Now, this is how you will write it," she laughed, and I laughed too. "Start with how we met. You do remember, don't you?" Of course I did. The chapters that she outlined to me that night have become the chapters of this book. Her words are their introductions.

As I write this to you today, Grandma just keeps talking on and on from the Spirit world: "Try the beginning! Stop wasting time," on and on. Feeling the swoosh and impending impact of the astral drumstick, I begin . . . .

> Thunder remembering Grandma Grace's words of how to write the book chapter by chapter per her wishes . . .

2

"START WITH HOW WE MET. YOU DO REMEMBER, DON'T YOU?"

The Sweat Lodge of Destiny

In the late 1970s, I was in a remarkable Sweat Lodge and ceremony with Leonard Crow Dog and his wife, in which I gave up a lifetime of grief for a mother I had never known. Grandma Mary and Grandpa Henry Crow Dog were there, as was a very old Lakota man named Grandpa Fools Crow. He didn't speak much English and so had an interpreter with him. This old man, Grandpa Fools Crow, was running the Lodge.

As my son Richard and I approached the Lodge, we saw that the fire was very large. I noticed that there was a rock in front of the lodge that had been left out of the fire. I had brushed this rock with my foot as I was helping to get ready for the ceremony, and it wasn't even hot. As I was putting wood on the crackling fire, I looked into the flames and was mystified that there were no rocks in the fire. But I quickly said shut up to my mind and did not mention it. Just who was I to mention to anybody about no rocks in the fire?

A lot of times, down in Lakota land, the Lodges are little. They fit maybe eight or nine people and you sit right up over the fire pit. Your face is right over the rocks. My apprehension was building, for I was quite heavy and was scared to sweat that night.

Soon it was time. Just seeing Grandpa Henry and this old man talk together was a special picture. Talking their own language, laughing, and kind of hitting their knees from time to time — I really did not have to know what they were saying, I was just honored to be there.

After a long while, they signaled that they were ready and that all would be going into the Sweat that night together. Usually, the men and women sweat separately, the women after the men. I felt my heart

Thunder in the Sweat Lodge

jump as I realized that we were all going to be sweating together and sweating right then. Fear raced back into my mind and my body was already sweating as I looked at my young son. I thought I might still have a chance to get out of the Lodge. Maybe there were just too many people, or maybe Leonard's mother needed some dishes done. The answer to my trying-to-get-out-of-the-Sweat-Lodge mind chatter came when Leonard said, "Niece, get dressed over there by Grandma." Resigned to my fate, I did as I was told.

We entered the Lodge. The old man spoke to the doorman in his native language and I was surprised to see him bring in that cold rock I'd noticed before. My mind raced. Where were the other rocks?

The old man started praying. He prayed and sang for half an hour, and Spirits came into the Lodge. It was warm in there, even without hot rocks, and I started to have again my not-knowing-if-I-am-going-to-live-or-not thoughts.

All of a sudden, he quit singing. He blew on the rock, and it turned red, fiery red. It became the hottest rock of the hottest Lodge I have ever been in before or since.

It was a miracle, a mystical sacred blessing in one of the highest sacred ceremonies, and I was so much in awe that I couldn't speak. Who was I to say something when there was this man who blew on a rock and it became hot? As each person prayed around the circle and it came my turn to pray, I just kept saying *Mi Takaye Oyacin*, for I could not breathe.

My head was swirling and aching, and it was so hot, it felt like the flesh was coming off of my body. I was scared, real scared; I thought that I was going to die. I heard my son crying and moaning. I hardly had the strength to reach out to him, and then I realized he was holding me.

Just then the old man, through his interpreter, said, "You are grieving for your mother. Why is that?" I heard him ask again. Someone nudged me. I still didn't want to say anything. I felt so heavy, and every breath seared my lungs. Finally, after several nudges, I realized that I had to speak, so I told them that my mother had left me when I was three weeks old. They talked in Lakota for a long time.

The interpreter told me the old man's words. He said: "You are ungrateful. You have always been walking on your Mother. You are sitting on her now, but you choose to grieve for somebody who isn't even here. You just came through that person, but you have always lived with your real mother, Mother Earth. She is Alive!"

I don't remember much after that because I cried and cried for a long time. They carried me out of the Lodge. All I know now is that, from the time of that ceremony, I have never grieved for a lost mother again. In that sacred ceremony, I found Her and She is with me — and all of you — still. Our Mother is the Earth.

I did not have much time to regroup after that Sweat Lodge ceremony, but before I left Crow Dog's Paradise, Leonard Crow Dog's wife told me, "You should meet Grace Spotted Eagle. I just have a feeling you and she would get along. Now, a lot of people talk about Grace," she said, "but I like her. She really tells it like it is. And it's been a hard road for Grace."

I left Crow Dog's Paradise that day with Leonard Crow Dog. I was driving this great Chief to the Black Hills Gathering where Indian people were coming together for maybe the first time in modern times to communicate with all on the planet about their plight as a race of people and about the planet's plight if we don't clean up our act and stop wasting our natural resources.

When Leonard addressed the Gathering, he said that seventy-eight percent of all of America's resources were on Indian reservation land. When the land had been forced on the Indians as a place to live, the white man did not want it because it was "poor, hard land." Guess why it was so poor and hard: it was full of minerals. Now the government and multinational corporations were wanting to assimilate the Indian and take back this mineral rich land.

At that Black Hills Gathering in Rapid City, South Dakota, I heard John Trudell and most all of the American Indian Movement leaders speak. Dennis Banks, Clyde Bellecourt, Vernon Bellecourt, Russell Means, Bill Means, Ted Means, Larry Anderson, singer Buddy Red Bow, and, of course, Leonard Crow Dog and Wallace Black Elk were there. It was also at this Gathering that I met Grace Spotted Eagle.

After Uncle Leonard spoke and visited with many groups of people, he and I were walking together on a hill above the camp smoking our cigarettes. He talked about many things. With Leonard, I never talked, I just listened. He was the Chief and I was just proud that he let me walk with him.

Somehow, the conversation turned to my not using the Indian name he had given me, not calling myself Thunder. He demanded to know why that was. I stumbled around and finally told him that I just didn't feel worthy. Then I took a deep breath and told him that I thought he had named me that as a joke anyway, because I snored so loud. Leonard got mad at that, really mad. Now we were all alone, standing on a hill on the other side of the Gathering, and out of nowhere a lightning bolt hit the ground twenty feet away. I freaked out. He said, "That's what your name means. Remember that." Now I ask you, Dear Readers, how could I ever forget it?

Then he went on to say, "This boy, my nephew, Buddy Red Bow, he has a song, and *that's* what your name means. You listen to it."

Crow Dog, Thunder, and Lightning Bolt

Leonard left me there, chastized and more than a little stunned by the crack of the lightning bolt and the feeling and smell of electricity in the air. It sure did move me out of my self-consciousness.

Shortly after that I saw Buddy. He was up on a truck trailer singing some songs. Buddy waved, for I had met him before and felt a wonderful connection to him. He sang his song, "Thunder Bird." It is a song about the prophecies and ancient wisdom of Native people. It is about our ancestors:

Thunder Bird

What's that I see
Circling over the Black Hills
Its wings expanded — slowly descending

Every time it opens its eyes
Lightning bolts fill the sky
And the Thunder it is crashing
It can be heard

It's a Thunder Bird
It's a Thunder Bird

Could this be the legend
My grandfather told me
When I was just a young boy
When I was only seven
Grandson, some day
When the dark moon
Covers the sun
And the Thunder Bird
Comes after you
Do not run

You're going to ride
On a Thunder Bird
You're gonna soar
On a Thunder Bird

Like my ancestors before me
I will take the journey
Back to the other world
Where I will be
Forever free
I'm gonna fly
Oh so high
I'm going back
To never die

I'm going to ride
On a Thunder Bird
I'm going to soar
On a Thunder Bird

Dennis Banks, Horse, Thunder, and Sundance Chief Buddy Red Bow after performing Thunder and Horse's wedding held at Big Indian, New York in 1989. Buddy is wearing Grandpa Fools Crows Eagle Bonnet.

As Buddy sang, I saw a vision from the Spirit. I saw a council of Elders — not Indian, not like any Elders I had ever seen before — in the space right above his head. They were smiling. This was my first encounter with my true home and Elders. I have now seen this vision many more times in my life, and the Elders are always smiling. They are always there to help me. From that time, Buddy and I became even closer friends. He told me that he was my brother and I just swelled with pride when he called me his sister. In April of 1993, Buddy passed into the Spirit World, but many times he and I talked about the story of this vision behind him and the Thunder Bird. He felt that these were ancestors from another place, Space Ancestors.

Buddy recorded that song on his tape, *Journey to the Spirit World*. Whenever I feel afraid or unsure of myself, I listen to it and think of the day with Leonard and Buddy and feel proud that I walk with this name, Thunder. And I thank you, Leonard Crow Dog, Buddy Red Bow, and Grandpa Fools Crow for bringing me back to my Mother and for the vision of my true heritage and Elders.

Crystal clear enlightenment — nothing does it like a lightning bolt!

Meeting Grace Spotted Eagle

It was a very hot day at the Black Hills Gathering. There were hundreds of people, and my head was spinning from all the information. My heart hurt, too; I seemed to be picking up all the pain of the people.

Leonard had gone one way, and Richard, my son, was off talking and playing with boys his age. He was so happy. I could see his genetic memory opening. I had always imagined him as a warrior, and that day I saw his true warrior spirit unfolding.

As he walked off and I found myself standing alone in the blazing heat, up popped one of my worst fears, being all alone right in the middle of Indian territory. I quickly walked to the nearest speaker for safety.

I stopped to listen to a magnificent, towering man with a great big hat. He looked ten feet tall. He was talking about the mysteries of the universe, the stars, and planets, and Mother Earth. I listened to him in awe and thought how beautiful he was.

Grandma Grace sitting with Eagle Fan

A lot of people were sitting on the ground, real close to him, absorbing every word he was saying. He kept talking and talking. My legs were beginning to ache and I felt hot and sick and tired and very heavy. It seemed too much effort even to sit at that point. I looked around, and an old lady sitting on a blanket, way in the back, caught my attention. I had a very strong impulse to go and see if this old woman needed some water or something, because the sun was so hot and she looked so alone on her blanket.

I walked that way, hesitated, and finally approached the blanket. Before I could say hi, she snapped, "What do you want?" A little confused by her angry, black stare, I told her that I didn't want anything, that I had just wondered if she wanted a drink of water. In a very loud voice she replied, "IT'S ABOUT TIME SOMEBODY THOUGHT ABOUT ME. I WANT A CUP OF COFFEE." Well, of course, the water stand was in view, but the coffee stand was about two miles away. I took off for coffee.

By the time I got to the coffee stand, I was so hot that I thought I would melt right on the spot. I got her a cup of black coffee. Half crazed from heat, I walked all the way back and gave it to her. She looked up, hateful, and said, "WHERE'S MY CREAM? YOU KNOW I DRINK CREAM IN MY COFFEE." I stood there looking at her, and then breathed deeply. Her expression was unchanging. I said, "Okay," and walked all the way back to the coffee stand. I got her another cup of coffee, this time with cream, *lots* of cream. I also got her another cup of coffee with not so much cream, to cover all my bases.

I took them back to her, through the two miles of heat and dust. My head was splitting with pain and sometimes my vision blurred. I could have sworn that little flames were shooting out from my body. I walked past that wonderful old man sharing the secrets of the universe with his rapt crowd. Why did I ever look around, I wondered. The old lady glared at me as I handed her the cups. "DOES IT HAVE SUGAR?" she demanded. As I stood there sweating, crumpled, and on the verge of heat stroke, I realized that I was pissed. Really pissed. In fact, I hated this little old lady.

Now she had three cups of coffee sitting in front of her, and none of them were right. I went back again. Not only did I hate this little old lady, I hated the coffee, I hated the cream and sugar, I even hated the blanket she was sitting on. However, I knew instinctively that I had to get rid of those feelings before I got the coffee or she wouldn't drink that cup either. I got her one cup with just sugar and another with just cream. And a spoon. I got her a donut, too, and anything else they had there that she conceivably might want.

I went back, past the beautiful old man who was still talking about the meaning of life, the destiny of the human race, and all those things I was really interested in. She was still sitting there. She put together her perfect cups of coffee, two spoons of sugar and quite a bit of cream, and drank them all down. I began to think I could finally escape. I said, "Here you are. I brought you a donut," — I knew it was fry bread, but my brain was gone — and got ready to make my break. "YOU ARE SO STUPID. THAT'S FRY BREAD," she snarled. Without breaking stride, she announced that she had to go to the bathroom and I needed to take her. Guess where the bathrooms were. Next to the coffee stand.

By then, I was so tired that I gave up any hope of sanity. I picked up all the coffee cups, and then she ordered me to clean up any litter that anybody else had left around and to carry her blanket. She marched off, and I staggered along behind her in procession. She went to the bathroom, then we trudged all the way back, past the old man still telling everyone else all the wonders that I longed to hear. No chance of stopping there. After she had me put the blanket down again, I just stood there, not knowing what to do. After another prolonged glare, she demanded, "Aren't you going to sit down? You are just *so* stupid!"

I did *not* want to sit by this little old lady. I never wanted to see this old lady again in my life. She must have read my thoughts, because she suddenly barked, "SIT DOWN!" I did.

She started talking and talking about the old man who was speaking and how no one ever paid any attention to her. I wanted to scream, "Just look at all the attention you got from me!" She went on in this way for fifteen or twenty minutes. Then she stopped and, looking closely at me as though she were reading my soul, she said, "You know, I need a daughter. I really like you." I thought, "Oh my God, please. This is *not* funny, Tunkashila. I don't *like* this little old lady."

By then, it had been many an hour since I had innocently offered to get this lady some water. The old man was still talking, and now half the people were asleep in the sun. She finally asked me my name. It was one of the few times ever I gave my whole Indian name to anyone. She then told me how people could take my whole name and use it as medicine against me. I asked her what her name was. She answered, "Grace Spotted Eagle. That is my real Indian name. No one gave it to me except my mother!"

She took out a cigarette and waited. It took me a few seconds to realize that she wanted a light. Wonder, my husband at the time, had just bought me a beautiful beaded lighter. As I started to light her cigarette with this lighter, she waved her hand at me like an Empress. She snatched the lighter from my hand, lit her own cigarette, and dropped the lighter right into her purse. This was the start of a trail of hundreds of beaded lighters over the years dropped into the bottomless pit of her purse, never to be seen again by my eyes. She loved it. God knows I tried to hide them anytime we were to see each other, but somehow by the end of every visit she would have my prize lighter in her purse.

Later that afternoon she said to me, "You're a very special soul. You have been sent to this planet for a specific purpose and will someday be a magnificent teacher. Now you and I have come together, and I am going to help you to get ready to do your work." Bless her heart, I remembered thinking, the heat has gotten to her. I looked at her as if she was crazy, and then I just knew my ass was grass. All of a sudden, I remembered something. I told her that I had just been over to Leonard Crow Dog's and his wife had told me that I should meet Grace Spotted Eagle. Grandma Grace said, "She and I get along, but Leonard and I don't." She told me that it was the women who started up Wounded Knee II, and that she and Leonard's wife had dodged bullets there together. She told me that she was with Leonard's wife when her son, Pedro, was born.

We spent a good part of the day sitting there and talking. All of a sudden, the lecture was over and that giant, towering man that I had so much wanted to listen to made his way through the crowd to Grandma Grace's blanket. It was then that I met Wallace Black Elk for the very first time and found out that Grace Spotted Eagle was his half-side (*i.e.* partner or spouse).

By then, it was quite late. Richard and I had to get back to camp and get ready to head home to Indianapolis. My son ran up to be introduced to Grace and Wallace. Grandma told Richard to call them Grandma and Grandpa, for that was who they would be to him from then on. As she looked at me and then at Richard, she said that she and Grandpa would be my Spiritual Parents and Richard's Spiritual Grandparents.

We hugged. If my natural parents had led me a merry chase, I had a feeling I hadn't seen anything yet. Grandma gave me her address and phone number and took mine. I walked away from that blanket dazed, exhilarated, confused, and awed.

Yep, I would say it had been one big day, that day in South Dakota.

Grandpa Wallace Black Elk

"Next tell them about my greatest speech, the one I made to the United Nations. Just think, me talking on the satellite for eleven whole minutes. They all loved it — well, the reporters did anyway!"

Grandmother Grace Spotted Eagle

3

✦ ✧ ✦

GRANDMA'S GREATEST SPEECH

Grandma Grace always seemed to be in the background at any gathering. Wallace Black Elk always took center stage.

It became one of my passions in life to try to get Grandma some time to speak. Not that Grandpa did not wish her to speak, but the sponsors seemed to want to hear only him. But every time she did speak before the people, those that heard her were awestruck. Living her life in the shadows, dancing with her pain, I don't believe she ever realized how magnificent she was as a speaker and how much hope she shared, especially with other women, when she spoke out.

My adopted sister and good friend, Nancy Moore from San Marcos, Texas, tells of the time she went to a World Conference of Women where Grace was scheduled to speak. Buddhist and Native American Elder women had come together to share their wisdom and concerns. Nancy said that a hush fell on the room as the men who had come with Grandma Grace cleared a large space to set up their drum. Grandma Grace was so small in stature that you hardly noticed when she took her place on stage with the other Elders. Each in turn, the woman Elders shared their stories — except Grandma Grace. Wallace spoke instead, even though all the women were wanting to hear Grace. Nancy watched Grace's little foot tapping as the frustration mounted throughout the room. Then the conference was over.

Nancy knew that Grace would not be there the next day, so she took a breath, climbed up on the stage, and asked Grandma to share her heart for all the other women. We had not heard one word from her. Grandma looked down and said that Grandpa had said everything that she had wanted to say. Nancy knew in her heart that the women were aching to hear more from Grace, but there was no time and she kept insisting Grandpa had said it all. I later explained to Nancy that

Grandma Grace at the United Nations

Grandma rarely spoke. Usually she just sat beside Grandpa while he did the talking.

What follows is what Grandma felt was her greatest contribution to the world by way of a speech. It is her eleven-minute address to the United Nations in which, for the first time, she not only got to say everything she wanted to say, but got it sent by satellite all around the world. I'll bet I heard about this speech hundreds of times during our time together, but I never heard or saw it until after Grandma had passed on, when a friend and student obtained a video copy from the National Congress of Records. It is a powerful presentation in which she asked women from all races to come together to stand up for their world. It was transcribed word for word by Pat Cross, my sister from Little Rock, Arkansas. As Pat said, "It was one of the hardest jobs I ever had to do because I couldn't quit crying."

Grandma's Talk to the U.N., Early 1980s

And my name is in Lakota Language, my name is *Wamblee Gelishka,* and that translates by English to Spotted Eagle, so Spotted Eagle is my name. And I've been here for the last few days and I've been waiting to say something all that time. And I keep all kinds of things bottled up inside me that I want to tell the U.N., the United Nations people, that they don't include us at all, so it seems to me like we're not of the United Nations, but we do own this Country. Even the white nation don't believe that is really true. Whether they like it or not, we own this Country.

We were here first, so in that line I will talk about [how] I was raised by Catholic people. And I love to hear their ABC and 123, which we never had, so I use their ABC. They always tell me about B.C., Before Christ, so I use their alphabet to come up with one of my own way too. I come up with B.C., Before Columbus. We had a good life here, you know, all these people. I used to look back over time and think about my people. They were so poor. They only lived in a tepee that's made out of buffalo skins, and they must be so cold in all this weather, and sometimes we have blizzards. And I think about my great-great-grandmother and wonder how they went through all this hardship.

I used to think this way because that's how I was told by the Catholic people. They used to make me denounce our own way, but now, today, I could compare. You know, it's a good thing I went there so I can be brainwashed into Christianity at the same time I could realize my old way of worship is very important, too.

We had our own way here, but they stomped us down for the last two hundred years or so, and it seems to me like we have to stay in the background and not say a word. We're good Indians, but once we get up and say something we're bad Indians, militants and all that, radicals and everything.

But today I look around and I'm supposed to be a savage. You know, it seems to me like today I don't know who the savage is. Look at all the things we have today, like my people had nothing, and he just mentioned we didn't have no gas. We didn't have no electricity, even no beds or pillows or nothing. We just slept on the ground, you know, and we were so stupid, ignorant, and pagans. That's what they used to call us, you know, and I look back at my people and I used to cry, thinking about how hard they had it in this western hemisphere before the white people came. And then, now today, I think about my people, and I want to say this: They're the smartest people that ever lived here in this western hemisphere because they lived without electricity, gas, or money. They didn't have no money, where they could go to a supermarket and buy anything.

So this is what I want to tell the white nation: that they could live without all the things we have today. All the things that you have today are so dangerous. Look at just what happened a while ago. You could read it in all the newspapers. Some of them died over there, gave their lives because of peace, which is not really peace that they take over there. You can't have peace with a gun over some people's heads, and that's the reason these people were killed, because they carry guns. Talk about peace at the same time they carry guns over other people's heads.

And so I would say to the U.S. government, I wish he'd have the common sense, you know, to bring those boys back over here. They have no business over there in the first place. The U.S. government sticks his nose everywhere and gets all our people in trouble. Some of our people are killed over there in war, First War, Second War, Korean war, and Vietnam. And we don't like that anymore. And we don't like this nuclear bomb that they're making right now. I just wonder sometimes if this government has a heart, you know, a mind and body and soul which he could use as common sense and think about his children, his grandchildren, and the unborn that are coming.

What is the matter with this United States not to think about his own kind, the persons that he calls minority: minority whites, minority blacks, minority yellows, minority red. What I said, one time, let's all us minority people get together and we will be a majority, for the people, by the people. If that's true, I want to find out. I want to find out if he does represent us, or is he holding us by the nose and make us jump around. That's like the kind of Government we have today.

And I would love to talk to that Reagan. Sometimes human beings, sitting down, talk about peace on earth and good will towards men, which has never been accomplished in this world at all. I hear about it all over the streets in Denver. I hear about peace on Earth, good will towards men, when Jesus Christ is born every year. Then we have, like I said one time, then we have people that live, colorful people, all kinds of colors live in colorful Colorado.

And we have this thing there called nuclear bomb there in the same vein, and we have Rocky Flats, and we have all kinds of dangerous things around us. And I said us people sitting here in Denver, Colorado, we're sitting ducks. And that's what we are all over this Country. We have a shadow of fear above our heads at all times because we have Christianity here. We have civilized people that don't think with common sense. That's what I've been wanting to say all the time that I've come to this place. I hear everybody talking about energy. Well, I'm energized right now, and I want to tell that government they're going wrong. They better, for once in their lives, listen to the people that own this country.

And I will say that these people that own this country, the Red People, the Red Nation, as one family, we don't have no arms against the Germans or the Russians, we only have some little arrow that they took away from us. So we don't have no arms against anybody. And we own this Country, and I think they better look back and say this people don't have no arms against anybody. So we shouldn't have wars at all. That's what I wanted to say to the United Nations.

And sometimes they say, the way you talk, you speak your mind, maybe some day the government will arrest you. I said, "Okay. I'll go to jail and convince all the policemen there. I'll get all the people that are incarcerated there to come back in a human way and fight for what's ours here." That's what I wanted to say. I keep everything bottled up inside me and I could just bust.

Today I went up into my room and I just sat there, and I started to cry, because I wasn't on any place, but I said as a woman I'm going to put in my two cents worth as to how this world should be run. And that's what I want to beg my white sisters, my black sisters, my yellow sisters, my red sisters, to let us women get together, because the men are not doing so good. I hope that someday a woman will be President of the United States. She will love her son and her daughter so much that she will not declare war. That's my prayer all this time.

I said that one time with women's liberation, but I will tell you again that women's liberation is going wrong because of birth control and abortions. They're killing our children, that they went wrong.

So I am saying to you white women, get together in a spiritual way. Come to our way of worship, which is not a religion. It is not organized like a church. You know, you have Bishops, Cardinals, and Secretaries in government. Well, we don't have that. This way of worship is our way of *life,* and the only direction we have is the Great Spirit. And He in turn cannot have no assistant directors, no treasurers, and no secretaries. That's who I speak for, and I said I speak for the Great Spirit. I'm going to be vicious about it. I'm going to be mean about it, and I'm going to tell them they better pray, because that's the only Person we need right now. We don't need no alcohol. We don't need no guns on His sacred altar.

That's what I tell the United States government. They're going too far. You know, they make all these lies, all these reservations, stuff my people in there in those concentration camps, and they never listen to us. But I beg them today to listen to me. Think about the lives that died, those Marines. Bring them back over here. Don't be sticking your nose where it doesn't belong. We want to live. We're talking about the Tree of Knowledge that they have that twists their minds, the Sun that we pray to. They take the atom from there and do destructive things.

And then I read in the newspaper, two people were talking, one of them was Anderson, and I forget the other one. And they said the Indian people don't care about energy at all, all they care about is shooting a couple of deer. They're nothing but mentally retarded children. But I will say today, I wonder who is the real mentally retarded children. That's what I want to say. I've been keeping that inside me all this time. And this white America stands there shooting at a human image. At least I shoot at deer to eat, not human beings.

Long ago, my people lived here without the CIA or the BIA or the FBI. We have our Chiefs and they are the smartest people. They are the overseers of our people and see that they have enough to eat, see that they have water, see that they have fire to keep our blood warm. That fire is sacred. I will tell you right now, United Nations, that fire is sacred, and you're playing around with it, and you're going to get burned. I hope that you come to realize that. I hope that these people here, the news people sitting here, are my eyes and my ears and will be a go-between and tell you that for me. I think of you that way, all of the news people, the press people. I want them to be our eyes and our ears.

Give a message to the United States government. Have them listen to us once in a while. For all those years that they have been here, they never asked if we liked these laws or not. They just placed laws and laws on top of our head and make us suffer. United States laws make people into criminals. That's what I said. If I go and eat one cattle of his, I will be charged "rustler" because I go there to eat, just like my Spotted Eagles come down to eat cows and they shoot them. Well, I'm not going to tell them they have a United States emblem as an Eagle, and they better take care of my Eagle.

So I beg my white sisters to take this message for me, please. *(She is crying now very hard on the tape.)* Excuse me, but that's the way I feel. I really feel for these people. I'm not going to judge or cast them aside. I want my little white brothers to come to our way of worship, to come to the Spiritual part of this world. The Spiritual part is the Great Spirit. He gave us everything. He provides everything for us. Nothing is man-made. Man-made alcohol and guns don't belong here on this sacred altar.

That's what I want to say. Help us. Help us to give a message to him so he will try to understand us. I hope that the next president will come out and talk to us, get his guidance from the Spirit.

That's what I want to say. I don't want to take up that much of your time. If I went over, I'm sorry. Thank you very much, I'm glad to be here.

The videotape showed Grandma finishing her speech and sobbing and wiping her eyes, while all the news and camera people crowded around her and hugged and comforted her. She may not have been a hit with the U.N. officials, but she sure was with the real people!

Dahyana Yahoo, Grandpa Wallace & Grandma Grace in a chapel at the Cathedral of St. John the Divine

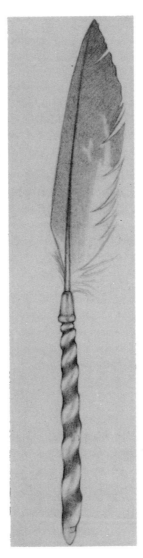

Thunder's Eagle feather

"We are taught that it is the Elders, the babies, and the children who have the greatest access to the Ancestors and the Spirit. The babies have just come from the Spirit world and so are fresh from the Great Mystery, while the Elders, nearing death, are heading back into it. There is much wisdom we can learn from both."Grandma paused, then continued, "Tell them about some of the lessons that I have taught you. You did learn something didn't you?"

I answered, "Yes, Grandma, you have taught me a lot."

"Yes, you silly, I sure have had fun teaching you. Actually, I have always known that you loved me and I want you to hear that I love you," she said, sitting back and smoking her cigarette. "You know I quit smoking, don't you." She went on, "Oh yes, I taught you everything, especially how to live, for I want you to live and to help others to live, too!"

Grandmother Grace Spotted Eagle

4

GRANDMA'S TEACHINGS

Grandma's Flowers

Over the years, the road led me many times to Denver, Colorado, to the little house that Grandma and Grandpa shared. What I had planned as a one-hour stopover on my way to Sundance or to a gathering usually became a four-day marathon of helping them get ready for a trip, move rocks, or whatever else they needed done. On these visits, from time to time, Grandma would gift me with small gifts, like the pair of earrings she had beaded as Grandpa Wallace talked in an Ashram. "Beaded in this holy place," she would say, "so the energy would be just right for you."

I always tried to have something special to give them. It is our way to honor our Elders. I got in the habit of arriving with the prettiest bouquet of flowers I could find for Grandma. As she took them, she would bawl me out for killing the flowers and ripping them out of the Earth where they belonged — how could I be so stupid. Then she'd arrange them in careful and perfect balance and set them in the middle of the table with a smile in her eyes. She always gave me this mixed message.

Any time that I showed up without flowers, her first question was, "How come you come in empty-handed?" Finally I asked her if she liked the bouquets of flowers. She told me that, although her heart felt happier when she drove by houses and saw flowers growing in the yard, just as nature meant them, she did enjoy receiving the flowers from me as a token of my love. After all, I was just saving them from the wanton cuts of the florist who did not even know the flowers had a life also. Then she always said, "People are like a bouquet of flowers: all colors together, pretty, getting along, all working together to create Beauty." I'll bet I heard her say that a thousand times.

As I have walked my path, I have found that the seven colors unify all the nations of the Great Spirit, past, present, future. We are children of the seven senses, seven chakras, seven rays. All nations of the world, from the beginning, have had the rainbow as our natural flag. All blood is the same color, the color of living fire.

As Grandma arranged the flowers, time after time, she always repeated that she wished that all people would get along just like a bouquet of flowers.

Blessed by Wamblee Gelishka

On one of these visits, when I was at a point of total exhaustion after helping Grandma get together a bunch of stuff for their next trip, she told me, "Sit down." She began to speak, saying that a long time ago, if a person had two Eagle feathers with the same markings, that person would hold onto those feathers for the time when a bonding between two humans needed to take place. A mother might give a feather to a daughter, a father to a son, a mother to a son, a father to a daughter, a man to his wife, or a wife to her husband. Then she took out two very beautiful, identical Spotted Eagle feathers. She said that she had planned to give one to her daughter, but her baby had died soon after birth. Now she was going to gift a feather to me.

Grandma said that sharing this feather meant that she loved me, that she was old and unable to fly on her own, and needed me to help her out. She said it was only when we joined hands and hearts that either of us could enjoy the soaring flight of the Eagle. Being physically together is not always possible or necessary when love is shared by two people. Love transcends all time and space. "Wherever I am," she said, "whatever I am doing, I will always be with you. As long as you have this feather in your possession, it will protect you from harm and will comfort you in loneliness. My spirit has been transferred from my body to your feather, and your spirit from your body to my feather. As long as either of us lives, we pledge ourselves to one another in time of need. Only burning the feather will break the bonds between us."

I still carry my feather on a staff that Grandpa Wallace carved for me that goes with me everywhere. Grandma had lost her daughter at birth and I had lost my mother when I was three weeks old. Now, in spirit, we were each other's missing pieces.

*Grandma Grace, Sparky, and Thunder in 1986 at
Grace's Mother's Give Away in Colorado*

Singing with Grandma

As I journey through this life on this road, many people ask me if I understand and speak Lakota. I smile and reply, "I understand it a little. I sing the spiritual songs in Lakota and I also understand them in English. But I do not speak Lakota." I have seen many Elders offended by non-Lakota people speaking fluent Lakota. I vowed early on not to become one of them, although I am part Indian. I have seen some people on the street speak Lakota better than some of my Lakota brothers and sisters. If I spoke fluent Lakota, it just wouldn't be me.

Learning to sing the songs took a long time. I traveled on the road with Wallace and Grace as one of their singers. I was first taught ceremonial songs by the Crow Dog family. I was even gifted with and allowed to sing a special song by Grandma Mary Crow Dog, Uncle Leonard's mother. Every singer puts his or her heart and soul into

Grandma playing drum and Grandpa singing with Thunder on the road in 1984

expressing a song. This can result in slightly different words, a different beat, perhaps a whole different interpretation. That's why learning the songs exactly as you are taught them is of utmost importance.

Now, having sung aloud only with Leonard's family and the Black Elk road crew, I was in for a major growth experience. Grandma Grace had her *own* way, handed down from the Spotted Eagle family. She was a marvelous singer and everyone loved to hear her sing. Saying, "I am singing these songs just like my father and grandfather taught them to me," she would hit the drum and start the song that would transport me through time and space. Even now, I can close my eyes and hear her singing and drumming. Those were happy days for me.

In the early days, as I began to sing with her, I always kept my voice less loud than hers as a mark of respect. Not knowing exactly how she would sing some of the songs, my inclination was to be very quiet. Unfortunately, you cannot always sing Lakota spiritual songs quietly.

As my cue to sing louder, Grandma would punch upwards into my ribs as I stood close beside or behind her. If I was singing one song and she was singing another, she hit me in the stomach with the drumstick.

I knew I was in trouble if she had me kneel down beside her at the drum. That was where she wanted me for a final refinement of the song. That's when the old drumstick would connect to either the right or left side of my head. Grandma and I soon sang perfectly together.

Sometimes, when Grandpa made a speech and went on a little longer than expected, Grandma (who often went to sleep) would wake up, grab the drum and start pounding on it. Grandpa wouldn't miss a beat in his speech, but at the end of the next sentence would say, "I think it's time now to take a break." One time when this happened, I too had fallen asleep, and when Grandma started pounding on the drum, I started singing the Four Directions Song very loudly in front of 400 people. It struck Grandma and Grandpa as funny and they started to sing also, just to cover up how stupid I was. For months afterwards, it was a running joke.

I learned a lot of my songs at the knees of those beautiful Elders. It was not just a matter of listening to a tape. It took many years. The sacred songs resonate to the Spirit with a certain vibration or energy and, unless you understand all aspects of the songs and why you sing them, they could cause harm. There is nothing more dangerous than opening the gates to the Spirit with a song and not knowing how to close them. Only the Elders know when you are ready to sing.

I learned lots of amazing things singing the songs. I found singing to be a really important aspect of following the Pipe, whether in the Sweat Lodge or the Sundance. If nothing else, the songs taught me what was going on.

After my first year of Sundancing, I was instructed by Grandma and other Old Ones to go out and share the Pipe with the people. Grandma Grace was worried because I would need a singer of my own. At the time, it was just my friend and student, Sparky Shooting Star, and I making up my road crew. After an adventure traipsing across Florida, Grandma and Grandpa woke us up one morning at four-thirty dressed in their ceremonial clothes. They wanted to make me a tape of Lakota songs so Sparky could learn them and sing for me in ceremony. I was in awe that they would sacrifice for me by getting up so early to make this tape. I cried all the way through the hours they sat there singing the sacred songs. I still have the tape and play it every once in a while just to hear their voices.

Today, I rarely sing out loud because there are so many beautiful singers around me and the songs now live in my heart! My sons Johnny and Richard, my husband Horse, students Sparky Shooting Star, Debbie Bonniwell, Augusta Ogden, Mike Hull, and Jimmy Schulman, and many more raise their voices to the Spirits' praise. Many of these people also were taught by Grandma. Often, when I pour water in the Sweat Lodge and one of these people is singing, no matter how beautifully, I still hear Grandma Grace's voice. And if I'm singing too and miss a beat, I still duck.

Grandma's Tobacco Ties

"Tobacco is the chief of the four sacred herbs to the Lakota," she would say. The other three are sage, which is used to cleanse the energies; cedar, to cleanse the Spirits; and sweet grass, which is braided like the hair of our Earth Mother and used to let the Creator know we are praying. Tobacco is used when we pray to honor the Spirit. When we pray with tobacco, we put the energy of our prayer into the physical world. One of the ways that we pray with tobacco is to make tobacco or prayer ties. We pray and wrap little pinches of tobacco in small squares of fabric, which we then tie closed, one tie after another, until a whole string of tobacco ties holds all our prayers together.

Grandma Grace had a very specific way of making tobacco ties. She got the most use and least waste from her material. Material was very precious to her. She felt very strongly about doing the spirit work of prayers in this way. She and I spent many hours together in the sacred space, praying and making "Little Prayer People" or "Spirits," as she would call them, according to "original instructions" from Grandpa Wallace, her own family's Old Ones, and the Spirit.

When making tobacco ties, Grandma always made these suggestions, which, to me, weren't just suggestions, but the way to pray: "Clear your mind of thoughts. Get in a prayerful state. Every tie should be a prayer. Be careful what you pray for. Know your own personal motives for a prayer, because this is your connection to the Spirit world. Live your prayers. Your actions speak louder than words." She also taught me to pray for the people before myself: first for the Elders and the children; then for others; next, for my family; and last, for myself. And she always reminded me, "Never add to or take from the original instructions from the Elders about the way of the Pipe and your Prayers."

I have included on pages 48 and 49 the steps for making tobacco ties, as taught to me by Grandma Grace.

In 1988, right after a New Years Eve celebration in Chicago, we went to Colorado and helped Grandpa clean out all of Grandma's things. She had been adamant about not wanting anyone snooping around in her "poor things" and laughing at her after she passed on. We took her mattress and burned it. Of course I had to look for all those beaded lighters that had disappeared into her bag. Grandpa told me that when she took a lighter from me, she usually gifted someone special soon after, telling them a whole story about how she had gotten the lighter from me and how I had not wanted to give it up.

Among her things, there were many little dresses that she had worn to the Sweat Lodge. I just could not throw them away. I asked Grandpa if I could keep the dresses and he gave them to me. Some beautiful friends from Houston — Kathleen Koerner, Kim McSherry, Lois Metcalf, Vicki Ghost Horse, and Jan Sims — and I sewed bags from the materials of her little Sweat Lodge dresses. On each bag, we sewed Grandma's Eagle (an Eagle getting ready to land) and Grandpa's Eagle (a beautiful Bald Eagle Head). At the Ashland Oregon Sundance, in 1988, those bags, filled with Grandma's instructions for making prayer ties, little squares of material, string, tobacco, and scissors, were gifted to the Sundancers. They were kits from Grandma, to help people make their prayers. At the Dance where a lot of people were dancing so her spirit would have a good journey, Grandpa and I gifted these beautiful bags to all.

Grandma's Pipe Advice

> *With all the flowery rhetoric that passes for enlightenment, truth is usually very simple*

It was only much later on down the road that I really understood many of my lessons.

Grandma Grace Spotted Eagle's Method of Making Tobacco Ties as Described by Mary Elizabeth Thunder

Grandma Grace Spotted Eagle had a very specific way of making her tobacco ties. She got the most use and the least waste from her material. Material was very precious. She felt very strongly about doing the Spirit work of prayers in this way. She and I have spent many hours together in the sacred space, praying and making "little prayer people" or "Spirits." As she would say, these are the original instructions from Grandpa, her Elders and the Spirit. Hope this helps you with your prayers. Some added suggestions are: clear your mind of thoughts; get in a prayerful state; every tie should be a prayer; be careful what you pray for; know your motives because this is your connection with and prayers to the Spirit World; act and live with your prayers.

Materials needed: Fabric: Red   = North
                                    Yellow = East
                                    Black   = West
                                    White   = South
                                    (100 percent cotton: ¼-½ yard each)
                          Cord: #12 heavy string (100% cotton)
                       Tobacco: Bugler or American Spirit (additive free)
                       Scissors

Directions:
  1. Lay material out salvage to salvage (one yard=36")
  2. Cut a strip 1½" (1¼") wide. (Strip is now 1¼" x 36")
  3. Fold in two, fold in four, fold in eight (i.e., half it, quarter it, then eighth it).
  4. Cut in 3 (three) pieces.
  5. You will now have 24 squares, each 1¼" x 1¼".
  6. Cord (#12 heavy string) should be the length of the blanket if ties are being prepared for Vision Quest (perhaps 74" long).
  7. Ties should be spaced 1" (one inch) apart on cord.
  8. If ties are being made for Vision Quest, you need 101 for each direction:
  9. If you have a pipe, you need 250 red ties to put around the altar on the blanket for the pipe.

NORTH
(Red)

SKY	WEST		EAST	EARTH
(Blue)	(Black)		(Yellow)	(Green)

SOUTH
(White)

  10. In your prayers, put other people first: Elders, then children, then your family, then yourself.
  11. Never add to or take from original instructions from Elders about the Way of the Pipe.
  12. Actions speak louder than words.

Tobacco Ties

Take material (100% cotton), salvage to salvage (edges) 36″ length of yard. Strip 1¼″ wide. Fold in two. Then fold in four. Then fold in eight. Cut in three pieces.

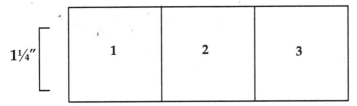

Each piece should be 1¼″ square. 24 squares per strip.

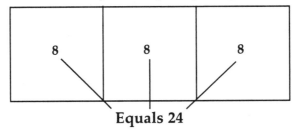

Equals 24

The string should be length of blanket. If doing Vision Quest, perhaps 74″ wide. Ties should be tied 1 inch apart.

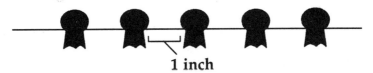

1 inch

Ties for Vision Quest are 101 for each direction, plus one of your choice. 405 total: for all the nations, winged ones, creepy crawleys, four-leggeds and those that swim in water.

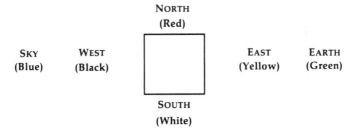

	NORTH (Red)	
SKY (Blue) WEST (Black)		EAST (Yellow) EARTH (Green)
	SOUTH (White)	

If you have a pipe, you should make 250 red ties to put around your altar for the pipe on the blanket.

Thunder's daughter Beth and son Richard

When I left my old life to share the teachings of the Pipe with the people, I was given many instructions by my Elders. Uncle Leonard Crow Dog said, "Follow the Pipe and hold it like a baby. Teach what you most need to learn." Another teacher said, "Be in service and watch the Hawks for messages." Grandpa Wallace Black Elk said, "Walk behind the Pipe — never beside it, or in front of it — and pray with the Pipe so that the People will live." Grandma Grace Spotted Eagle said, "Be sure to make your bed every morning."

I'd been walking, following, holding gently, and learning for several years before, on a spring morning at Rudi's Big Indian Ashram in New York, I finally learned the wisdom of Grandma's advice.

I was making my bed that morning and one of our students, Linda Saxton, a teacher of Eastern spiritual disciplines, told me how making my bed proved that I was a humble Spiritual Master. I leapt over the bed to sit on its edge all in one move — pretty good for a chunky gal. I had waited a long time to hear this one, but I tried to remain calm as I asked Linda to explain. She told me that Swami Rudrananda, "Rudi," taught that if you did not have your physical act together, if, for example you could not make your own bed or keep your own space and personal life clear of dirt and clutter, then you shouldn't waste your time — and his — studying spiritual disciplines.

Spirituality is a *total* way of living. Much of my training in the "secret" medicine ways has been from washing dishes and cleaning house so that Spiritual Light could impregnate the home and living space and enhance ceremonial energies. Order in your personal life reflects out to the world around you. Getting your thoughts orderly, clean, and impeccably pure is the first step. If you can't keep the bed you sleep in well made, perhaps someday you will suffocate in your own mess. Thank you, Grandma. You are still walking with me! Thank you, Linda. Thank you, Rudi.

Grandma's Dress

From the North comes the wisdom,
the compassion, the inner peace and knowing.
Our elders are examples of this.

In 1985, a wonderful group of people in Indianapolis put on a gathering called Celebration of the Sacred Earth People. Grandma and Grandpa, Wonder, Charles Lawrence, David Bratcher, and I were among the featured speakers.

Grandma was always very sensitive when working with people, and she always seemed to have a problem with those she called "fancy-dressed white women, who know the Indian way better than I." She always felt that other women were trying to take Grandpa from her. So it was always my thought and prayer to walk a step behind Grandma, in honor and respect, and never to outdress her. Being a poor woman, she never had any fancy clothes or special Indian dresses to wear out in public. She usually dressed in slacks and a blouse with a sweater. In those days, when I was traveling around with Grandma and Grandpa, I wore blue jeans, cowboy boots, a t-shirt, and a blue jean jacket. I wanted Grandma to be the one that people looked at, so I was never fancy or flashy. I had beautiful clothes that she and another Elder had hand-stitched for me, but I never wore them. One of my beloved Elders from Indiana often made me outfits, praying over every stitch of the blouses and long skirts she created and painted with beautiful designs.

At this particular gathering, one of the committee leaders, Denise Diegs, gifted me with a very beautiful long skirt and blouse she had sewn using one of my old dresses as a pattern. I asked her if she would make another outfit for Grandma and called the Elder who had made so many of my other dresses to ask her if she would paint on the dresses for Grandma and me. Denise and the Elder got busy and created two of the most beautiful outfits I had ever seen.

On the first night of the gathering, I presented Grandma Grace with her dress. She didn't seem excited at all. She barely looked at it, but just folded it and put it aside. I felt heartbroken that she didn't like it. And if she wouldn't wear her dress, I couldn't wear mine! I often wonder what Denise and the Elder felt.

I carried a resentment about the dresses around with me for a long time, but I never talked to Grandma about it. In 1987, Grandma told me that soon she was going to pass on. As she explained her wishes for the ceremony of putting her body away, she told me that she would be buried in the dress I had given her, and that's why she had not worn it before. She called it her Rainbow Dress. She wanted to be buried with my love.

Sometimes we can only see things as they really are after time has passed. What I thought was rudeness turned out to be the greatest of honors.

Grandma's Praise

> *It seems the elders*
> *can look into your heart and mind*
> *and offer the lesson*
> *that will ultimately change your life*
> *and bring you closer*
> *to walking within the spirit.*

In 1986, my beautiful adopted daughter asked me to perform her wedding. Since I always go to the Elders with any new request for the sharing of spiritual energy, I called Grandma and Grandpa on the phone to ask what they thought, and if perhaps Grandpa could come down to do the wedding.

Unfortunately, I got Grandma first. She spent an hour-and-a-half lecturing me on just who do I think I am to be thinking about marrying people. I am a woman, and women don't do that.

Then she handed the phone to Grandpa, who spent another hour telling me exactly how to do the ceremony and that, as a Sundancer, minister, and counselor of these ways, it was one of my spiritual duties.

I hung up the phone, totally confused, and then called them right back. Grandma answered again. This time she told me that Grandpa had told her that I was going to do a wedding, so she would make and send me the shawl I would need for the ceremony.

When I asked her what had happened to change her mind, she said, "Oh, I still don't think you're worthy of marrying anyone, but if Wallace thinks you are, I'm going to help you out."

I did perform the wedding of Doug and Linda Hamdorf, and it was a truly remarkable happening. During the ceremony, it thundered, and lightning veered off in all four directions. After the ceremony was over and all the people had a chance to get into the house for the reception, it rained quite a downpour. At the end of the storm, three rainbows appeared outside the front door, overlooking Lake Superior. I figured the Spirit, with me assisting, had done okay.

When I told Grandma about this great happening, she said, "I bet you think you did that. Well, you didn't. The Spirit did. And that's that."

Thunder (with broken foot) giving a lecture before the beginning of Sundance, 1988

Remembering that it is Spirit who does the work has been the cornerstone of my life, working wonders to keep me out of my ego.

About Being a Medicine Woman

Late one night, Grandma talked to me about the energy of the body, what others call *chi*. She took her hands and formed a ball of energy that shined very brightly in the dark. She placed it in my hands so I could feel its raw, body energy. Mystified, I handed her back the ball. Then she took the ball and placed it on my chest so its energy would enter my heart and heal the places that she said hurt so bad. But her story to the public was that she was *not* a medicine woman, that you could not be a medicine woman until you could grow plants out of your body like Mother Earth. According to Grandma, Mother Earth was the only true Medicine Woman.

But to me and to a lot of others Grandma was a great medicine woman.

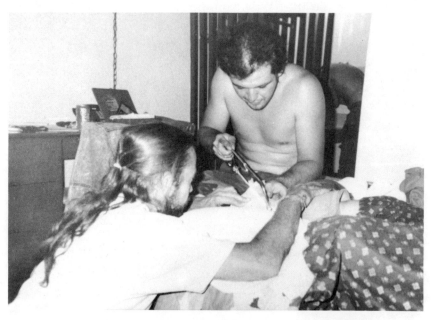

Warriors, Butch "Buffalo Horse" Hennigan & son Richard Grimes, after the dance in 1988, cutting the cast off of Thunder's leg

Medicine Woman

"Well, be sure you tell them that you knew the Spirit even before you came back to this way of life. You could tell them that we found you and helped you in these Indian ways to relearn of yourself and your own Spirit connection. But make sure you tell them that you were already special and that no one person can take credit for 'giving you a Spirit . . .' What you know is beyond this Indian way. You are more universal, accepting of all ways. Yep, tell them about the Spirit you knew when you were young, and also tell them about you trying to commit suicide. That's important for women to know . . ."

Grandmother Grace Spotted Eagle

5

I Knew the Spirit When I Was Young and the Spirit Took Care of Me

Spirit Friends

I spent most of my young life alone. I always seemed to be afraid, afraid of the dark, of my father, my step-mother, my foster parents, and even of going to sleep at night. But I always had my Spirit friends.

When I was small, I used to think that there was a monster or great big snake under the bed, so I would take a quick peek and then call in my great big White Wolf Dog. One day, I overheard an Aunt saying to some other people, "Do you think Mary is okay? She is always talking to make-believe friends and animals. Should we do something for her?" I took a quick look to my left, and there sat the Wolf, and then I looked back at the room full of people, and I realized that they could not see her. That was when I first knew that I was seeing things that others could not. From then on, I was more careful about sharing what I saw. I just took silent solace in having my Spirit friends around me.

One of my favorites was a Spirit Horse who lived in the basement. I would go down and visit him and feed him, and sometimes we would go on Spirit journeys at night, riding the plains and letting the wind blow through my hair. I had whole tea parties and games with my Spirit friends.

Every week in the second grade, we had Show and Tell. I loved it. I would tell stories that, to me, were absolutely true. I shared things I saw the Spirits do at my home, or messages that had been told to me by the Spirits, like what the teacher was thinking, or about how we all should go to a small grocery near school because they had a lot of newspapers that we needed for our newspaper drive — and they did!

Without fail, the teacher would get mad. She would tell me to take my chair and go to the boiler room. What she didn't know was that my step-mother's Uncle Cedric worked down there, and he would bring me funny books and candy. This went on for two or three months or more.

Then one day the teacher called my parents. I knew I was in trouble then. First, my parents came into school. Next, they called in a school psychologist. My little inner self told me I was in big trouble. As I walked into the school psychologist's office, I decided I had to tell my Spirit friends goodbye. I still remember how they looked as they faded away from me. I cried, wiped my tears, and headed into the office, somehow knowing life would be very different from then on.

Although I felt that I could not continue to play with the Spirits, they never really left me. Several times, when I was still very young, they told me I would not die, that it all was going to be okay. I remember telling them that I didn't think I had chosen this planet. There had to be a mistake, because I didn't seem to fit into life here. Even at the time, young as I was, I realized my thoughts would be considered strange and that I must tell no one I had them. The Spirits just smiled in a loving way. I did not understand.

Church

I always loved church. Going to church was my escape from life at home on Sundays. I would go to as many churches as I could —Baptist, Nazarene, Lutheran, Catholic — any church that was close to my parents' home. I have gotten saved and baptized many times, for I loved Jesus and knew that He loved me. I also loved Mother Mary and spent hours sitting beneath her statues anywhere I could find them. I also loved to go to church because I could see the Spirits and angels and beautiful lights there. Once I got into trouble for going up to take sacrament/communion. I wanted to take communion because there seemed to be a Spirit standing with the minister and I wanted to be blessed by the minister and the Spirit. The church fathers and mothers went to my home and questioned my parents about my taking communion when they weren't officially "saved" members of the church. I did not get in trouble with my parents for lying to the church to take communion, but I did get in trouble for bringing those holy rollers into our home. Even today, on the road, when the going gets tough for me, I (the tough) go to church. I have stopped at many a church on many road journeys to help calm my distraught soul.

Nature

Although life was unpredictable and violent as I grew up, my dad and I found common ground in Nature. I loved to walk through the woods by his side, imagining myself an Indian princess or a great warrior. He and my grandfather were master hunters, and though I was a poor excuse for a son, they took me hunting with them. By the time I was eight or nine, I was carrying a gun with them into the forests of Indiana. They trained me to track all kinds of animals, large and small. I learned how to listen to the stories the woods and animals were telling us. I learned to watch how the leaves go up when the rains are about to come, and about how my awareness of the way I came into an area was the key to finding my way out.

I skinned many a rabbit and deer in those days and carried thousands of birds and small game for my father. My dad, part Cheyenne and Mohawk, knew instinctively those old ways. He never left a kill behind and hunted only what we needed. The only animals I ever killed were a fox and a wild dog, because I loved animals so much. But

Thunder and Dad, hunting

I knew that if I had to, I could feed my family by hunting and killing game.

One time we found a mother raccoon who had been shot, killed, and left to rot. All her little baby raccoons were around her. We were very upset. We buried the mother and collected all the babies in a box to take to an animal shelter. The babies were wild. Papaw, my grandfather, warned me that grown ones could kill a shepherd dog quickly and easily, so not to be deceived by their cuteness. They had very sharp teeth and claws. When Dad and Papaw were not looking, I stuck one in my shirt. Later in the car, it squealed and they bawled me out, but then they laughed and said, "Well, I guess he's yours." Little Bandit stayed with me for years as my best friend.

Gift of the Snakes

Another time when we went hunting, I got separated from Papaw. It was spring and the ground was wet. All of a sudden, a copperhead snake struck at me. It was shedding, and when a copperhead is shedding, it will strike at anything. I was wearing blue jeans and long johns and, as the snake struck, it got caught in my clothes and just kept biting. For the first time, I heard Spirit speak to me very clearly, "Don't look down, don't get scared, just call your Papaw." I called Papaw over and over again very calmly. He was a little irritated because he could not see anything wrong with me until he got right to me. Then he started to cry. He took out his knife and cut a huge gash clear across my left knee to release the poison. I passed out and became violently ill and delirious for four days. Today I still carry the scar from Pawpaw's cut.

Snakes became my worst fear. The last time I walked through the woods with Papaw, I saw and killed seven snakes. I bet I have sent more snakes to the Spirit World than St. Patrick of Ireland did. I could smell them, feel them, and taste them. My hands would swell when I was near one.

Years later, an Elder told me that when I had passed out, I had gone on a shamanic journey to the Spirit World. He said I had gone through an initiation and become a sister to the snakes. I remember thinking, "Oh God, that is the worst thing I have ever heard." The old man said that the snakes came to me to give me messages, and he wanted to do a thank you ceremony to them to help me out. I remember thinking, "Oh God, this is the second worst thing I have ever heard of."

It took a while, but I did start feeling guilty about all the snakes I had killed on their way to give me a message. I had a funny vision of a teacher snake before a classroom of student snakes saying, "Who wishes to take this message to Mary?" All the snakes shook their heads no. Then one poor snake was chosen, a kamikaze snake sacrifice. This sacred snake came and tried his best to give me a message. Then I killed the messenger.

The Elder said I would have to go through a ceremony with a snake to see if the snake nation had accepted my apology.

Elders don't mess around. In about two or three hours, I started noticing a lot of people gathering from who knows where. Since I did not understand Lakota, I had no idea what they had in mind except, when they called to me, my blood suddenly ran cold and I started to sweat bullets.

I waited with several other people in a tepee as a rattlesnake was brought in a bag. As it was dumped out, my heart dropped, because it looked very mad. Then the drums started and I was told to calm all my emotions. The snake would be thrust into my face. If it bit me, then I would fail the test and die. If it did not, I would live and have power to communicate with the snake nation. A tear rolled down my cheek. I had not asked for this ceremony. How could they do this to me? Then I surrendered, breathed, and started to pray.

After about an hour of singing and praying, the old man picked up the snake, which had been curled in front of him, and he quickly thrust it right up to my face. I saw its eyes looking into mine and then saw no more, for I was taken by Spirit to another dimension. I guess I passed the test, for it did not bite me.

Even today, at a Vision Quest or other ceremony in places where there are lots of snakes, I talk to them and tell them human beings will be walking there and, because human beings are afraid, they might hurt the snakes. Our camp never seems to have any trouble with snakes.

An Attempted Suicide

There came a time in my life, after the birth of my three children, when nothing seemed to be going right and I was running out of solutions. It seemed, among other things, that my husband had found

Bob Green and daughter

another woman. We had lost our house, and I was really fat and really depressed. One day, after listening to my father yelling at me about how no good I was and then finding a note from a girl to my husband, I decided to commit suicide.

I had thought about suicide many times before and this time I was ready to return to the Great Mystery. I was not any good for anyone. I put the children to bed, kissed them goodbye, and cried a lot. To complete my preparations, I wrote notes saying goodbye and that I was sorry, but I just could not live anymore. Then I took a whole bottle of aspirin. It just hurt too bad to live any longer.

As I lay down on the couch and began to drift away, I heard one of my children wake up and cry out for me. I still can't say which one it was. Somehow I realized that I was in trouble, that I had to take care of my children, and that I wanted to live. I called the hospital. While I was still on the phone — in an altered state — I saw my door bowing from someone's pounding on it. The police barged in. I hardly remember the trip to the hospital.

Bob Green, Angel of Light

Later, I will tell you about an eleven-year-old boy who found me on a very messy pillow after I had been left by my mother for over eight days at three weeks old. The little boy's name was Bob Green.

Throughout my childhood, Bob and I were together a lot, since both his father and my grandfather were sheriffs. There used to be a dirt race track where midget Indy race cars ran every Saturday night on 16th

Street right across from the fabulous Indianapolis 500-mile track. Bob and I would go to work with Papaw and hang out in the pits with midget car drivers and mechanics. My Nanny had many pictures of me in race cars as a little girl. Those were fun days. Nanny would pack a picnic lunch, Papaw would work at the track, and I would go adventuring with Bob Green. I thought of him as my older brother.

I had not seen Bob for years, except to tell him I was married, and once to show off my kids to him and his mom and dad.

But the night I tried to kill myself, Bob, now a police major, heard the call over his radio, and entered my life again.

As soon as I reached the hospital, I was put in the prison section. I lay there terrified until Bob walked in. He sat on the side of the bed and hugged me. Then we talked and talked. He told me that, because of my political background and connections with the city, he was having me taken upon release to a psychologist instead of to jail, to avoid embarrassing the city fathers.

At this point, dear Readers, I feel a need to finish my story of Bob Green. He and I remained close until his last days. Again and again, he entered my life as a wonderful big brother.

Thunder, Grandfather and race car driver, Dick Fraizer at the "Old Indy 500" in the 1940s

Once, while I was at home cooking dinner and taking care of baby Beth, I received a call that Daddy was shooting at Wonder. I got the neighbor's wife to watch my baby and asked her husband to drive me to within a block of my parents' home. My neighbor had heart trouble and I knew what the scene would look like. To someone not brought up in a dysfunctional family, some of the scenes could just scare his/her pants off; while to those of us who have grown up in total chaos, nothing is unusual.

As I ran that last block, worried about my husband and baby boy, I saw lights flashing and police car after police car pulling up in front of Mom and Dad's house. In the driveway was our cherry red Mustang. I looked into the driver's window as I approached the house and saw that the key was broken off in the ignition. Dad had done this once before. Policemen were everywhere. As I walked into the house, I heard my father telling the police officers that I was a prostitute working the streets. My father had been subdued by the officers, but, as I walked in, he somehow got free, grabbed a rifle from a place the police had not checked, and began to hit me with its butt end. I fought for my son's life and my own as well. The police restored order and told me they were taking my son to Juvenile Court until they were sure of the truth.

Then in walked Bob Green. He took Richard out of the policeman's arms, put him in mine, and told me to get out. I was running down the driveway just as a wrecker hitched up our Mustang. Wonder came out from hiding and we both jumped in the wrecker to be driven home.

It seems that Dad had been really drunk, and when Wonder had come from work to pick up baby Richard, an argument began. Dad started shooting at Wonder, and Wonder ran away. When he thought he was safe, he circled back and got in the car to drive away. That's when he found that the key had been broken off. Dad shot at him again. Until the day we traded that car, it carried two bullet holes on the driver's side, just above the front windshield.

My life was crazy chaos. At the time, I had no concept of my own part in this situation, of how I was addicted to the emotions of the drama, to being the victim and the martyr, nor did I have any idea about how I could break the pattern. All I could see was that life did not make sense and I felt trapped. One moment I was at home, very much in love with my husband, cooking a good dinner, watching my

Thunder and Richard G. Lugar, Mayor of Indianapolis

baby girl sleep; fifteen minutes later, my dad was hitting me and calling me a whore, and I was looking at the possibility of my son being taken away from me. If it had not been for Bob Green, I wonder what would have happened.

Like an angel, Bob just kept appearing whenever things looked hopeless.

In later years, I had a job as Secretary to the Board of Public Safety, working closely with the Mayor of Indianapolis. Bob had become Deputy Chief of the Homicide Division of the Indianapolis Police Department. We were best friends and enjoyed many lunches together. When Bob was nominated for Deputy Chief, I felt good that I was in a position to add my good recommendation to his list of many who thought him deserving of the position. He and his beautiful wife Tony adopted seven children. He was a loving father, devoted husband, and he always honored his mother and father, Jake and Gladys Green.

One day, after delivering a message to the police chief, I stopped by the Homicide Department to have my usual chit-chat with Bob. Our conversation started at about three o'clock in the afternoon and at five we sent out for Chinese food. Now, I did not usually spend my work day chit chatting, but I felt something ominous hovering around him and I suddenly felt concerned. I called my boss and asked if I might have some free time to talk with Bob. During those hours that we sat together, we recounted almost all of our life together. He had been invited to go on a trip to Florida with his brother and a former mayoral candidate to check out a land investment deal. He was very apprehensive. He became more and more scared — terrified — to go. He told me how much he loved his wife Tony and stories about each of his kids. I remember him looking at me and saying, "Don't you ever give up hope, Mary, for you have come a far, far way in this life, and you have a far way to go." I shall never forget leaving Bob that night, telling him how much I loved him and thanking him for all he had done in my life. We hugged, and I was sure I had convinced him not to get on that plane.

After arriving home that night, I still felt apprehensive. I tried to call Bob and Tony. About nine o'clock that evening, a female police officer called and asked that I call the Director of Public Safety and other city officials. She told me that a high-ranking police officer had been killed in an airplane accident. This was the way communications of this sort were handled within the city structure: as Secretary to the Board of Public Safety, it was my duty to inform the members of the Board of Public Safety of any immediate changes or developments that might affect the city's business. My breath stopped within my body and tears started streaming down my face, but keeping my professional voice, I said, "Yes, please give me the information." I knew what was next. She informed me that Police Major Bob Green had been killed in a plane crash just minutes before. I cried for a second, then got on the phone to the city officials to share the message. Bob was so loved by all. It was really a hard message to deliver to his friends.

At the funeral, I found out that he had been so frightened before the plane hit the ground that his hair had turned completely white. I found out that either his brother, Don, who also died in the plane crash, or the other man who had gone on the trip had called Bob at the office and talked him into going after I left. Bob Green saved my life as a little baby. Later in life he probably saved my son's life, as well as my reputation. I wondered if perhaps the white hair that they said came from fear was only to show that he really was an angel!

Remembering back to the ominous cloud that I had seen around Bob when I had visited him earlier that day, it was my first clear understanding of what a forboding of death image looked like.

Now, I take you back to the hospital and Bob telling me to go to a psychologist.

Meeting the Psychologist

I was driven directly from the hospital after my suicide attempt to the home of a very beautiful man, the psychologist. I stayed with him and his wife for three days. I was going to stay longer, but my great-uncle died and I needed to go to the funeral.

I went to the funeral home, and right away the whole family started yelling at me. They said I had no right to show my face at the funeral when it was my father who killed my great-uncle. I was already back in the chaos! But my grandparents quickly put me between them. Later I found out Dad had not really killed Uncle Virge, but they had been drinking together and had gotten into a fight the night of his death. To say the least, I quickly returned to the psychologist's door and asked to stay the rest of the week.

I was in therapy with the psychologist for over three years. One day, upon arriving early for my appointment and seeing my file on his desk, I had to snoop. The file said he did not believe some of the outrageous stories I had told him about my life and family. I was crushed; for the first time I had trusted someone with the story of my life, and he had not believed me. Then I got mad.

When he came into the office that day, I confronted him. He explained that, in his professional opinion, I could not have experienced all that I said I had and still be as sane as I was. I wrote out ten names and telephone numbers and told him to call me to apologize after all of the stories were confirmed. He did make the calls and immediately came to my home to make his apology. From then on, he gifted all my therapy to me. He said that if I had survived all that, then he wanted to learn from me. After about one year of being in therapy, I actually started facilitating one or two of his therapy groups a week. I shall never forget him and feel that this man provided the cornerstone for my healing. I am eternally grateful to him.

It wasn't until fifteen years later that I was able to start understanding and defining how Spirit had been working in my life the whole time. I did see the Spirits and Spirit did take care of me during those times. I think that I have had many "Spirit interventions" in my life, from physical angels, like Bob, or etheric angels that have talked with me. But I think, from some of the stories that I have just shared, it also must be clear that I did not know how to live a happy, healthy life, even with this help and knowledge.

For me, the native ceremonies were what began to define, redefine, and clarify this gift of Spirit sight for me. I began to realize all the stuff that comes with Spirit sight is great, but I feel that one must do a lot of other work — have an inner discipline, live in integrity, and know how to discern good spirits from bad spirits, for example.

Spirit told me in the Sundance one year that we live in a world in which we have to take full responsibility for the creating of our own realities. All the chaos we experience is of our own creation, created by our own thoughts. Now, let's think about this for a moment.

In a private counsel with the Hindu Master Swami Rama, back in the '80s, he redefined this same truth by saying, "Yes, I chose to come into this life, be deserted, have a crazy father, and live in chaos!"

"Why," I asked?

"For growth of the soul. You see, we live in a world and an illusion of our own making," he said, sitting on a deer skin rug on that beautiful autumn day. "Thunder, close your eyes. For just a second, when you re-open your eyes, there is a black "blurry" space. That is the real world. Very soon after your eyes open, the illusion that you have created will reappear. It is as if, every time you look at someone or at a rose in bloom, you discover this person or rose for the first time. You give them life in your world. You expand your reality!"

The idea that I had chosen all that had happened to me in my life, that it had all been in the interests of certain lessons and energy for my growth, and that how I acted or reacted to those choices, energies, or lessons reflected my soul's growth potential was pretty amazing to me.

From the ceremonies and Spirit's sharing, I have learned that I have to stay centered and grounded in awareness of my own emotions before I can live in a state that the Native calls the Flow of the Great Mystery.

Remember, I said I was always afraid. I have learned that fear is a limitation, and that the opposite side of fear is faith. I made some little wooden coins I used to give out to people that say faith on one side and fear on the other. I always carry one in my pocket, and whenever I feel fear, I just flip the coin! I have learned that I have choices and have become a much happier person. This is what the ceremonies have done for me.

I am on a journey of discovering my own patterns of creation. I feel this journey will transform me from a victim to a master of my reality. The lessons set up by Spirit in my life have facilitated transitions in consciousness that have taken me beyond my accustomed levels of awareness.

Once I began my spiritual walk, I moved deeply into the workings of the subconscious mind to create bridges between ordinary consciousness and the sacred dream time of magical existence and power. I've worked hard to get in touch with Spirit, God, and my inner self.

I learned about true introspection, or pulling energy inward to discover the secret and hidden places of our "self wounds," the hidden baggage that no longer serves us, the passion that we have denied, and other parts of ourselves that we have disowned.

Create the Lodge of the higher self. Devour your problems — eat of them, digest them, and transform them so they no longer have dominion over you. Connect the mind with the heart. This is what I have been told to do. This is how I have learned to deal most effectively with my inner spirit and self, how I have come to understand my own life in my effort to know better the Source of All Life.

Thank you, Spirit!

Sparky, Thunder, Grandma, and Grandpa at Sun Bear gathering

"Tell them that story you told me about how you found out you were Indian, or part-Indian."

Grandmother Grace Spotted Eagle

6

✦ ✦ ✦

WHERE DID ALL THIS INDIAN STUFF COME FROM?

The links and pieces that make us whole choose their own form and time to appear. The lessons that change our lives seem to reverberate through both the past and future. I have learned, through many hours spent at my Elders' firesides, that a teaching in the Native American way is not chained to the illusion of time. The Elders tell stories within stories within stories. Just as these threads of tales tie together to create a whole, the lessons and healings we receive are reactivated over and over again in our lives. In fact, that is what healing is: the use of our painful lessons to heal others and thereby heal ourselves. I've heard it said that the word *Shaman* means *injured healer*.

To tell my story, I will borrow from my Elders' way and jump to February 1989. I was in Houston, Texas to address the National Conference of Astrologers from an indigenous perspective. One of my female students, a warm, loving wife and mother, was in major crisis in her relationship with her husband. She had begun to grow within herself while serving the Spirit. Although I had a hectic schedule that day — television interviews, a lecture to the Conference, and a ceremony for the people — I agreed to meet with my student and her husband to try to help them.

I soon realized that before me was a replay of my own life. The man was frozen in indignation and anger. He demanded his way and his rights, without any signs of caring about his wife or children. He said to his wife, "Unless I get my needs met, your lifestyle could change just like *that*!" The man was scared because his wife was growing and changing.

The woman was struggling to make everything okay, to be a "good" wife and mother, but also to find some spiritual enlightenment. She wanted to "fix" the situation, but she was having a hard time dealing with his feelings.

Their postures as they sat on the couch perfectly illustrated their problems: he was stiff and separate; she was slumped and reaching out to offer comfort to him, which he would not accept because he was too involved in "I, I, me, me." He had shut down his emotions out of fear. She, too, was in great pain from fear. They were reflections of each other.

I knew they wouldn't move from that stalemate until one or the other wanted and demanded health. All I could do for them was to share my own story. The man and woman were reflections of each other and of my years with my former husband. I looked at her and saw myself. I breathed and prayed and decided to tell them of the crucial lesson I received so long ago.

The Key to the Past

I hardly could have been less prepared to receive the key that would unlock a big piece of my life than I was on a tear-sodden, dismal Friday in the late sixties as I drove out of Indianapolis. My husband had encouraged me to go to French Lick, Indiana, about 100 miles away, to attend an Astrology Conference. I was pretty sure I knew the true reason he wanted me to leave town: he planned to spend the weekend with another woman.

I was crushed, but this time I decided not to stay home and cry or chase all over town trying to find him. I got a sitter for the kids and took off.

I cried old, old, tears on that drive out of town. I knew in my heart what was happening at home, but I did not want to face it or call him on it because I might lose him and I had three children to raise. So I just kept on driving to that stupid convention.

Then, through the tears, I suddenly had a vision. A friend of mine appeared and showed me the face of the girl my husband was involved with. In the vision, I saw the girl and my husband together.

I pulled off the road and sat there stunned. I wanted to go back and fight, or catch them, or something! I was fat (up to 250 pounds at this point) and scared to go to a new place and be with a lot of people I didn't know who would be talking about a subject that bored me to tears. A woman can tell when a man, her man, is drifting away. It's her choice as to how long she will wallow in the pain.

I turned the key and started driving again. I had made arrangements to stop off in Paoli, Indiana, to pick up my mother-in-law who wanted to come with me. She was a lovely person who seemed happy anywhere. To this day I still remember her dearly. She never really believed in any of the New Age lingo, but she was game to go to the conference, any conference, and have fun.

I was going through all kinds of fears on my journey to pick her up, so I stopped for a Pepsi and prayed that she would not be able to tell that I had been crying, for I did not want to tell her the truth about her grandchildren's father, her son whom she so loved.

Calmed down and more firmly committed to having fun on this New Age adventure, I arrived at her home. We got into the car and hit the road for French Lick.

We finally arrived at the French Lick Sheridan, a grand old hotel that has seen many presidential visits. It flourished in the old days when there was gambling in Southern Indiana. You can feel the memories of horse-drawn carriages and women in beautiful dresses etched in the wood and marble of this hotel. You can still hear the arguments of past passions and glimpse the faded scenes of rage and love.

Mother-in-law in hand, I plunged into the convention. We had arrived very late. As we moved through the darkened corridors to a lecture, I had the feeling that someone was watching me. I glimpsed a tall man with long dark hair in the shadows. He wore blue jeans and a blue jean jacket, and had around him an energy of pride. We went into the lecture, but it passed in a haze, and I had no idea what it was about. I never could understand astrological terms and, besides, my mind was preoccupied.

The next scheduled event was a meditation to be led by a man named David Bratcher. We moved again through the eerie passages of the grand hotel. Again I felt a presence and saw the man watching. There were prickly feelings all over my skin. I decided not to mention it to my mother-in-law, but it seemed very strange to me.

We entered the room where the meditation was to be held. There was a huge dome, the largest unsupported dome in the world at the time, and this dome arched over a pool. My mother-in-law nudged me and said, "Look, Mary. There's that man who has been watching you."

There was the man from the shadows, David Bratcher, leading the meditation. As the meditation progressed, the energy was so high that the dome made cracking sounds, and we all stopped at once and ended the meditation laughing. David seemed completely secure and powerful in that situation, and he laughed very easily. He was a Native American and I could feel his pride in being so.

The next day passed for me in a blur of meetings, pain, and boredom. Wonder had not called and I felt hurt. Wonder's mother was having fun. I was in so much pain that I couldn't even decide which lectures to attend. Every so often during the day I saw David Bratcher, and his eyes were always fixed on me.

A banquet was scheduled, and I decided to go. I met some nice people there. Up at the front of the room was a speakers' table crowded with all the astrology sages. One of the girls nearby pointed at David and said, "Isn't he beautiful?" As I looked up to see to whom she was referring, to my horror, he rose and, looking right at me, approached our table. The women I was sitting with were all just gorgeous. Everyone's mouth gaped when he approached me and began to speak.

"You are Indian. You don't know it. Six months from today you will hear from me again and by then you will know the story. You are a Spirit Interpreter and a prophet and you have much spiritual work to do. We have been in many lives together and will work together again in this one. I love you as my sister. If you need me, call me." He kissed me and gave me his card. His words opened a flood of images for me. Everything seemed to stand still. I kept hearing his words: "You are Indian." The mysteries of my life were caught up in those words, "You are Indian."

Needless to say, the girls at the table were chattering with amazement. I vaguely heard them talking about this man and how he was an Indian from California. As they talked, I seemed to go through a gate someplace else, into my past and future. I was seeing and remembering being an Indian.

The convention ended the next day, and I left for home without seeing David Bratcher again. His words had opened a burning need to know inside me. This was the start of my search for my spiritual heritage.

Back in Indianapolis, the waiting game went on. I actually saw my husband with the woman I had seen in the vision. I desperately tried to be "super-wife" and make it all work. I wanted to be perfect so Wonder would not leave. I kept trying to figure out what I had done wrong so I could make it right. I was working now as a counselor, and my days were busy with my career and with raising my kids. Through it all, however, the light from the opened gate streamed in.

I began to read everything I could get my hands on about American Indians. And I began to question and gently probe for answers from Papaw and Nanny, the only Grandparents I had been raised with, my father's parents.

Every Friday of the week, I took the kids out to their house to go shopping with Nanny at the grocery store. Then I would spend a good evening with them.

Papaw finally took me aside to answer my questions. He told me we had Indian ancestors, Cheyenne and Mohawk. He said he believed that my mother had been part Indian also, as well as being part Irish. He showed me an emblem of my dad's and her legacy to me. It was a beaded headband, blue and red, with red crosses. I held it to my heart.

He told me that this headband had been found inside my crib. He took me to the garage to show me that very crib that since had been painted over, but still had little bumps where they couldn't scrape off the infant's poopoo. Everything inside me cried as Papaw told me how I had been left alone in that crib, with the headband beside me, for eight days, until I was finally discovered and carried out.

Papaw told me that he was part Indian. Suddenly his stories and his love of the wilderness made sense to me. He also warned me to be careful of Indians, because he thought they drank too much and were lazy. I loved him so and felt for his fears, but nothing could now deter me from finding out all I could of my heritage. He told me that I was the only one to have felt his love of "Indianness" and to have loved to hear him tell Indian stories. He talked of how the Miami Indians had walked the very river, the White River, that he and Nanny lived on to that day.

The very next weekend, Wonder took us to a shopping center where we heard a man talk about Native Americans. In the wonderful way the universe has of making connections between past and future, the shopping center was called East Gate. Later, I would many times enter through the East Gate of the Sundance into the Mystery Circle to begin my dance, to learn from the Great Spirit.

Wonder was very supportive of my search, for he also had Native lineage. He and the kids plunged right in with me. We met people who were setting up an Indian center in Indianapolis. Wonder and the boys helped to build that center, and we helped to raise money and obtain materials to create a place where the Indian people could come and learn. My kids learned lessons, heard the Elders talk, made costumes, learned dance steps, and did beading. I met many wonderful people there. It was there that I met the first Elder I would call Teacher. She was and will always be my first teacher, and truly she changed my life and the lives of others with her work.

Our family grew stronger and closer as we shared with others, learning of our Indian heritage. True, many Indian customs and tribes blending together did cause some ego in-fighting, and there was not too much nitty-gritty spiritual work going on, but it was there that I first experienced the sense of community and shared purpose of the Indian way of life. I will always be grateful to the American Indian Council of Indianapolis for that early help in connecting to my roots.

Six months later to the day, David's letter arrived. He was going to be in Evansville, Indiana, lecturing on American Indian Karmic Astrology. Of course, I called and made arrangements to meet him there. To my surprise, Wonder was upset because I wanted to go. He decided that we *all* would go.

We arrived in Evansville. As we walked into the lecture, David came up and embraced me. It felt so good to see him again and, of course, I was full of stories. Wonder became upset and David tried to explain that I was his sister from a past life. Wonder was not handling jealousy very well, and this reaction from him was new and strangely gratifying. He left with the kids. The Karmic Astrology lecture was really interesting. At lunchtime, David and I walked over together to a Chinese restaurant. I told him a little about what had been happening.

For some strange reason, I had never liked Chinese food or restaurants. It had always caused me problems when the high officials of the city or other business lunch partners wanted to eat Chinese food. The gaudy red and gold made me queasy, and I always imagined the food would poison or kill me. I had tried and tried, but I had always gotten sick. I'd gotten to the point where I'd order only a coke, thinking at least they could not mess with that. I never understood those thoughts or why I had such strong reactions.

Once again, I began to get sick. There were lots of people from the conference there, and David and I ended up at different tables, our backs to each other. My head was beginning to swirl. David leaned back and said, "I'm picking up on a past life for us in China. I'll be over in a minute to tell you about it." I just kept getting sicker and sicker. Pretty soon I had to jump up and run out of the restaurant. I became violently ill, throwing up and losing all control of my elimination system, right in front of this Chinese restaurant in ritzy downtown Evansville.

As I was going through this awful cleansing, Wonder and the kids walked up. I had to ride about eighty miles to Macy with my husband and children watching and smelling me in that condition. The kids sure had fun with that one.

Later I called David. He was grateful to hear from me, for he had been worried about me. He told me to be sure to come up early in the morning so he could help me understand what had happened.

Early next morning, we drove back to Evansville, and David offered to do a karmic reading for me. As my daughter Beth was with me, I asked David if he minded if she stayed. He said, "No, in fact I'll have her read my shield for me." Beth proceeded to read his personal Indian shield verbatim. He said, "She is very psychic and is going to be a great teacher some day. Take care of her." David also said that Beth had been with me in many lives.

He explained that the day before he had seen me as an Empress in China. Plots and coups were so common that I was afraid to eat because the food might be poisoned. In fact, I had died from a slow-acting poison. "Yesterday," he explained, "you had all the symptoms of poisoning. That intense cleansing," he said, "cleared the karma of that life." Now I was free to enjoy China. Now I love Chinese food and delight in red and gold silk. Thank you, David, for bringing China back to me.

David went on to say that I had been reborn on this planet to help out humanity. It was hard to understand right then. He felt that I had been one of the original souls to come here to Earth and that I had chosen to come back now to help further the consciousness of man, lifting it up to God. I remember thinking to myself, "Right, sure, boy has he made a mistake." He felt that he and I had had many lives together, and we would write a book together someday.

I left, feeling he had gotten the numbers wrong or confused me with someone else. It was hard for me to accept his words back then in the sixties, feeling as I did and with the responsibilities of three small children, a husband, and a full-time job. He gave me his home address in California as we were leaving and said that if I ever needed him, I should just call out his name on any level and he would hear.

A few months later, I did need him. My husband had left our home to move in with the other woman. I was in complete panic. A psychic named Gracie Manuel, an older lady whom I loved, called me at work one day and said, "You must come straight here. I have an emergency. Don't even go get your kids. Come right here." She made me promise I'd go to her place, but when I got there, she wouldn't answer any of my questions. I just sat there and watched her think. If I tried to get up to go, she made me sit back down. After an hour or so she said, "Okay, now you can go home. There was a lady with a gun, the lady Wonder is seeing. She was coming to kill you. Now go home and write down all of your feelings." She said she had not told me what was threatening to happen because my energies would have gotten involved and brought it about. "Today," she said, "I have saved your life. Now go home and get your life together and save many more, for you are a grand and wonderful soul." I left thinking, if I am so grand of a soul, why does it hurt so much right now?

That day my two boys were staying with my parents in Macy, and Beth was staying with a friend in Indianapolis. Because of the danger of an enraged woman shooting me and because the heat, lights, and water had been turned off (my husband had had them turned off and taken back the deposit moneys), I went by to visit Beth and tell her I'd pick her up the next day. I wanted her to come home with me, for I felt all alone and lost, but I could not chance her precious life.

When I got to the house that night, my neighbor, Charlotte, ran out in great excitement to say that Wonder's girlfriend had been there, and — she knew I would not believe this — she had had a gun. Charlotte had seen it and was afraid for my life. She wanted me to call the police.

Thank God for Gracie Manuel and how she handled those energies that night. She has passed on now, but her memory is always alive in me.

I went home, lit a candle, sat in bed and cried, wrote in my diary, and talked to my dog, Harry. Sometime during the evening I thought about David. I tried to find his number, but with only a candle in the dark, it was a fruitless search. I just sat back in bed and prayed and called out his name. About an hour later, David called. I was amazed, happy, and confused. He talked to me for two hours, and the things he said made a lot of sense.

I did not see or talk with David again until the eighties, but that night he gave me the wish to live again. I will always be grateful. My wish to die had been answered by the lady with the gun. With the intervention of Gracie Manuel and David Bratcher, I had changed that wish into wanting to live. Right on cue, just as my energy changed, my husband returned. He always held over me that I could not make it without him, and I always believed him. I played the same game of trying make it right for over twenty-three years.

I told this story to my troubled friend and her husband to illustrate the great lesson that had come to me at that time. The Universe manifests around us the people and circumstances best suited to bring crucial lessons to our awareness. My husband was used to receiving nourishment from chaotic energy and my pain. I was used to being a victim and a martyr. Because I wanted to change, the Universe manifested David Bratcher, who showed me another way, that I was a person worth supporting and nourishing. Dark and light in balance— the Universal flow. I had been able to change my energy. My husband immediately felt that change on some level and rushed back to try to re-establish the old link, but, for the first time, I really *saw* the co-dependence and negativity and was able to shatter the old pattern. And the keys to my Indian heritage had turned in the lock of my past. Now the future would begin.

I watched my beloved student and her husband sitting on that couch, he in anger, she in fearful dependency, feeding each other's negativity. I felt grateful for that lesson I received so many years ago and to all who participated in it as my teachers. With Spirit's help, the old lesson would bring healing to the children before me. I looked into their eyes and thought, "As she is now, I was then." Every experience we have always circles back around to bring higher levels of understanding.

As I began writing about my student and her husband, my son Richard called to ask for prayers for the family. My daughter had just left the father of her children that night after being hit and knocked unconscious. Here I was in Houston, talking with my student and her husband about their stuff and reliving my own, while Beth, two thousand miles away, was dealing with hers. Always the patterns and cycles.

In the Native American way, it is said that when we heal our own lives, we heal seven generations forward and seven generations back.

The day I wrote this, I called Beth. She said, "Mother, it took you twenty-three years to see the light and demand to be treated like a human being. I have spent six years with a man who has always hit me, and now I want to laugh and feel worthwhile and live a good life."

As I prayed for Beth and my grandchildren, Spirit made sure I remembered: it took me twenty-three years, Beth six years, and maybe Heather Emory and Marissa Er'rin, her daughters and my grand-daughters, won't have to experience the pattern at all.

Today, having finished writing this chapter, I asked my student in Houston to type it for me. I received the finished pages in record time with a note thanking me for letting her type this material and for helping her to learn the lesson and heal her relationship with her husband. I am grateful to be able to share these words. Thank you, Spirit!

Isn't the Universe wonderful? Some twenty years later, circumstances permit me to see, feel, hear, smell, taste, all of the old emotions of one of my original negative patterns.

Through all those years, I never took another astrology class nor attended another astrology convention, and then there I was, about to be a featured speaker at the Houston Astrology Convention.

Now, it's not that I don't believe in astrology, for I truly do. I just can't understand the mathematics of it all. But I have world famous astrologers, like Kim McSherry and Dr. Christopher Benton, to understand all of that stuff for me. This ancient art of stars has been a great teacher for me, but please don't ask me what a Saturn/Neptune conjunction is.

Sacred Medicine Wheel, Big Horn, Wyoming

Grandma slurped her coffee and reached out to hold my hand, "You know that I do love you, don't you."

It was hard for me to speak with the lump already in my throat from her telling me she was going to pass on. Now hearing this, and writing in the dark, I just nodded and smiled.

"When I pass into the Spirit World, then I will be with you in all of the directions, and especially in your heart of hearts. Now, talk about the directions of the hoop of the Great Mystery."

Grandmother Grace Spotted Eagle

7

THE SACRED HOOP

Over the years, I learned from Grandma that Life, the Lakota Sacred Hoop of the Pipe, and the Medicine Wheel are all circles. The Medicine Wheel Circle is a way to look at self and experience in the world. The essence of the Medicine Wheel is movement and change. To walk this earth and pray in this way is to walk and progress around the wheel and experience as many manifestations of human nature as possible. The way to understand the Sacred Hoop is to enter into the Sacred Circle and begin the path of self-exploration that leads to the Primordial Source of all life — God, Creator, or what Grandmother Twylah Nitsch calls "the Within."

In all cultures, three natural cycles are clearly recognized and often compared with each other: The Day; The Lunar Month; The Solar Year. When you put the cycles side by side, this is what you get:

PHASE	DAY	MONTH	TIME OF YEAR
I.	Sunrise	New Moon	Spring
II.	Noon	Waxing Moon	Summer
III.	Sunset	Full Moon	Autumn
IV.	Midnight	Waning Moon	Winter

All this also correlates to the cycles of a lifetime.

East, the Beginning of Our Lives and the Beginning of the Wheel of Life

The time of day is sunrise and the time of year is spring, when the light returns. On the Wheel of Directions, we are born here, in the beginning. The Sun rises in the East. It is the beginning of the day and also the beginning of life.

It is said that the White Buffalo Maiden (the sacred one who brought the Pipe to the People) stands in the East, and so our human symbol is a young girl.

The animal totem for the East is the Eagle and also, many say, the mouse. The Eagle has the ability to see high and far, and the mouse can see what's small and close. As above, so below. It is said of the Eagle that it is the bird that can fly closest to the Great Mystery and take our prayers to Tunkashila, the Source. The Eagle is the Messenger of the Great Mystery. The element of the East is air. The sacred herb is sweet grass, braided like the hair of Mother Earth. It is in the East that we make prayers for Illumination and Enlightenment. Bright golden yellow is the color of the East, Grandma's favorite color, the color of the Sun.

South, the Growing and Learning Time of Our Lives, the Adolescence Time of the Wheel of Life

The time of day is noon, the time of year is summer, when the Sun is most intense and the Moon is waxing. It is a time of increased growth, maximum activity, and learning. The South brings the good things of life, the warm winds of summer, and the growing season.

The Owl flies, the Coyote howls, and the Swan swims. The color is white. This direction represents adolescence, when we look all around us to find our place in the family, community, and world. The South teaches us trust and our relationship to all things with life.

The element is fire, which brings with it the heat of passion and emotions that become our inner barometer. When we learn to trust our emotions, they lead us into right relations with other people and all beings with life.

The sacred herb is Sage, which cleans and purifies. The human representative is an Old Medicine Woman. The words of our prayers should be about Trust, Relationships, Innocence, and Risk. Grandma liked to use snow white sheets for her white prayer ties.

West, the Going Within Space of the Wheel of Life

The time of year is autumn and the time of day is sunset, when the light begins to fade. The Sun sets in the West and brings the end of the day, or the end of life. The West is where we go inside ourselves to meet the teacher within.

In the West, the Horse, Thunderbird, Raven, Dog, and Bear walk. The color is black. The element is Water. This direction represents adulthood, when we take on responsibilities for home and family.

The West teaches introspection. We face the West to learn how to go inside ourselves to find out who we are, what we came here for, and how we do what we came here to do. We go through our fears, face ourselves, and take responsibility for our own lives. Grandma always said that the human representative of the West is a young boy. We can pray for Introspection, finding the teacher within, Intuition, Change, and Contemplation. The sacred herb is Cedar, which clears the Spirit realm.

North, Where We Are Taught Wisdom by the Elders and the Children, the Old Age Time of the Wheel of Life

The time of year is winter and the time of day is midnight, when darkness takes over. North brings the hardships and discomforts of life, the cold winds of winter. North is the place we go to talk with our Elders.

In the North live the Red-tailed Hawk, the Buffalo, White Buffalo, Elk, and Snow Goose. The color is red for the blood of the Ancestors. The element is the Earth. North is the direction of old age, the time when we complete our Earth walk.

The North, like the Elders, teaches us wisdom. The wisdom of the North is of our genetic heritage. We look to our ancestors for guidance and to heal ourselves from unhealthy family patterns. The sacred offering is Tobacco, the Chief medicine plant, which, when offered in prayer, nourishes the Earth Mother. We pray for Wisdom, which Grandma used to say comes from the Elders and Children, who are our representatives here.

The Center, the Space Within

The center of any wheel is always the catalyst for all other parts and aspects of the wheel. It is to the center we go for the learnings from the walk of all four directions. At the center is the Witness Within.

The Above, Our Masculine Representative of the Universe

The Tunkashila, Wakan Tanka is represented here through our sacred Father Sky and Father Sun and the Star Nations. We pray upwards, towards our source of Life, the Fathers and Grandfathers who provide us with the sustenance needed for our growth here on our Mother Earth.

The Below, the Feminine Aspect of Our Universe

Mother Earth is our feminine nature. She is our home, the only one we know. She gives us all we need to survive. She provides us with every medicine for healing. We keep our feet firmly planted on our home, in our physical bodies, our gifts of Life. We chose to come to this Earth plane to learn our lessons of love and growth and to ensure the lives of generations to come.

I have included three charts to help you see and feel the different qualities of each direction.

At the Path of Maximum Service gatherings, I love to ask the large groups to divide into four smaller groups representing the directions, East, South, West, and North, and to create a play or message from each direction. Some great messages have come from these gatherings.

Grandma would always quote the prayer in Old Man Black Elk's book: "Within this sacred pipe you will walk upon the Earth; for the Earth is your Grandmother and Mother, and she is sacred. Every step taken upon her should be as a prayer. All the things of the Universe are joined to you who smoke the pipe all send their voices to Wakan Tanka, the Great Spirit, you pray for and with everything." [Black Elk, *The Sacred Pipe*, 1953]

"Now, remember that the seventh direction in the Sacred Hoop of the Pipe is upward to the Universe, whose color is purple. Through this Pipe, the People are connected to the *Universe* and the Great Mystery forever and always," said Grandma.

There are Seven Circles

Woman is the Vibral Core
  Man is the Prime Protector
Children are the Future
  Aunts & Uncles are the other mothers & fathers
Grandparents are the Prime Teachers
  Community and Clan all together are Wholeness,
The Sacred Hoop

Four Winds

May your path be under the protection of the Four Winds.
  May your path have Strength and Creativity.
May it strengthen your faith, and through it may it strengthen your goals!

The teachings of the Seven Circles and Four Winds are shared with the permission of Grandmother Twylah Hurd Nitsch, Seneca Wolf Clan Teaching Lodge.

Horse doing Morning Meditations by the Medicine Wheel

Path of Maximum Service

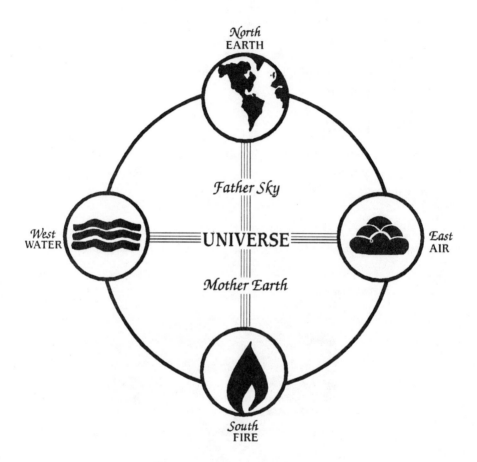

Path of Maximum Service

POWERS OF THE FOUR DIRECTIONS

Color : RED
Animal : WHITE BUFFALO
ELK, SNOW GOOSE
Element : EARTH
Person : OLD MEDICINE MAN
Sacred
Offering : TOBACCO
Pray for : WISDOM IN OUR WAY,
WISDOM CAN COME
FROM ELDERS & CHILDREN

Color : BLACK
Animal : BEAR, HORSE
THUNDERBIRD
Element : WATER
Person : YOUNG BOY
Sacred
Offering : CEDAR
Pray for : INTROSPECTION,
GETTING TO
TEACHER WITHIN
INTUITION, CHANGE

Color : SUN-YELLOW
Animal : EAGLE, MOUSE
Element : AIR
Person : YOUNG GIRL
(WHITE BUFFALO
CALF WOMAN)
Sacred
Offering: SWEET GRASS
(Hair of Mother
Earth Braided)
Pray for: ILLUMINATION,
ENLIGHTENMENT

Color : WHITE
Animal : COYOTE, SWAN
Element : FIRE
Person : OLD MEDICINE
WOMAN
Sacred
Offering : SAGE
Pray for : TRUST, RELATIONSHIP
INNOCENCE, RISK

Path of Maximum Service

SELF-ACCEPTANCE MISTAKES WHEEL

**LEARNING FROM
OUR MISTAKES**
Contemplation
Integration
Old Age

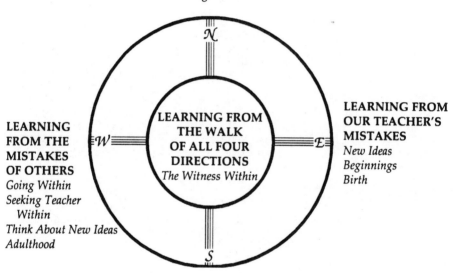

**LEARNING
FROM THE
MISTAKES
OF OTHERS**
Going Within
Seeking Teacher
Within
Think About New Ideas
Adulthood

**LEARNING FROM
THE WALK
OF ALL FOUR
DIRECTIONS**
The Witness Within

**LEARNING FROM
OUR TEACHER'S
MISTAKES**
New Ideas
Beginnings
Birth

**WILLINGNESS TO MAKE
AS MANY MISTAKES
AS NECESSARY
TO GROW AND LEARN**
Doing — Action
Doing the New Idea
Adolescence

Medicine Wheel at Thunder Horse Ranch

"Tell them about your childhood and your life growing up," Grandma said.

"Oh, Grandma, I don't think so."

"Of course! People need to see where you have been
to really see just how far you have come! You know
that I was raised up Catholic." she said. "If I spoke
my own language, they made me scrub the floor on
my knees with a toothbrush. That's why I have weak
knees today. They made me pray to plastic and plas-
ter-of-paris statues and I did not want to, but I never
forgot my language and I never put God in those
statues!"

Grandmother Grace Spotted Eagle

8

THE EARLY YEARS

Dear Readers,

This chapter contains my remembrances of a not-so-happy or functional childhood and early married life. I want to make it clear that the purpose of this book is not autobiographical in the classical sense; I share these stories for the sole purpose of demonstrating how the events of one's life are not random, but hold crucial lessons for spiritual development. It is important to remember, as you read this chapter, that I am not writing it to make anyone wrong. Instead I wish to illustrate that while during the early years, I did not know any better and felt myself a victim, later I learned that I had *chosen* to share the energy of my love and service in a way that fed the chaos around me, so that then I could try to "fix" it. Later, I came to believe that everything that had happened in my life had happened as a lesson. From that time on, I felt lighter and better. When I stopped judging others and let them live their own choices in life, and began to focus my love and service on the Creator, I was able to move out of the victim or martyr role. I began to honor everything that happens in my life as a *gift*, an opportunity for spiritual problem solving. If I create it and manifest it in my reality, it is to learn its *lesson*.

When I began to see that everything in my world is of my own creation, and that everyone is showing me a piece of myself to handle in whatever way I choose, I began to forgive, love, and celebrate my own father, mother, step-mother, and ex-husband, and to see that all the other people in those early experiences were reflections of *myself*.

A psychic once told me that my father had sacrificed his own joy in this life to present me with the opportunity of becoming an impeccable teacher of the fact that we choose our emotions. I saw my father as a living example of what I didn't want to be, and so I strove to live my life as his opposite. If he drank, I was involved in recovery. If he hated

Thunder, Dad and brother

blacks, I worked for the Civil Rights Movement. If he hated women, I became a spokesperson for women's rights. His prejudices were my loves. His prejudices gave me the desire to remain open and work for the rights of all people, no matter their race, party, or sex. I walked through the streets with Mayor Richard G. Lugar and Dr. Martin Luther King during a race riot in Indianapolis. I have been able to meet and talk with every president and presidential candidate since Eisenhower. Yes, my father was an impeccable teacher. Everything that he hated, I chose to investigate and decide about for myself.

I can now look back on the experiences of my early life that, at the time, had made no sense to me and see them as amazing training. Now when people come to me in trouble, I can draw on those experiences and hold their hands and perhaps say something to give them insight to help heal their lives.

I am now able to salute the example in my life of the ultimate Warrior, my father, whom I honor for putting me through his own personal school of Spiritual Warrior Training. I have learned one thing: whatever situation life throws me into, I can and will always survive. Right now, there are a lot of other folks who, after surviving a dysfunctional background, feel that same strength. At a time when the whole planet's survival is at stake, I don't think that is a bad asset to have.

The great east Indian swami, Swami Rama, once said to me that it was not my destiny to sit on a blanket and meditate. He said that I had chosen the path of action. I believe I am a warrior of action. To me, the journey to God is merely the reawakening of the knowledge that we already hold deep inside of us, but have forgotten. This is the time of remembering what we really are, forever. Our image of God is what we are becoming at each and every moment.

My Birth

I was born Mary Elizabeth Crickmore in June, 1944, in Indianapolis, Indiana, during a thunder and lightning storm. In the world's time, it was less than two weeks after D-Day. It was a desperate era of struggle and death, but there was a sense of new hope as well. Many years later, Hugh Lynn Cayce (Edgar Cayce's son) told me that many "original souls" had reincarnated during that time to help the planet avoid creating a third World War that could possibly end the planet's life as we knew it. He called us "zone people."

I really don't think that is too far off, since my heart prayers are and have always been for Peace — Peace in the World, Peace in my Family, and Peace in my Heart. In 1991, on the Cattaraugus Indian Reservation at the Wolf Song I gathering, Grandmother Twylah Nitsch named me a Peace Elder. I can't share how that made me feel, except to say it was the return of an old knowing or memory. In 1992, we held Wolf Song II at our ranch in West Point, Texas, where "many relations" helped create the beginning of the teaching lodge and passageway for over seventy Elders from all over the world to come together in joy and celebration to talk about Peace.

In 1993, I journeyed to Australia as the representative for both Grandmother Twylah and Grandmother Kitty at Wolf Song III, which was attended by 200 Peace Elders from all over the world, with 150 representatives of different Aboriginal ("Original People") tribes. On the return flight from this most auspicious gathering, we had a layover in Hawaii. This was the first time I had ever been to Hawaii and I wanted to pray at Pearl Harbor. A cousin of one of my Warriors picked us up at the Hotel and drove us to Pearl Harbor on the way to the airport that last morning. There were many flowers and offerings there, and I thought to myself that, even after so long a time, many people had not forgotten.

On the plane, as I read the paper, I realized it was Veteran's Day. It was good to see the flowers and the remembering of the 2,400 of our men and women who were lost at Pearl Harbor. It was a fitting way to end my long journey as Peace Elder at Wolf Song III.

I like Peace now, but, as you will see, in my early years I would not have known Peace if it came up and bit me. I was truly a most troubled soul.

I heard stories of my early life from my beloved grandparents, Ernest and Mary Crickmore. My dad was overseas in the Navy. My birth mother became the great mystery of my youth. She was described to me by my grandparents as a no-good whore and an alcoholic. I never knew her as I was growing up.

When I was three weeks, she supposedly got amnesia and just left. I stayed in a crib for eight days, alone. This story was later told to me by Bob Green who had been our eleven-year-old neighbor. The story goes that he kept hearing a baby crying somewhere downstairs and told his dad and mom. As the cries got quieter and lower, they became more worried, and finally they broke down the door and found me. Bob carried me out on a pillow covered with poopoo. Because my dad was still in the service, they took me to my grandparents. I don't know how I survived those eight days, except by my intense will to live.

Apparently there had been another little boy at the apartment who had tried to feed me, but hadn't really known how; I carried a scar on my arm for years from the burn of a hot bottle. This boy was my half-brother, Danny; but it would be many years before I learned he existed and we met again.

Early Life

My early life remains a confusing set of tales and, at this point, I have resigned myself to never really knowing the truth of it all. Sometimes I lived with my grandparents, sometimes with my Dad, and sometimes in foster homes or with other relatives. I dearly loved my grandparents, Nanny and Papaw, and felt safe with them. Yet I loved my Dad, too, and longed to be with him.

It seemed there was always chaos and confusion. One time, when my dad came to get me, Papaw shot at him with a gun. Dad came in, fought him, and grabbed me. We left in an old car, with Dad shot through his hand and bleeding all over the car and me. There was always a fight going on, and I always felt I was to blame for it. And then there was the unspoken thing, the mystery.

I had many visions of my mother. She was beautiful and carefree and wore a blue checkered dress. I always saw her that way. But I was not allowed to talk about her, and it was many years before I was able to find out some truths. One Christmas, I saw Nanny burn a big beautiful doll, almost as tall as I was. Years later, I found out that the doll had been a gift from my mother. At least once she had tried to contact me.

While I was still very young, my dad remarried. My stepmother, Mumsey, is the only mother I've ever known. I love her so very much. She was thrilled when anyone said we looked alike. She did the best she could, yet chaos continued to rule. My Dad was violent, resentful, and a full-blown alcoholic.

Family

In remembering my early days with Papaw, who loved to tell me Indian stories, and my Dad, who taught me how to hunt, I realize I was raised more in old traditional Indian ways than white.

The details about my dysfunctional life matter less than the awareness I have now of the patterns that I learned then — the great lessons, or "opportunities for growth," as crises are sometimes called. I honor my father for his tough love and the lessons he provided. He was my greatest teacher.

During grade school I was smart, but my grades never reflected it. I went from one school to another, a different school almost every year, returning only to the school in Lawrence, Indiana, for parts of two years when I stayed with my grandparents.

In high school, although I was barely passing most subjects and flunking algebra, I scored 171 on an IQ test, the second highest out of 2000 kids. They called me in and bawled me out for under-achieving. I hated that school. Everybody fought and there were frequent riots. The next year, I moved to Warren Central, where I graduated in the upper third of my class and served as representative for the Heart Board and secretary for several organizations. My grades were great, because I was happy at Warren Central.

It was during my junior year, in a class called Family Relations, that the Universe brought me the first clue to my mother's family. One of the cutest girls I had ever seen — short, dimpled, with a beautiful big smile — came up to me and said, "Are you Mary Crickmore?" "Yes," I answered. She said, "I am your cousin Barbara."

She told me that my mother, Gladys, had told her about me. I was stunned and so very happy. I got a beating at home for talking to her, but I had to know more. She said that my mother was an artist, sensitive and beautiful, and that she had always missed me. She told me good stories of my mother's parents, the Grandma and Grandpa I had never met. She also told me that my mother had once sent me a big beautiful doll for Christmas. It sounded just like the doll Nanny had burned.

Barbara told me my mother had drawn pictures of me at different ages. I wondered, had she been watching me? How had she known what I looked like? Had my father gone to see her? I had a thousand questions, but I never got the answers I needed, because Barb soon graduated and went off into married life, and we lost contact. I missed her, and the hollow place inside me ached even more. I really wanted to see my mother, but where was she? Sometimes, just remembering my cousin Barbara's face was the world to me.

Dating

I began to date in secret a boy named Mike, and even planned to marry him. Then one day he was killed in a fiery car wreck. My already bruised heart was broken. After some healing time, along came the next love of my life, Willard. For some unimaginable reason, Dad and Mumsey seemed to like Willard. Once they even went to the drive-in with us.

Another time, though, as I was leaving for a date with Willard, Dad turned on me. In a rage, he fired a gun. The bullet flew right past my head, into a plastic red cardinal bird. Reeling from the shock and almost deafened by the noise of the gun, I watched in amazement as Mumsey rushed in and screamed, "Richard! You broke my bird!" I realized I better get out quick, so I ran out the front door and dove into the bushes, just as my date was driving up. I was not the best date that night.

Nearing graduation, I qualified for a college scholarship; but Dad's view of me and college was that it was just a place where I would have sex with as many guys as I could. So I turned down the scholarship and got a job at Hook's Drugs. I had worked at different jobs from the age of fifteen. My grandfather was a judge and Dad was a Constable, so I had also done paper work in the courts.

In 1962, I graduated from high school in the top third of my class and got a full-time job in the Marion County Clerk's Office typing jury rosters for the judges. I could type up to one hundred and twenty words per minute. After work, I attended college at Indiana University Indianapolis Extension, and then I worked at Hook's Drugs until seven o'clock the next morning. There was no time for sleep or dating, although I weighed 115 pounds and was looking good. Through the pain of losing Mike in a car crash, not being able to go full-time to college, and living in an alcoholic home, I worked continually day and night; but somehow I was happy, because I was creating my own freedom.

Marriage

In 1963, I met and fell in love with Wonder. Not long after we first met, he and Dad got into a fight. Apparently, Wonder had called my father "Daddyo," a phrase popular at the time, but not with my Dad, who promptly threw the love of my life out the front window. Wonder needed some twenty-three stitches over his right eye. I decided he would be the hero to save me. I moved out of my Dad's house and Wonder and I were immediately married by a Justice of the Peace. I did love him so. Interestingly we were married twenty-three years. I've often wondered about the parallel between the twenty-three stitches and the twenty-three years, and who was saving whom.

My First Child

In 1964, I became pregnant with our first child, Richard Earl. What a change came over my life! For the first time, I felt responsible for another life. The miracle of creation was at work inside of me and I felt I would no longer be alone. I ate good food, did not smoke, and really took care of myself.

But then the pattern of turmoil reasserted itself. I was terrified to be pregnant and my family was still crazy. My weight shot to over 200 pounds. I felt no support from my parents, and my husband was given to calling me "chocolate chubs" and "balloon woman." The pregnancy had become a struggle, and I could not wait to see my little son or daughter.

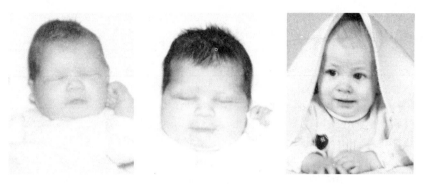

Richard Earl Grimes, Beth Evelyn Grimes and John Eric Grimes, III

After he was born, I lay in the hospital and dreamed beautiful dreams of his future. Once home, a severe depression overcame me. Even though Richard was only ten days old and I had thirty stitches in me from the birth, I was forced to return to my job as a secretary because our financial situation was so bleak. My first day at work, all my stitches broke. No problem. I got stitched back up and returned to work. I missed being with my newborn son. My parents had had a change of heart and were taking care of him during the day. At noon and then again at night I would race home to breastfeed him. My life was hectic to an extreme.

My Real Mother's Death

When Richard was only a few months old, Wonder and I took him on a trip to southern Indiana, about one hundred and fifty miles away, to visit Wonder's mother. It was snowing as we headed out, and soon we were in a full-fledged blizzard. About halfway there, the car broke down. We limped into a filling station, where Wonder called his cousin in Indianapolis. I bundled up my baby and we waited in the cold while Wonder's cousin made the journey in the middle of the night to get us and drive us back home in the blinding snow. It was a horrendous trip.

It was about 4:00 a.m. when we finally got home. As we walked in the door, a picture over my living room altar burst into fire, and a voice told me, "Your mother has died." I still had not had any contact with her and I did not want to believe what I heard. I became very upset, and I couldn't sleep the rest of the night. The next morning, I took my young son to Mumsey's house. As I walked in, the phone rang. I already knew what the caller would say. I overheard my stepmother say that she would tell me and Dad. She walked into the living room and looked at me. I was holding back the tears before she said a word. "Your real mother has died, honey," she said.

My father did not go to the funeral, and Wonder, who had recently lost both his real father and stepfather, God bless his heart, couldn't bring himself to attend either, so I went to the funeral alone. As I walked through the door, there stood my cousin Barbara and a very handsome man in a Naval officer's uniform. They looked up at almost the same time, smiled, and I heard him say, "Hi, Sis." I had heard by then about the little boy who had tried to feed me as I lay for eight days alone in the crib, and there he was, my half-brother Danny.

I was breathless for a few moments, but then we talked for a while, and then up walked my mother's mother. She held me and cried, and said how good it was to hug her granddaughter again. She seemed so loving and warm; I instantly loved her and yearned for all the time together we had missed. I also met my grandfather and my mother's sisters, Dorothy and Effie. Then they asked me if I wanted to see my mother. I really didn't. I knew that seeing her would crush all of my dream visions of her, and they were all I had.

I had always pictured her in a blue dress and in the casket, I saw a woman in a blue dress with a high neck and long sleeves. Her beautiful brown hair obviously had been dyed, but had not been touched up for the funeral. The woman I saw in the casket had clearly lived a very hard life. I could tell that she had died in a toxic condition and that she had been alcoholic. I later found out she died from an overdose of heroin. They found her with the needle still sticking in her arm. She died in California, and they shipped her body back home. Going to her funeral was never the way I had dreamed or imagined that I would meet my real mother.

She was buried under my father's name, Crickmore. I was told that she loved him until the end. I was also told that he had been very mean to her, that even when she was carrying me he had beaten her, and that she had almost lost me twice. The two families' versions of what had happened always seemed to conflict.

That Christmas, my father, stepmother, husband, small son Richard, and I spent Christmas Eve at Grandma Crystalbel's. I was able to be with my cousins, Barbara and Donna. I was so happy. But it was the first and last Christmas I spent at Grandma Crystalbel's home, for the next year she died. She had been very heavy; it took nine men to carry her casket. There had not been enough time to get to the truth of my mother or to know my grandma. I saw my brother Dan at Grandma Crystalbel's funeral, but I would not see him again until I was thirty-seven years old.

Barbara and I continued to get together, and we remain very close to this day. It's interesting to me that from a family ripped apart by dysfunction, there were three girls born to three sisters in one year, 1944 — my cousin Donna, born in April, Barbara, born in November, and I, born in June. None of us drink, and all of us try to live with integrity and caring for other people and have had to overcome much adversity. All three of us have been college-educated, have held highly responsible jobs in our communities, and take an active interest in serving our world. Although the circumstances that first brought us together were very sad, I am very grateful that part of my mother's family has been restored to me.

The House Explodes

In 1966, I became pregnant with my daughter Beth. I was working as a group supervisor in systems analysis at RCA in the manual data processing department. I left work in my eighth month of pregnancy. About one week later, as Wonder was leaving for work, I told him I thought the furnace sounded funny. He said he'd call the furnace company when he got home and have them come back to check it, as it had just been serviced. I went back to bed after getting Wonder off to work, but again I heard a voice, and the voice told me, "Get up. Something's wrong. Go get Richard."

I quickly woke up my baby son and had dressed him completely, except for his shoes, when the kitchen ceiling fell in on the other side of the house. The house immediately filled up with smoke and fire. I could not see. If Spirit had not awakened me, no doubt I would have been killed. At any rate, I could never have found my son in that smoke.

Again the Spirit spoke: "Get to the floor and crawl to the front door. Hurry." I did. I grabbed my son and prayed to God. Just as I was reaching for Richie's jacket and opening the door, the furnace exploded, throwing Rich and me out the door. We were very lucky. The explosion ripped off cabinet doors and blew the whole kitchen right out the back of the house. Our home burned down to the ground. All that was left were two Bibles. The firemen could not believe Rich and I had made it out alive.

The Birth of My Daughter

After the house was rebuilt, we moved back in, and Beth was born on January 15, 1967. Her hair fell in natural Shirley Temple curls and to me, she looked like a little goddess. One day, before she was a year old, she said, "I chose you, not him," meaning her Dad. I asked her to repeat what she had just said, and she told me, "I said, `I chose you as my mother.'" At first, I thought she was angry because her Dad had just scolded her, but later I realized she was telling me she had chosen me as her Mom before coming into her body. From day one, she had not wanted her Dad to hold her, even though he adored her and never abused her. If anyone held her except me or Nanny, she would cry and scream and make herself sick. Today she and her Dad seem to enjoy a good relationship, but it took lots of effort between them to make it work.

Beth was really smart. When Doctor Parr, her baby doctor, tested her at two years of age, she scored at the third-grade level in vocabulary and in some relationship skills. Beth was born with a birthmark of a flame on her wrist, maybe because I was carrying her inside me the day we escaped the fire. She and I have always shared a close relationship.

The Birth of My Second Son

In 1968, John Eric Grimes, my third and last child, was born. He was a little ray of sunshine, but the pregnancy had been difficult for me. One beautiful summer day, when I was about seven months pregnant, I dropped the kids at Sunday school and then returned home to sew a pair of checkered shorts for Wonder. Later, we went to a family reunion in Fishers, Indiana, where we saw some of our favorite relatives. It was a time when we were all happy. As we drove home in our Chevrolet convertible, Richard stood in the back seat and Beth sat in my lap in the front. We had no seat belts. Wonder was driving about 45 or 50 mph. Suddenly, a car turned into us from the opposite direction, caught the front of our car, and sent us flying into an embankment. I grabbed hold of Richard and squeezed Beth close to me. Seconds were like hours. The car finally came to rest. We were lucky that it had not flipped over. With one hand on Richard and another arm around Beth, I must have flown all over the inside of the car. My body had broken off the gear shift and the steering wheel and cracked the windshield. Richard had a bad bump on his forehead. Beth had a broken arm. Wonder was not injured, but I had a brain concussion, several broken and cracked ribs, and a broken sternum bone. My pelvis was chipped, and I was bleeding everywhere from cuts and scratches. Beth would not let anyone else hold her, and, not realizing the extent of my injuries, I tried to carry her to the ambulance. I passed out on the way.

When we arrived at the hospital, they took my children from the ambulance and a priest came to give me last rites. I told him to stop because I was American Indian, as well as Christian. Days later, I woke up feeling all the pain in my body and believing myself back in time five years, when I was still dating Mike. I later found out our accident had happened about two blocks from where Mike's car had crashed in 1962. It was only by concentrating on the checkered shorts I had sewn for Wonder the day of the accident that I was able to remember who and where I was.

The doctors said that, because I was pregnant, I couldn't be medicated for the pain. After the accident I had several false labors and became severely depressed. I gained a lot of weight again and started to smoke. I was afraid the baby would not be born at all or that he would be born handicapped because of the wreck. On September 4, 1968, at 1:00 a.m., John Eric came into the world naturally, even though I was due to have him delivered by Caesarean section later that day. I was a very happy mother, to say the least, when they laid my healthy, blond-headed baby in my arms. Thank you, God.

We Lose Our House Again

When John was about three weeks old, our home was taken away from us again. After the fire, the insurance company had rebuilt the house from the ground up. It was a beautiful job. But then they said we had been one year behind in payments before the fire, and, since we could not prove otherwise, they took us to court. We were so young and stupid then, we did not think to sue the furnace company or in some way fight to prove our truth and keep our home.

After we moved to an apartment, Wonder went back to working nights and I got a job at a hospital as a unit clerk. First, though, I had to take a class to learn what a unit clerk does. On the third day of class, it was icy and bitter cold. Carrying John Eric to the car, I slipped and fell on top of him. Terrified, I quit the job. I had always wanted to be home with my children, to cook and bake and watch them grow, but we couldn't afford for me not to work. I took another job, this time with the city of Indianapolis.

My husband had found another woman, we had lost our house, and I was really fat and really depressed. It was during this time that I attempted the suicide.

I feel now I need to apologize to my children and former husband. I was a workaholic, I was always tired, and I never could get it all done at home. And the demands of my career continued to grow. I worked for the Civic League and almost had a park named for me. I was a city ward chairman. I worked on the Human Rights Board. While employed at the Department of Public Safety, I received seven keys to the city and was named Chairman of Women in Government. I received a Governor's Award for Human Rights Service. I was also involved with church activities, Cub Scouts, and the American Indian Center. In addition to my professional life and trying to care for my husband and three children, every Friday I took my Grandmother Nanny to the store. I really did love everyone so very much. I tried to make it all work, and more and more found that nothing was working.

My husband and I never seemed to be happy together or able to handle success very well. Every time we got comfortable, something would happen — fire, repossession, or accidents — and we would lose it all.

Through all those years, I still went to college, taking classes in many forms of therapy. My career was taking off. I was made Executive Secretary to the Board of Public Safety and, at times in that job, I also served as Assistant to the Mayor of Indianapolis, sometimes carrying a gold badge from the police department.

Working for the City,
or Civil Service Training

Working for the Department of Public Safety, my education in psychology found a practical application. Sometimes, when a complaint was made about a police officer, I'd be disguised as a college student and sent out to ride with that officer for a shift. I would then prepare a psychological profile and present the results to the department director or the Mayor. This work lasted only about six months before the officers found out what was going on, but I gained from it a healthy and positive opinion of policemen. My investigations found most of the officers to be dedicated to their profession and good servants of the city.

But there were exceptions. One night, I was to meet the officer in question in the basement of the City County Building and start the shift at 6:00 p.m. I knew I was in trouble when, over the roof of the police car, I saw a fellow just about my height. There seems to be an unwritten rule in psychology that short men in authority are aggressive. I swallowed my heart back down, quieted my stomach, and got into the police car. The officer informed me he had several relations also in the police department. He seemed to think he could do anything he wanted because his relatives would cover for him. We spent the first two hours riding around the streets of Indianapolis while he told me about his life, all of his "hates," and how he dreamed of dying and being laid out in his casket with the best stereo and headphones, a can of Pepsi in one hand, and a gun in the other. I took four aspirins and prayed.

All of a sudden, for no apparent reason, he stopped in front of a house in the black community. He grabbed his shotgun, ran up the walk through the front screen door, and began to shoot. People seemed to be flying from every window. He came back out, got into the car, and we drove off. After a few minutes, I asked him, "Well, gee, what happened there?" He said, "That's a suspected drug house, and we have to keep them on their toes."

Later, after dark, we pulled over a young kid and his friends, and I got a great view of police manhandling. When he could not find the teenager guilty of anything, the officer threw him back in his car, bloodying his nose, and sent him on his way. I wanted out. As that thought was magnifying in my head, a call came over the radio:

Thunder with Richard G. Lugar, Mayor of Indianapolis, accepting award of being Chairwoman of Women in Government in the 70s

"Robbery in progress." A car chase, then a running chase, the beating up of the suspect, and finally taking the suspect to jail ensued. But, after all, there had been a robbery.

Once at the jail, I thought I could try to get away, but he told me to get back in the car and shut up. We went out again, and soon we ran into another disturbance. He realized he had forgotten his gun at the lockup, so he handled things with his fists and then went back for the gun.

Then on Indiana Avenue, in the middle of a rough black district, the young officer came upon a bus that was double-parked. He proceeded to arrest the bus driver at gunpoint, instantly creating a riot. This was the first and only time I ever used my radio code name. I grabbed the mike and announced, "The chicken is in trouble. This dumb sonofabitch I'm riding with is going to get us both killed." Twenty police cars immediately descended on the scene. I was taken in another police car and driven to station M, where I got in the car with another officer who took me home. The officer I was investigating is no longer working for the Indianapolis Police Department; before I could even make my report, he shot and killed an unarmed civilian and was discharged.

The officer who drove me home impressed me very much with his concern and gentleness. He asked me if he could make his usual rounds before taking me home. He seemed to be a friend to everyone, and people genuinely liked him. In the two minor disturbances we encountered, he handled all parties fairly, while still being firm and responsible.

After he'd settled a family disturbance and we were back in the car heading home, he began to talk about a man who had lived at 22nd and Leslie in Indianapolis and used to chase his family and relatives down the street with a gun. He said he was in terror of this man, of having to confront either him or someone like him. Of course, this officer was talking about my father. And *I* was in terror that he would know that I was the man's daughter. I sat silently as he recounted my own memories of family confrontations. Then he added, "And this man had a daughter. I hate to think what she's going to turn out to be. Domestic disturbances still scare the dickens out of me."

The officer insisted on walking me in my front door. He stayed for a few moments and talked with Wonder while I sat in mortal fear that somehow Dad's name would come up and he would find out the daughter was me. There was a picture of Dad on the wall. Thank God he never saw it.

From then on, I followed this officer's career, and I learned that he received several commendations for good deeds to the city. Only five years after we met, however, he was shot and killed in the line of duty by a man who also had shot his wife, his mother-in-law, and his daughter. What we fear truly will kill us.

At that time, I was very involved with civic and political committees, and outwardly my life seemed to be going well. Inwardly, however, I was desperate, because I knew my husband was seeing other women. I continued to seek comfort in food and gained weight at an alarming rate. It seemed that the emptiness inside me was never really filled. I still felt I didn't belong anywhere. I still didn't know who I was. I was still haunted by the mystery of my birth and wondered why I always felt different. Where was my heart's home?

Yet almost every psychic I met would say, "You are very special. You have a grand purpose." "Okay," I would mutter to myself. "What's the joke? When will this grand purpose be revealed?"

But soon my awareness of my Indian heritage that had been awakened by David Bratcher would be heightened by meeting a man who would irrevocably alter the course of my life: *Leonard Crow Dog!*

Leonard Crow Dog

Grandma reached into her pocket and took out a dark but familiar lump. "Well, I guess you had better talk about Leonard and his wife," she said, looking at the lump. "You know what this is?"

I said, "Yep, it is the medicine that Leonard made for you."

"Yes, that is right. It has a face on it. It is very powerful and he is a very powerful man. He does not like me, but he did make me medicine."

Grandmother Grace Spotted Eagle

9

LEONARD EMANUEL CROW DOG

The first time I met Leonard Crow Dog was in the 1970s, when he was in federal prison in Ft. Wayne, Indiana. He had been arrested for holding a Pipe for the people at the Wounded Knee standoff, where the Indian people were protesting injustice, abuse, and the outlawing of their sacred traditions.

I went down with a Medicine Elder and some other supporters to visit Leonard in prison. Through the glass separating him from the world, he was like a god — grand, proud, magnificent, and humble, all at the same time.

As he talked with the Elder by telephone, he looked directly into my eyes and said, "Please help my family back home . . ." He was like a proud lion in a very tiny cage. He thanked us for coming and told us not to worry, because he was going to the greatest school ever. He said we must sacrifice to know what this American Indian Movement is all about.

Some of us waited outside for several hours while the Elder did ceremony. When he came out, he told us to write letters to the people to help free Leonard. A lot of thoughts, energies, and prayers went out for this beautiful man.

He had asked us to help his family, so I started sending food, money, and clothes down to Rose Bud, South Dakota. Later, I visited them and became good friends with Grandma Mary and Grandpa Henry Crow Dog.

On these visits, I heard many stories about the morning when the authorities came to arrest Leonard. The Spirit had told him the FBI agents would be coming; he would have had plenty of time to run. He chose rather to call his people together to do ceremony to ready himself for this next part of his journey. His former wife told me of looking out her window that morning to see 100 to 150 FBI agents coming over the

Leonard Crow Dog with 100-year-old Zen Buddhist man

hill. They stripped Leonard naked in front of his people and took him to prison. I could still hear the horror and pain in her voice as she talked years later about that morning at sunrise when they took Leonard away.

In 1978, the Long Walk for Survival came through Indianapolis. My family and I were so excited, we wanted to help in any way we could. Four days before 700 Indians were due to arrive in town, I got a call asking me to find a place for them to stay. Imagine finding accommodations, food, blankets, and clothing for that many people in four days! Elders of the American Indian Council in Indianapolis, my family, and many other people rushed around and finally made arrangements with a Church retreat on the edge of a big lake.

The Walk members began to arrive. There were the 700 Indian people, Tibetan Buddhist monks, eight of whom had been sent from a Tibetan monastery to live the rest of their lives here working for American Indian causes, Zen Buddhists, Sufis, and all kinds of other people.

The advance group, including Clyde Bellecourt, Mary Jane Wilson, John Thomas, and Ted Means, stayed in our home. We all gathered that first night at a nearby church. John Thomas stood up and announced that this was an *Indian* function, and that all those in the room who were not Indian should get out. A third of the room stood up and left. I did not know what to do. My friend Jan, seeing my confusion, took my hand and said, "You stay . . ." Mary Jane Wilson also looked over, smiled, and whispered, "Stay . . ." As I listened to the speakers, I saw that they were magnificent warriors, with lots of radical anger and also lots of heart. There were lots of songs and laughter along with the serious speeches about what had happened to the American Indian people.

With 700 people, major problems, or "opportunities," arose, like the Omaha man who wore size 54 jeans, split his pants, and had no others to wear. Somehow I found him a pair of jeans that fit. Then a child was hit by a car. The Indian people were hysterical and spoke very little English. At the hospital, they cried that a white person had tried to kill their child. I had my hands full working with the two worlds, Indian and White, trying to get medical services and to balance everyone's emotions.

There were also wonderful opportunities to test personal faith and to see the Creator at work. A rumor was started that Leonard Crow Dog had been killed. All the people began to scream in fear. The next day, we learned that the rumor was false and that, in fact, he was on his way to Indianapolis meet up with the group. Indian dignitaries came from all over the country to meet and be with their Indian brothers and sisters. Indiana again lived up to its name, the Place of Indians, and Indianapolis lived up to its name, City of Indians.

But prejudice was rampant. The local government declared they would arrest the Indians if they walked on the highway. State and city police were mobilized. Newspaper headlines screamed of "700 Angry Savages Descending on Indianapolis." This did not help public relations. Because I was a part of the city's political structure, I could move easily within the different departments, trying to get proclamations made and letting city and government officials know what was really going on. Doing all this in addition to my full-time job in the mayor's office and taking care of my husband, kids, and distinguished guests really fried my brain.

After an exceptionally heated discussion at the State House, the Indians put up a tepee on the State House grounds in protest. I too handed out papers and held a big sign that said, "The Government hates Indians. Will prejudice ever stop?" I did not realize at the time that the T.V. news cameras were zooming in on the sign — and me.

As fate would have it, earlier that day I had made another T.V. statement on behalf of the City and Mayor of Indianapolis concerning a police officer involved in a citizen's complaint. The evening news showcased me, Mary Grimes. I was pretty well known in Indianapolis at that point, as I often had occasion to discuss Human Rights on T.V. The news commentator began with a report on "angry Indians protesting at the State House" and a very good shot of me, and then moved on to "city employee discussing police officers" and my little fat face again and in the same outfit, too.

While my family sat there stunned, I told myself that no one would notice the coincidence. Then the phone rang. The next morning at dawn, the Big Cheeses wanted to talk with me. What made it worse was that I loved my boss in the Department of Public Safety and the Big Cheeses and the man who was Mayor of Indianapolis. I had walked with him and Martin Luther King through the streets of the city back in 1967 when there was a lot of unrest in the black community. I had helped him and my boss hand out ice cream during a major riot when the gays and the straights were fighting over Holiday Park. Mayor Lugar was a Rhodes scholar and absolutely one of the most humane men I have ever met. When I think of city governments, I think they all should have a Richard G. Lugar. Actually, I think he should run for president.

The next morning, I sat in his office, really scared, and listened as he and other city officials did a lot of good talking. In the course of this conversation, I resolved to go on the Long Walk. The City did not fire me, but I felt in my heart it was time to go home. They were correct in talking about my responsibility as a city employee, and I was correct in my feeling of responsibility as an Indian. Deciding to go on the Long Walk for Survival to Washington, D.C., was a difficult decision to make with a family to raise, and I did love my job; but the truth in my heart would not be denied.

Meeting Leonard Again!

After that meeting, I went out to the park where the 700 Indians were gathered. The Indian Elders reported that Leonard Crow Dog was on his way in. They gave me the honor of greeting him at the entrance.

A car pulled up, full of Indian people, and one man got out. By now I was pretty used to cars with Indian people coming and going, and I didn't think too much about it. The guy said, "Hey, you know where a bunch of Indians are camped out around here?" I said, "Yeah, this is it." We discussed how many people there were, and this and that. I told him I was waiting for Leonard Crow Dog. The guy asked, "What do you think he looks like?" I said, "Ah! Leonard, yeah. He's got white hair and he's real old." It had been several years since I had seen him, and that had been in prison, so I was sure he had aged quite a bit. Then the guy asked, "What's he going to be driving?" I answered, "Oh, probably somebody's driving him." He said, "This guy's pretty special." I said, "Oh, yeah." The guy was beginning to irritate me. He just wouldn't leave, and I had an important mission to take care of.

Then he said, "I'm Leonard Crow Dog." My heart stopped. I couldn't even look at him. I raised my arm, pointed toward the camp, and said, "That way!"

He laughed and said, "Don't you have no tobacco or nothing?" I took out my cigarettes, tore open the pack, and cigarettes went flying everywhere. My eyes were glued to the ground. He said, "You better come with me." I frantically gathered up cigarettes and began stuffing them in his hand. He smiled at me and said, "You're going to be okay, I just know it. Come on, ride down with us."

From that point on, I couldn't get away from him. Every time I started to get up, he'd say, "Oh hey! Sit down, sit down..." He remembered that I was the one who had helped out his parents and family while he was in prison.

Leonard ran a Sweat Lodge that night, and finally I got away. Sitting up on a hill talking with some friends, I could see down the hill towards the Sweat Lodge. A guy came out of the lodge and ran across the lake right on top of the water. He was a long way across that lake before he finally sank. I'd never seen anyone run on water before. Everyone still talks about that sometimes when we all get together.

Everyone in the camp really loved hearing what Leonard had to say, but soon he had to leave to go on ahead and take care of other Walk business.

My oldest son and I got ready to join the Long Walk. Wonder prepared the truck. Richard and I traveled with the Walk from Richmond into Washington, D.C.

Tipi and Warriors on the Long Walk for Survival

At the front of the Walk, all the Warriors and the Spiritual Leaders took turns running and carrying the sacred staffs and tribal flags. One of the leaders handed Richard a beautiful old staff covered with Eagle feathers and robes and belonging to a traditional medicine family. That staff was the staff of life, the tree of life, the symbol of the Nation. Richard, who was fourteen at the time, ran and carried that staff thirteen miles across the entire northern point of the state of West Virginia. He later said, "Mom, I did it for our family and our Nation to live." He almost had to quit the Walk, he had so many blisters. I knew then I had a true future spiritual leader as a son.

At the time of the walk, I weighed nearly 300 pounds, and it seems I had a very loud snore. As a result, there was the Cheyenne camp, the Lakota camp, the Arapaho camp, and then there was the Thunder camp, which consisted only of our truck. I snored so loudly, they wouldn't let me sleep in any of the other camps.

Leonard did a huge ceremony of honoring, taking Richard and me into his family and giving us each a name. This was when I received the name Thunderbird. He named my son Wolf, because of his Warrior tendencies.

We walked all the way to Washington, D.C., where the people pitched tepees on the White House lawn. The president had left town and so could not talk to us, which was frustrating, but I think we made our point.

When we returned home, I quit the Department of Public Safety, after working there over eight years. I took a position in a CETA program to get counselling experience. I worked with 450 blacks, twenty-six whites, and one Indian — me! I moved from the twenty-fifth floor of the City County Building to a basement office across the street. One day I had a gold badge and could take policemen out of their line of duty if they were doing wrong. The next day, nobody would even talk to me. It was a great humbling. I was surprised to find myself going through power withdrawal.

In 1979, I worked with an Indian sister to bring $750,000 into the state of Indiana to start a Native American CETA program. I was the first Director/Coordinator of the American Indian Business Office in the State of Indiana. At one time, we had 127 Indians receiving educational and social rehabilitation through our program. We also instituted a paralegal program to work in connection with Juvenile Hall. It felt good to be using my abilities to help out Indian people.

Then, for some reason, my Indian sister coworker and I got into a big argument. She felt she could do the job better than me, and I felt betrayed. Lies were told about me, and finally I resigned. It was the first time I felt firsthand the results of prejudice turned inward, of Indians fighting Indians. As I look back, I was as guilty as she was of creating discord.

I didn't know it at the time, but I was getting very sick. Later I was told I had Pickwickian's disease. The stress of the argument seriously worsened my health.

Wonder and I sold our home and bought a huge house in the inner city. We wanted to make it an Indian Center. It was not immediately livable, so we stayed in the attached Carriage House, without heat, water, or lights. There were countless obstacles in creating the Center. To top it off, I broke my leg. Wonder said we had to give up our dream and move into an apartment. At that point I agreed the dream might be better fulfilled in some other way at some other time.

I next saw Leonard in 1980, when he came through Indianapolis on the Second Long Walk for Survival. I was in the midst of yet another typical family crisis. It was Richard's sixteenth birthday. He had decided to run away from home, and had managed to get himself arrested and detained. He spent his birthday in Juvenile Hall eating bologna sandwiches and tomato soup. Richard was not pleased with either of his parents at that point, and he was particularly angry with me.

Then Leonard came onto the scene, immediately sized up the situation, and announced, "I think he should come with me." Richard traveled with Leonard for some time, and finally Leonard flew him back from Pennsylvania. We went to meet the plane not quite knowing what to expect. My son came up to me, dropped to his knees, and started to cry. He told me how ungrateful he'd been to me, that I was his mother and I had given him life, and he wanted to thank me for that. I had known Leonard could work miracles, but this was amazing! I thank Leonard for that, as for so many gifts.

Richard and I met up with the Long Walk in Greenbelt Park, Pennsylvania, and went on into Washington, D.C. There, I helped the advance people get food and money and fix cars, and do whatever else needed to be done. When we got into Washington, we had a huge ceremony led by a Zen Buddhist who was over 100 years old. He blessed each one of us. Then we walked into Washington, D.C. Dick Gregory, Marlon Brando, Muhammed Ali, Buffy St. Marie, and all kinds of other celebrities were there. But for the second time, the President of the United States left as soon as the Indians came into town.

Chicago Grass Story

In November of 1980, Leonard came through Indianapolis. Being a master teacher, Leonard always gave us wonderful examples of experiential learning.

One time, I was supposed to drive Leonard to a big conference in Chicago. As usual, we left late. Leonard was scheduled to speak to an audience of thousands of people at a big stadium. We had fourteen people in the station wagon, all talking at once, including kids throwing candy and popping balloons. It reached a frenzied pitch as we hit Chicago freeway traffic. My nerves were frayed. We were nearly an hour late already. You can imagine my amazement when Leonard pointed to the side of the road and said, "Pull over."

I couldn't help but think of the thousands of people awaiting his arrival — not to mention the fact that I was in the far left lane and he wanted to pull over on the right. However, I also had a recent memory of an incident involving a driver who had ignored Leonard twice when he told him to turn right. The guy finally got the message when Leonard's fist impacted his head. These Lakota warriors don't mess around.

I veered across three lanes of traffic. He said, "Back up." I backed up for at least a half mile on the freeway until he told me to stop. He got out and the rest of us followed. We worked our way across the rushing traffic and walked down the median. Leonard pulled out his tobacco. It is fair to say that I was berserk.

Leonard looked down at a little blade of grass struggling through a crack in the cement. I couldn't imagine how he had seen it He started to pray . . . and pray . . . and pray. He talked about how nature would always overtake the cement highways and cities. He said the little blade of grass was just like a man, growing up through the cement. He said this blade of grass was a warrior and it would be the first of its breed. There would be more grass which would grow, but first this one had to be honored.

Now you have to understand, as beautiful as that concept was, at first it just didn't impress me. Luckily, I had ample opportunity to grasp the beauty of the lesson, because we stopped eighteen more times on the Chicago Freeway. By the time we got to blade of grass Warrior number four, I was seeing Chicago covered by grass and grass taking over cement all over the world.

We arrived at the conference at least two-and-a-half hours late. The set-up people were in a rage, and of course they just tore me apart. They threatened to sue me because people had already left. At that point, I just didn't care.

Within fifteen minutes from the time Leonard started talking, the crowd was in tears and remained so for the duration of the night. Spirit has its own time. When Spirit wants to come through, no matter what the situation, it's always perfect timing. I wasn't sued. In fact, I received a commendation. I'll never forget the Chicago grass story.

About this time, I began to have trouble sleeping lying down. I slept all night sitting up in a chair. The doctors said I needed to buy a water bed and my little daughter took to sleeping in the room with me, so if

I stopped breathing during the night, she could shake me. Besides, Leonard always loved the water bed so when he visited I always slept in a chair. One morning I woke up in the chair to find a sign on my chest that read, "Bless This Mess."

On December 15, 1980, Leonard started the Native American Church of Indiana, Inc. He made adoptions in the name of the Church. He adopted my husband and children. My adoption papers said that I wished to follow my Indian heritage, to join with my husband and Chief Crow Dog, and that I dedicated my life to the Great Spirit and the way of sacred ceremonies.

We spent the day typing these papers and having meetings. As Leonard left, he gave us copies of his Certificate of Ordination signed by Reverend Eagle Bear and copies of the Peyote Papers signed by Frank Fools Crow, Wallace Black Elk, Chief Eagle Feather, Francis Primo, Sr., Chief Iron Shell, and Juan Ederacanto Aguilar. I signed all these papers as resident agent. Leonard said that, because I had been adopted into his family and had a good heart, he knew the Church would always be in good hands.

Sometimes Things Were Strange When Leonard and the Spirits Came

Leonard often stayed with us when he came through Indy. I set up lectures for him. It was always an adventure to have him around. My family and I learned the true ways of the Warrior. Leonard always traveled with Warriors, and I was amazed at how they functioned as a unit. Soon he began to call us his warriors. Warriors' eyes were everywhere, covering all contingencies in the crowd. Leonard trained his Warriors in telepathy. Soon I could be anywhere in a room or even anywhere around him and hear his voice in my mind: "Go sit behind that man there; he's having bad thoughts," or "Get ready to move out soon." Leonard said the keys for a Warrior are to be aware, open, and organized. Sometimes he would have his Warriors walk down the street and make a list of everything they noticed. Then he would send them back out again to see all the things they had missed. He told us if we would get out of the way and create an open space, information could be received. Everything talks to us, but we don't know the languages. We have to clear our minds, let go of expectations, and then

Leonard Crow Dog in New York City back in late 60s or early 70s

we can hear the languages of the birds and trees, or solutions to problems and situations.

Whenever Leonard was on his way into town, we'd know he was close because the cabinet doors and the front and back doors of the apartment would open and close at the same time, all by themselves. It freaked us out at first, but in time we came to know of the great compassion that accompanied the amazing feats of this man. One night at supper he prayed over the food and waved the Eagle Fan, and the room filled with the sound of Eagle cries and wings flapping.

Living With the Spiritual Things

Usually when Leonard came, he would put one of the four Pipes smoked at the Battle of the Little Big Horn in our bedroom, high on a chest. Many times we would see it glowing at night. My instructions were never to touch it. One time, after he had been at the house for a month or so, I was cleaning and forgot the Pipe was on top of the chest.

I reached up to dust and there was a barrier — it felt like someone grabbing my hand. I went to Leonard and told him what I had done. He smiled and said, "That's good. It stopped you."

Later, he put me on a Vision Quest in South Dakota. I stood for four days and four nights holding one of those sacred Pipes. The pain in my body was severe. I couldn't sit down and I surely couldn't let go of that Pipe. Sometime during the third day the pain eased, and I truly believe I could have stood there forever.

It was Leonard who first told me I was an *Iyeska* (Spirit Speaker). Later, Leonard's mother, Grandma Mary, explained that it meant that I had the ability to converse with the Spirits. She said that she and Leonard would help me make sure I talked to the right ones. Leonard told me to bathe in the water at Crow Dog's Paradise, because it had been flowing forever. It was as if the water was alive and talking to me, and becoming a part of my body. Crow Dog's Paradise is beautiful, sacred land.

On many of our family trips to South Dakota, Leonard honored us with a peyote ceremony. One time, a former Warrior of his gifted us with the peyote altar of his mother who had passed on that year. Leonard did a ceremony to honor the altar itself and to bless me, praying to bring in the right vibration so I could walk with the altar. This ceremony took a lot of preparation and lasted several days. Wonder and I had brought lots of food and gifts for a feast.

During the ceremony, I was in the tepee with Grandpa Henry Crow Dog, Leonard, and several others. Suddenly, Jesus Christ appeared in full sight of us all to do healing. Leonard and Grandpa Henry sang. Later, I was given a tape of their singing. To this day, if I play it, I'm transported back to that sacred event. Even though I've been in many ceremonies, this is the one that always stays foremost in my mind.

Being and traveling with Leonard and his family changed forever my ideas about what is possible — and impossible — in this reality. I have never been with this man when I have not seen the utmost compassion from him. He would take the last money out of his pocket or the shirt off his back to give to someone in need. I have seen him bring lightning out of the sky and rain to parched lands. I've seen him heal people with hot coals in his mouth. I've seen his Eagle Sticks become alive and fly around the room. I am only one of many people who are better off because of Leonard Crow Dog.

Thunder at 300 pounds (Inset drawing: "Bless this Mess" sign that Leonard Crow Dog and Warriors put on her chest as they were leaving — the trip where he prophesied her heart attack)

"Okay," she said. She was getting tired. I could see that as she held her head in her hands. "You got very sick — you know, your heart attack. It was like you were tired of living, but the Grandfathers, they had another thing for you to do, right? Tell about Leonard telling you that you were going to die."

Grandmother Grace Spotted Eagle

10

The Heartbreak Hotel

In December of 1980, before Leonard Crow Dog left our home in Indianapolis, he called me over and said, "You are going to have what white man calls a heart attack. You are going to die. You are going to come back. Your life will change. And you can no longer be in what is called Today World. You'll be fully in the working Spirit World. You have much to do, so you must prepare yourself for death."

Something like this is great news, right? I tried not to take it seriously, because I didn't want to believe it. I asked him if something couldn't be done. He said he could take me to Crow Dog's Paradise and put me in Sweat Lodges for nine months. At 300 pounds, this did not sound like a whole lot of fun either. Like a fool, I laughed and said, "Oh, okay. I'll take the heart attack." I could not help noticing that Uncle Leonard did not seem amused.

As he left, he wrapped a beautiful Pendleton blanket around my shoulders and said, "This blanket will protect you. Keep it with you and be surrounded by our love." He and his wife blessed me. He said that I had to walk into my destiny proud and face death like a Warrior. I just looked at him and said, "Uh huh."

They left and, in one week to the day, Uncle was proved right. It was New Year's Eve. I was really sick that day, too sick to go out and celebrate. My husband went out, my daughter went out, the whole family went out. I stayed home alone. For some reason, never once did I remember Leonard's words. I sat in my chair all evening long, thinking about all the events of my life. I was very lonely that night.

Beth and the young Indian man she was dating came home. They went down to the club-house in our apartment building to meet my sons and attend a party. Somehow, a disturbance ensued. Beth's date knocked someone's windshield out with a stick. All of a sudden, police officers were running through my place searching for him. The next thing I knew, they had Beth's friend in a police car. They had beaten him up and he was acting crazy, kicking the roof and windows of the car. It was about midnight. I remember hearing the guns going off to celebrate the end of the old year and the start of the new. I went to the car window to try to calm the kid down so that he would not be beaten anymore, for he was really a nice kid. Nice kids on alcohol don't always act very nice.

Suddenly I felt as if somebody had hit me in the chest with a baseball bat. I fell backwards into another car. The police officers grabbed me and asked what was wrong. I couldn't talk. They wanted to take me to the hospital, but I didn't want to go; so, with my children, they helped me back to our apartment.

I sat in a chair. I kept praying and hearing the Spirit say, "Don't go to sleep." I knew if I slept, I'd never wake up.

The next morning, Beth's friend had to be in court. I knew the judge, so I went with him. As I approached the bench with the young man, this wonderful judge leaned over and said, "You're not breathing. What's going on?" I said that I had a cold, but I must not have been convincing. He told the bailiff to call an ambulance.

I was taken to St. Francis Hospital, where they told my husband that I had suffered a heart attack. They gave me oxygen and transferred me to Wynona Hospital. During my first night there, people kept running into my room. I thought, "Gosh, these are nice people." I found out later that my heart had stopped and the nice people were the Code Blue team trying to keep me alive. The next morning I met Dr. Cook, who, in addition to the heart problems, diagnosed Pickwickian disease, caused by my being overweight. Dr. Herd also came into my life and told me that my stomach should be stapled. Surgery was scheduled for January 19. My husband, God bless his heart, kept the home and kids going.

John Crazy Horse helped out with my children and visited the hospital almost every night to pray. I will always be so grateful to John, and also to John Macri, whom I think of as my Italian spiritual father. John Macri owned an Italian restaurant where great metaphysical people, like Kreskin, a mentalist, Yuri Geller, Jeanne Dixon, Hugh Cayce, and many more used to gather. I went to John Macri's group every week for years. I would sit in the back of the room to listen to all the great speakers. John himself is a master of numerology. All aspects of the metaphysical and psychic realms were investigated by his group.

During the Longest Walk in 1978, John Macri brought all 700 of the Walk participants into his restaurant and fed everyone a great meal. He personally brought out lots of food to the walkers camped at St. Maury's Church Retreat. I cannot honor this man enough, not only as my teacher, but as a great humanitarian.

During the time I was in the hospital, from December 31 to January 19, the day of the operation, John Macri and all the beautiful people from the Macri group came every day. They gave me Bach Flower remedies, foot rubs, Reiki treatments, and anything else that could be done for my physical body.

Indians from the Center and other friends came, smudged with sage smoke, and prayed. A few days after the heart attack, John Crazy Horse brought me a full Eagle Wing from Uncle Leonard. I was not supposed to touch it. Uncle's instructions were to focus on the Eagle Wing to give me incentive to fly like an Eagle. The Eagle flies closest to the Creator, and thus can carry our prayers to the Great Mystery. In this way, I was to pray for my life. Soon the Eagle Wing got its own table, and there it lay for the duration of my hospital stay. You can imagine how the hospital felt about this "dead bird's wing" in my room, but eventually everyone relaxed and enjoyed having it there.

My cousin Barbara came and brought pretty things and lots of laughter.

Mayor Lugar called and wished me a speedy recovery and shared that he had found out how to reach my brother in the Navy. The Mayor had arranged to let him know I was sick, and one day I answered the phone and my brother Dan was on the other end of the line. He and his wife Barb sent flowers and called almost daily.

But not one member of my father's family came or called.

On the Scam in the Hospital

After three days at Wynona, I was transferred to Methodist Hospital. There I spent the remaining sixteen days before the operation, on the research floor, where they put the terminal cases. I had met and done some work with Elizabeth Kübler-Ross, whose views of death and dying were now invaluable to me, for every other day in the bed next to me someone passed on to the Spirit world. I remember thinking, "This is not real good for me," particularly since the doctors said I had only a twenty percent chance of surviving the upcoming operation. Those were not great odds!

Every day my daughter Beth came. Daily she brushed my hair, which was so long I could sit on it, and, God bless her heart, she listened to me each day as I made a new plan for my funeral. One day I was going to be cremated, the next I would go with conventional burial. It must have been so very painful for her to go through this. I apologize to her now for having been so thoughtless of her feelings.

Even in the hospital, I did manage some outrageous behavior. One elderly soul's dying wish was to curse out the husband who had taken her children away some forty years before. Guess who made the call and held the phone up as she made her last statements? At the end of this tirade, she started to cry. She told him that she loved him. He got to tell her that he was sorry and that he loved her, too.

Then there was the lady who had a cancerous rib. She had her operation, but unfortunately, they got the wrong rib. I had to intervene for her with the doctors to get the right rib removed.

Another lady's dying wish was for pizza. I ordered the pizza and had it delivered to the receptionist downstairs, and then slipped off the floor with all my monitors, wires, and tubes, slowly creeping my way down to get the best pizza I have ever tasted in my whole life. The lady actually sat up and wolfed down her share. Of course, I was on a restricted diet, so it was a no-no for me, too, but we still had one hell of a party. Finally, the smell drifted down the hall, and we were busted by the nurses. That lady was still alive when I left the hospital, no small miracle, since the doctor had said she had only a day or so more to live. I concluded that with an Around The World Pizza, you could add a good month to your life.

By the night of the 18th, I was well prepared for my final meal. I had ordered everything that anyone could possibly want — steak, pizza, chicken — and had hidden it all over the room. After the operation, when my stomach was stapled and I could take no solid food, the food was still there to haunt me and drive me crazy.

On January 19, 1981, I was awakened early in the morning so that they could start administering drugs for the operation. I was happy, because my Grandfather, Papaw, who had been in the Spirit world for several years, came to me during the night. I had been frozen with fear about the operation until I saw Papaw. He sat on the end of my bed, just as I remembered him, and told me everything was going to be all right. He said that I would die, but I would come back to a new world, and he would be with me all the way through. He told me he loved me so, and that felt so good.

Wonder and the kids came in that morning and were surprised to see me drugged, but still happy and kidding. I tried to tell them about Papaw's visit. John Crazy Horse came and led my children in prayer with the Pipe in the chapel. The Sacred Pipe was out during the whole operation and recovery. My husband stayed just outside the operating room.

The Operation and Death Experience

The lights went out in the Operating Room and, the next thing I knew, I was awake and seeing myself on the table. I wasn't sure it really was me, but I felt a lot of compassion for that body down there. There were five doctors working on the body. One of the doctors stood on a milk crate. I could hear them all talking and laughing and making a fifty dollar bet that I wouldn't make it. Then a buzzer sounded and I faintly heard someone say, "We lost her!" Then ZOOM. I went down a tube of light very fast. Someone came to meet me, a very pure, very precious essence. It seemed to me to be Jesus. He talked to me about my purpose on the planet and what I had done to try to avoid it. He said they were sending me back to fulfill my purpose.

I thought, "What a rip! I worked really hard to get up to 300 pounds and make myself sick, and I have lots of pain. I'm tired of life. I know that it must be time to go on to the Other Side." Obviously, my timing and theirs were not the same.

He took me to other essences — to the Buddha, to the Indian Elders, and to many other swirling light forms. They all placed golden things in my body. Then they told me they loved me and that it was time to go back. I cried out, because it was agony to leave. I was pulled backwards, fighting an inexorable force.

Immediately, I was awake and aware that they were finishing the operation. I kept trying to move and to scream, but the eyes above said, "Go to sleep. It's okay." But I never did, as far as I know. In the Recovery Room I tried to take a tube out of my throat. A doctor ran over and said, "No, we'll just have to put it back in." They restrained me. I was so awake and aware — and it hurt so bad.

I remember, so strongly that it is like reliving it as I write, the peace of the Other Side, the most genuine peace imaginable in the beauty of lights and music, in the oneness with all things, in the joy and celebration. I also remember the awesome heaviness of returning to the physical plane and coming back into my body. The heaviness, lack of freedom, and agony of this plane were so horrible that I screamed.

Coming Back

My life had been changed forever. Now I had an idea of the meaning of true peace and love. We can only attempt to approximate it in our lives on this planet. This world is only a pale reflection of the voices and thoughts of the Elders. They watch us as we choose pain and lack of love in our lives. For myself, I could no longer deny that we can **choose** to have love and peace in our lives. The Elders sent me back and gave me another chance to actualize this great truth. And so, in so many words and thoughts, that day the Sundance trail began.

I later told the doctor that I had seen him on his milk crate and I apologized to another doctor for losing his fifty dollar bet for him. He turned very pale and said nothing. I thought it was funny, but I guess he didn't, because he did not come to visit me again. None of them seemed to want to admit what had happened. The anesthesiologist said there had been no vital signs for forty-seven seconds. He was the only witness who would acknowledge that I had actually died during the operation.

This is the first time I have put in writing my vision during the death experience. For about a week or so after the operation, I had a tube down my throat, tubes coming out of my stomach and my side, a heart monitor, continuous IVs, and all kinds of wires sticking out of me. Even though, with the tube in my throat, I couldn't speak to tell anyone about the vision, I thought constantly about it. Right after I returned to my room, the very first night after the operation, I was filled with gratefulness for being alive, and I finally knew that I had a purpose in life.

I tried to get doctors and nurses to confirm that I'd had a death experience, but I soon realized that I shouldn't mention what had happened during my visit down the tunnel. As I lay there thinking about it all, I heard the Spirit speak, very loudly: "Remember that you were told not to reveal what you experienced when you visited Home. You must keep this to yourself, never speaking it out loud until another human being repeats to you your experience word for word. This will mark the start of another phase of your work in this life." I heard the Spirit speak very clearly, and so did the lady in the other bed, for she hollered out, "Was that on your T.V., or is someone in our room? What experience?"

I never uttered a word about the vision, not even to my family, until the spring of 1986, when Kim McSherry, my newfound friend and student, whom I lovingly call my world-famous astrologer, did her first of many astrology readings for me. I had been told in the past that I had a very unusual astrological chart. Even taking that into account, she seemed extremely nervous. It was almost as if I was sitting before a gypsy tea reader who had just seen a star in my hand and knew I was about to be eaten by a werewolf. She sat down, breathed, and started to cry.

Finally, she began: "In front of me is the chart of a New Age prophet. I am honored to have the opportunity to do this reading." I started to laugh. She then proceeded to share, word for word, the vision I received during my death experience. As she began to speak, I felt my heart open, and tears streamed down my face. I knew I was now free to share the death experience that had changed my life and that a new phase of work was beginning.

❀ ❀ ❀

The operation had been a long and horrendous one. They had opened my chest cavity, cleaned the fat from around my heart, and checked the auricles and ventricles for any damage. They had stapled my stomach so that I could only consume two ounces of liquid at a time, six times a day. I hurt all over. I just lay there looking at the Eagle Wing, not able to talk or move. Soon the tube was removed from my throat, and then they began to take the other tubes, one by one. One day, they removed the tube from my stomach. That really hurt. I was given a two-ounce portion of Welch's grape juice to drink and had the amazing experience of seeing it spurt out of my belly like a little fountain. I called the nurse and told her I had sprung a leak. They got kind of excited, and I was laughing so hard that it only made it worse.

I got tired of lying in bed with all the monitors, and one day I decided I would get some exercise. Since I was hooked up to a huge board that continually monitored everything, the minute I moved to get up, I disconnected one of the cords and my heartline went flat. As I lay back down and leaned backwards to hook the cord back into the machine, one of the nurses ran in gasping. I popped my head up to ask her what was wrong and she screamed. Then she began to cry. She poured out her heart to me about the stresses her job caused in her life. This led to my bringing all the hospital nurses together so I could talk to them — while still hooked up to all this machinery — about their emotions and feelings and stress, and how they could ease the situation. It was the first time, as far as they knew, that the hospital had a speaker who was one of the patients.

I also spent a lot of time in the sleep lab. "Pickwickian's Disease," which is similar to Sudden Infant Death Syndrome or crib death, is caused by excess weight on the throat cutting off the air tube. Many people with this condition die in their sleep. I loved the sleep lab. I had great dreams there. They would wake me up at certain intervals so I could see what a scary dream, or a sexual dream, or a beautiful dream looked like on the brain pattern monitor. There was a definite variation in brainwave pattern when the Spirit was talking to me versus when my subconscious was at work. The lab technicians did their testing and I did mine.

I was in the hospital a total of thirty-three days.

During that time, I managed two furloughs. On the first one, Barbara took me out for a haircut. My hair, which I could sit on, had become badly matted from the operation and from lying in a hospital bed. My hair was cut and I got an afro perm. Now, Barbara would look good with her head in a paper bag; I would not look good, ever, in this afro. But it made life easier in a hospital bed. I also got to visit at home.

On my second furlough, Wonder, the kids, and two of my former Indian counselors took me to see *Windwalker*. I went nuts in the theater smelling the popcorn, the hot dogs, the Pepsi, and hearing all those people munching and crunching around me, but the show, the story of an old Cheyenne man who died and came back, was great. The old man felt it was his time to die, but the Spirits just would not let him. He fell off his death pyre, was attacked by wolves, fell into a cave, fought a bear to the death, and returned home to find that no one believed it was really him. Somehow I identified with his story. I was the only one laughing in the theater; everyone else was crying or scared.

Hereby Gratefully Acknowledges The Outstanding Services Of

FIFTH FLOOR NURSES AT METHODIST HOSPITAL

Whose Contribution Toward The Betterment Of The Community
Has Been Conspicuously Demonstrated In The Role Of

ACCOMPLISHMENTS MADE IN THE MEDICAL FIELD AND
GUIDING MARY GRIMES THROUGH HER WEIGHT LOSS PROGRAM

William H. Hudnut III
_____
MAYOR CITY OF INDIANAPOLIS INDIANA

JANUARY 19, 1982
_____
DATE OF ISSUE

During my hospital stay, I lost forty pounds. I was most anxious to go home. My husband and children were having a hard time keeping it all together, and they too were anxious for me to come home.

On day number thirty a Warrior shown up to get the Eagle Wing for Chief Leonard Crow Dog and John Crazy Horse. Then I knew that I was going home.

My Right-Out-of-the-Hospital Adventure

My daughter Beth had shown up at the hospital every day to comb my hair, braid it, and talk; but on day thirty-one she didn't come. No one seemed to know where she was, or they each told me a different lie. I started to get uneasy.

Day thirty-two, Beth still did not show up.

Day thirty-three, I went home with my beautiful sons and husband. I was so excited. I ran into the house and called out for Beth. It was then that my husband told me that she had run away with an Indian man — the one, by the way, who had created the scene on New Year's Eve. I started right away to try to find my daughter. It seemed that all roads were blocked; none of my phone calls brought any information.

For maybe the first time, I asked the Spirit a specific question. The Spirit answered that she was in Oklahoma. Within three hours, I had raised enough money from friends to fly to Oklahoma. My sister-in-law and her husband in Dallas agreed to pick me up at the airport. I called my husband at work, refused my sons' request to go with me, put on a poncho over the one suit of clothes that fit me, and got myself to the airport, not even two days out of the hospital.

After landing in Dallas, I hit the road with my sister-in-law and her husband. By 3:00 a.m., we were at the Oklahoma border. All I had to go on was a photo of Beth and the guy. By 4:00 a.m., we were in a motel room in Oklahoma City. By 4:30, I was already tired of watching my brother-in-law sleep. Soon my sister-in-law and I were out scouting the streets. I asked a lady where in town we could find a large Indian population and learned of a Shawnee reservation. I asked Spirit to show me the name in the phone book that I should call. At 6:00 a.m., I called the number.

An old man answered. I asked for the young man by name. I was told he was just walking in the door. The young man who had "kidnapped" my daughter was very surprised to hear my voice. I asked him if Beth was with him. As he hesitated, I heard my darling daughter in the background demand, "Is that my mother? I want to talk to my mother. I want to talk to my mother *right now!*" He wouldn't allow me to talk to Beth, but we proceeded to negotiate the best way to get together and transfer Beth from him to me. I realized then that this was not really a kidnapping; they had run away together. He was as scared as I was, and even more so when he heard I was in Oklahoma.

We set a time of 10:00 a.m. to meet at the Little Ax Grocery. After hanging up the phone, I felt suddenly afraid I would never see my daughter again. I immediately had my sister-in-law take me to the Shawnee tribal police. At first, they were totally disinterested in what I had to say, but when I told them that she was fourteen and he was twenty-one and that, if they did not take some action, I would then proceed to the FBI, they became *very* interested. It was only a bluff, but it worked, because everyone knew that the FBI was just waiting for any excuse to get onto a reservation and bust Indian people.

When I got to the meeting place, many of the roads were already blocked off by police. I stood in the freezing cold, terrified. I've never seen a more beautiful sight than the old Indian car that drove up with Beth. She jumped out and ran to me, and then I knew that everything would be okay.

We went to a restaurant and Beth ate everything in sight, while the guy cried a lot. We discussed what should be done. It was very clear that Beth was coming home with me, and the guy seemed ready for her to leave. We parted as friends, and our group started back to Dallas in the truck with my precious daughter between us. I gave my word that I would not press charges. It all ended in a very good way.

It seems that Beth had not taken to traditional Indian life very well. She had experienced many traditional Indian Church ceremonies held in a tepee, but she'd also had to wash the dishes fifteen minutes after every meal and scrub the floors several times a day. It hadn't taken long for her to realize that this fellow was not the true love of her life.

On the way out of town, we were stopped by the local sheriff. He interrogated us for a couple of hours, trying to force me to sign papers to have the young man arrested, not because of what he had done, but because he was Indian. It was my choice, I had given my word, and

I was not about to have anyone arrested. We continued on our way to Dallas, very happy to get to my sister-in-law's home and into a bed.

Somehow, while I was sleeping, the little bed I was in flipped over, and I landed belly down on the floor. I felt as if I had torn everything. My doctor in Indianapolis told me to rush back to the hospital; I told him I was in Dallas, Texas, and that I would see him Friday when I got back to Indy. He told me to go immediately to the nearest emergency room. A brief check-up determined that I had done no damage, but my doctor was sure furious when I next saw him.

At home, I continued my massive weight loss program, consuming only two ounces of liquid at any one sitting. I suffered frequent "pork chop attacks." My husband tried everything, including sticking the pork chops in a blender, but we could never get them into my stapled stomach. Fudgecicles tasted good and helped my stomach feel better. They slowed down the weight loss process somewhat, but, within six months, I had lost nearly 150 pounds and was down to about 160.

It seemed that almost every day I needed new clothes. I was not working and the doctors had told me to walk a mile every day, so I took to collecting cans and going through people's garbage, in which I found whole wardrobes. A County Courthouse judge, who had come by to visit, found me on my route, just as I was popping my head out of a garbage dumpster. She couldn't believe her eyes.

With so much spare time on my hands, I began to give lectures and presentations for Leonard Peltier, Yellow Thunder Camp, and other Indian Movement causes. [I have included in the Appendix some reprints of newsletters and flyers about Yellow Thunder Camp and the Leonard Peltier fund. Both still need our prayers, help, and contributions.] I went to Ohio to take part in a panel discussion on human rights with one of my former bosses, William H. Hudnut, III, then the Mayor of Indianapolis. They introduced me incorrectly as "Mary Jones" from Cleveland, but I just got up and said what I needed to say on behalf of my dear brother, Leonard Peltier.

After the lecture, Mayor Hudnut came up to me and said, "I used to know a Mary Grimes in Indianapolis who talked about a lot of the things you talk about." Not realizing at first how much my looks had changed, I thought he was kidding. After I told him I *was* Mary Grimes, the Mayor graciously sent a proclamation acknowledging the outstanding service of all the nurses and doctors at Methodist Hospital and their contributions toward the betterment of the community in guiding Mary Grimes through her weight-loss program.

Meanwhile, I kept going to the weekly meetings of John Macri's group. Once in a while Uncle Leonard would call to see how we were doing and to gently remind me that I should soon start to think about Sundancing. I did not want to think about Sundancing.

The Indians at Yellow Thunder Camp were preparing for a standoff on April 4, 1981 to protest the government's purchase of the Black Hills for twenty-six cents an acre. They refused to leave their 800 acres. I made speeches in Ohio, Illinois, and Kentucky, and raised several thousand dollars for the cause. My husband got the UAW-CAP union office to donate printing. The AFL-CIO union office donated a tremendous amount of time, energy, and money.

On the night of April 2, my son and I left with a convoy of eleven other vehicles for Rapid City, South Dakota. We were stopped at least eighteen times on the way down to Yellow Thunder Camp. Many of the vehicles were completely unloaded by state police and reloaded by us. At one point, my son had to watch as I was body-searched by the National Guard. Because there were so many vehicles, we had to travel slowly. The journey was hard. We arrived at Yellow Thunder at night, and I instantly fell in love with this beautiful camp.

The leaders knew we were coming, so we were taken directly into the camp. My son Richard was put on Warrior duty. I was put on Women duty, i.e., cooking. In addition to the confusion, anger, and fear, racial prejudice was rampant, both from White to Indian and Indian to White. As I walked into the kitchen to offer help, a full-blooded Indian woman threw a knife so that the blade penetrated a cedar post just to the side of my head. I grabbed the knife and threw it back to a cedar post just to the side of her head. She smiled, handed the knife back to me, and graciously asked, "Will you help us cut up the meat for dinner?"

Later that morning, I was told to take breakfast up to the Warriors keeping watch on one of the hills. The walk was hard going, but finally, at the top, I saw a little wickiup-type building. As I hollered at the door, I looked down and suddenly realized I was standing at the edge of a three-thousand-foot cliff. I froze in terror. A Warrior came out laughing at the look on my face. He thanked me for the food and then suddenly barked, "Stop, don't move," and started yelling as hard as he could. I was still scared about the three-thousand-foot cliff and this was not helping to ease my mind. Then the Warrior started laughing again. I didn't see anything funny. I turned around to look behind me and caught sight of a six-hundred-pound bear loping off.

I saw no reason to stick around and was heading back down the hill when the Warrior yelled out, "Watch out for rattlesnakes. They're pretty mean right now and will strike at anything." I stopped for a moment, breathed, then took off running at breakneck speed straight down the slope. Russell Means was standing with a group of people on the road at the base of the mountain, but it was too late for me to stop. I came charging out of the woods yelling, *"Hoka Hey!* [a good day to die]," right into Russell, knocking him flat. I didn't stop to apologize, but kept running straight to my truck to hide.

I was still catching my breath when Russell came around to the back of the truck, opened the door, and asked me what I thought I was doing. I told him, "Well, you guys have your way of protesting, and I have mine. Because of the extreme rattlesnake problem, I am now in protest in the back of my truck."

Eventually I did leave the back of the truck to sit on the hood and get some air, only to have my son Richard and his good friend, Frankie Drennon, throw a black snake my way. I jumped at least twenty feet in the air and came down beating on both their bodies.

On April 4, Russell made an eight-hour speech that I shall never forget. Hundreds of newspaper men, reporters, and cameramen were there to hear it, but when I finally telephoned Wonder, I learned that not one word of news about Yellow Thunder Camp had been published. I wondered what all those media people were doing there if they weren't giving our news to the people.

After a week-and-a-half in camp, I got very sick. On a trip into town for supplies, I collapsed on the street. Richard carried me back to the truck and took me into a tepee where the Greenpeace doctors could work on me. They said I was suffering from Toxic Shock Syndrome, and they wanted to take me to a hospital in Rapid City. I wanted Leonard Crow Dog to doctor me, but he could not be found. Instead, Buddy Red Bow and Grandpa Fools Crow did a doctoring on me. My son Richard says that I answered Grandpa's spoken words of Lakota perfectly, apparently understanding everything in my fevered state. The songs began, and I received a tremendous healing with the Eagle Feather.

That night, they had a huge ceremony, with baby namings, healings, and a marriage. Indiana had brought in lots and lots of corn that year, and they could finally do these ceremonies in gratitude. That night and the next day there was lots of singing and drumming and fun. I felt great after the doctoring and was really enjoying myself. Buddy said, "Well, sis, I guess you're going to live. Again."

Grandpa Fools Crow told me to come to a ceremony in Pine Ridge in the next few days to receive additional healing. I couldn't make it, but as soon as I could, I did go to a Sweat Lodge near his home. I was honored to be in the Lodge again with this old sacred man who could blow on rocks and make them hot.

In November of 1981, we brought another caravan to Yellow Thunder. Wonder came with me, and he and I were invited backstage at the Willie Nelson concert, which Willie gave for the Indian people out of the kindness of his heart. Willie is such a wonderful man. He did not break even financially from that concert. He was picketed by the Ku Klux Klan, which kept many people from attending. I got spat on by a KKK member. Willie took money out of his own pocket and gave it to the Black Hills Alliance to support their cause. I will *always* be a fan of Willie Nelson.

In December of that same year, I happened to turn on the radio to hear John Macri, numerologist, and Jan Moore, astrologer, on a show on which listeners could call in for readings. Neither of those personal friends of mine recognized my voice when I called. In their reading for me, they said that soon I would be journeying to the west to start work at a new job. After a short while at the job, I would quit it to begin a more focused spiritual education. They talked of a great purpose and prophesy that I had to fulfill, of my being a bridge between many races of people. I asked them over the radio if they knew who I was. Both said no. When I told them, they were amazed.

A year later, I came in, unannounced, to John Macri's noontime session on numerology. They just happened to be replaying the tape of my reading as an example of a good astrology and numerology reading. When I filled them in on what I had been doing, they realized *how* good a reading it had been. By then I had moved to Dallas, Texas, and begun a whole new phase of my life.

Coincidence? I don't think so!

"Well, let's see, read the list back to me." Grandma said. In the dark with a Bic lighter for my light, I read back to her the chapter headings that we had come up with so far. "Well, tell about the Indian Center and all that healing there in Dallas," she said, as she took her cup and yelled at Sparky Shooting Star to get her one more cup of coffee.

11

Dallas

In late 1981, I was asked to go to Dallas, Texas, to talk about Yellow Thunder Camp. I talked to six different community groups, and the talks were very successful. I was also asked to speak at the Dallas Intertribal Center. About 100 people showed up to hear about the Lakota camp of resistance. After the presentation, the director of the Center told me that he was looking for someone like me to help save their Native American alcohol counselling program, called Tribal Concern. Tribal Concern was the only agency in the Dallas metroplex that maintained the culturally sensitive network of services required to follow the recovering Indian alcoholic from the first stages of awareness, through treatment, rehabilitation, and sobriety mainte-nance. The program also provided public education to various com-munity organizations and schools. It was the only agency of its kind in the whole state of Texas. The director had my interest; but when he offered me the job, I had to explain that I lived in Indianapolis and would need to talk to my family. Also, I didn't know if I wanted to go to work for another Indian agency. I was tired of the way the Indian people tore each other apart instead of helping to support each other. He handed me an application. I filled it out in pencil and handed it back to him. He said that he would present it to the board with other applications and get back to me in about a week-and-a-half.

Since all the money that was collected at my speaking engagements was sent directly to the Black Hills Alliance, I had absolutely no money of my own. I still was walking a mile every day as part of my physical rehabilitation, so I explored the streets of Dallas, as I had back home, picking up cans to pay for my cigarettes. The walks gave me time to think about this possible change. After a few days, I flew back home and talked to my family about taking the job in Dallas. My husband, who was laid off at the time and collecting unemployment insurance, wasn't thrilled with the idea, but the kids were all for it.

A week later, the director called to ask if I could fly down for an interview in another week. We had no money to fly, so Richard and I caught a ride to Texas with John Crazy Horse. I interviewed for and was hired for the position. I didn't even return to Indianapolis, but started work in December 1981. As my intuition had warned me I would, I quickly became a controversial character at the Center, but the Tribal Concern program took off immediately, and I really enjoyed my job.

As my clients resided in the poorer sections of Dallas, one of the first things I did was to fight for the right to wear blue jeans to work instead of a dress suit. I wanted to go out into the community myself, rather than to sit and push papers in an office.

After three months, Wonder, Beth, and little John moved down to Dallas to the apartment that Richard and I had rented. Although my job was fulfilling, our family life was becoming more and more dysfunctional. Wonder never seemed to be really happy. He would find a job, and then it just wouldn't work out, so then he would go back to Indianapolis. This happened several times. We were pulled further and further apart.

One morning after praying to get closer to my kids, I came into my office and a flyer fell off the desk onto the floor before me. The flyer announced a meeting of people interested in building a Sweat Lodge. Rich and I joined with this group, helped build the Lodge, and we began to have Sweats. We brought many speakers and teachers into Dallas. I myself was still making speeches about Indian issues. We went to a lot of local Indian functions and powwows. My daughter ran for Miss Indian Dallas and came in third.

I became more and more despondent about my relationship with my husband. By then I had made a lot of new friends, one of whom was a gay Indian brother who worked at the Center. We went out once a week to talk and dance. In my ignorance, I believed that Wonder would know not to feel threatened or to worry that I was cheating on him because my friend was gay and his brother had a very handsome lover. But unfortunately, the lover developed a crush on me. I did not know that a man who was in a love relationship with another man could also love women — in this case, me. Before I knew it, I was totally embroiled in a big mess. Wonder was jealous, my friend from the center was angry, and his lover would not leave me alone.

Although the relationship was never sexual, it was completely out of control. Until then I had no idea of how damaging jealousy could be. My work suffered, my children suffered, my husband suffered, and I suffered.

Eventually, my friend was fired, I was put on probation, and my friend's lover continued to harrass me day and night. The director of the Center told me to take three days off to get my head together. It was an embarrassing mess, particularly since I had never actually been unfaithful to my husband.

On the three-day break, I went to Galveston Island to think it all over: the death experience, being told to Sundance, and why my life felt so crazy. Nothing seemed to be working. I wanted so to be a spiritual person, but I felt like anything but. I took a fourteen-mile walk in cowboy boots down the beach, badly blistering my feet. When I finally got back to my hotel room and collapsed, I heard the Spirit say in a very loud voice, "This time, you hurt other people; they didn't hurt you." As far as I knew, until this incident, I'd always been on the receiving end, never the giving end, of thoughtlessness. *This* side didn't feel so good either. I vowed to live within the teachings that I had thus far received from my Elders, to clean up my act, and to live in personal integrity.

On a last visit to the beach before leaving Galveston, I lay down on a rock in the sun. I pretended I was a seal. I prayed and felt truly at peace. When I looked up, I saw what seemed to be a snake swimming directly towards me. I had heard stories of horrible sea snakes that were very poisonous; but I also remembered that snakes brought me messages from Spirit. As it got close, I reached out to take hold of a perfect wooden staff. I prayed for healing and began to think about going to a therapist. I returned to work with a mission to make as many amends as possible to all parties involved.

"Snakey," as I called the wooden staff, stayed with me for many years. Whenever I looked at it, I would know I had the power to keep my sexual energy under control and not ever let it run rampant again to hurt people.

*Thunder talking on phone at work at
the Dallas Intertribal Center*

The Grass That Grew

As you have probably gathered already, my life at the Dallas Intertribal Center was a mere bit hectic, what with gathering support for the
Center, often feeling misunderstood, Indians fighting Indians, and
nobody happy with anything. Not that we didn't help a lot of people,
it's just that it was always hard.

One day, I was very depressed for a mother of five children I'd just
talked with. She was out of work and not able to receive compensation.
I went outside to smoke a cigarette. All around the Indian Center, there
was nothing but cement, but that day I noticed some children sitting
in a little triangle of dirt right in the middle of the city block. I'd never
really noticed the dirt there, but these little children had found a piece
of Mother Earth that they could touch and play on. Grandma had a
therapy for depression: to adopt a live thing, pray to it, be with it, care
for it, and, as it grows, so would I, out of my despair. As I watched the
children play, I decided the next day I would bring some tools from
home and start working on that little triangle of dirt.

For several weeks, on lunch breaks, I dug up the dirt, mixed it with
bags of potting soil, and, as money was available, planted grass and
flowers. I sat every day on the curb, my feet on the small plot of Earth,
and I prayed. I really loved that little triangle of grass. I began to notice
other Indians praying on this grass. Every once in a while, someone
would add a plant. The Indians in the neighborhood became as pro-
tective of the small plot as I was, picking up cigarette butts, pop cans,

or any trash — but only from the triangle of dirt. The rest of the block remained trashed.

Then word came down that the utility company would be repairing the sidewalk, which meant they would cement over our piece of Earth. A group of us journeyed down to a Dallas Council meeting to ask for leniency for our little triangle, and it was granted. The workmen were very careful of our piece of Earth as we all stood and watched them work. When I went on the road in 1983, I made my prayers and left food and gifts as I said goodbye to that piece of Earth.

Five years later, journeying through Dallas at about 9:00 at night, I stopped by to see the little triangle, to see if it was still there. As I got out of the van, the door to the Center opened. A sister, who turned out to be the new Deputy Director, greeted me: "You must be Thunder." Every once in a while I hear about how you made and prayed for this place of Earth in the sidewalk." I told her that in the dark I couldn't even find it. Did it still exist? She got a flashlight and showed me that the little triangle had grown into half a city block.

A Chief Auto Parts had taken the building next door, and, in the process of repairing their sidewalk, decided to bring back the Earth and flowers and grass. When we love something living, it can grow.

Contained within every seed is a flower that needs love for growth and blossoming. Within us, as well, is a flower — wisdom — a gift from Nature. If we nurture and love the seeds of our own inner beauty, we can experience the blossoming of our full potential.

The Deputy Director took me on a tour of the Center. She told me a lot of people really missed me there and remembered times that I had helped them. That made me feel really good.

The Spirit Gifts Me Health

One day, Grandma Grace called to tell me that Grandpa was going to be in Houston with Sun Bear. She asked me to help take care of him, and especially to make sure he didn't fall in love with any of those cute Texas girls.

So I went to Houston, where I met Dee Kendall, Scout Lee Gunn, and Brooke Medicine Eagle. Grandpa Wallace Black Elk was happy to see me, and we had a good time together. My ride to Houston decided to stay longer than we first planned, so someone hooked me up with a very interesting lady, Shirley Barclay, who drove a big RV.

By the time we got back to Dallas, I had time only to take a shower, change my clothes, and get to work. Shirley Barclay is one of the world's great psycho-dramatists. She invited me to come that evening to her psychodrama therapy group.

At the time, I had no extra money, so she included me in her weekly women's group at no charge. Those women helped me see who I was and gave me the encouragement I needed to start walking my spiritual path. This was the first of many opportunities the Creator has provided to help me sort out my life. I thank Shirley Barclay and the Dallas Metaphysical Center for all the love and support they shared over that next year.

A few months later, I received another gift from the Creator through a beautiful couple named Tom and Catherine Adelstein. They allowed me to attend their Prosperity Workshop on a scholarship. As I entered the room on the first day of the workshop, I saw that it was filled with people holding Gucci handbags and wearing Tony Lama boots and other elegant clothes and jewelry. I felt very out of place, since my best outfit at the time was a good pair of jeans and a t-shirt. Tom Adelstein asked, "What's prosperity to you?" I answered, "Everyone happy, everyone with enough food to eat, and everyone's needs being met." I sat and listened as 148 other people answered, "a Mercedes" and "fur coats."

Several times I fought back tears of embarrassment, and I seriously thought about walking out the door. On the third day, Catherine Adelstein opened a discussion called "Dressing for Success." It was the straw that broke the camel's back. She said, "Never, ever, wear stop-light red, green, or yellow." At the time, I was wearing a t-shirt from Santa Fe that was stoplight red, green, and yellow. I couldn't keep back my tears any longer.

When the presentation was over and the break was announced, I headed out. Catherine caught me at the door. She said, "Seeing your tears really made me think about what I was saying. If you will stay for the rest of the workshop, you and I will find a way to turn the pain we're both feeling now into something wonderful for the people. Two weeks ago I saw you speak on behalf of the Indian Center at the National League of Women's Group. You were impeccable. Please, don't leave and ruin your chance of picking up one more piece of information for your future."

*Catherine Adelstine, Thunder and Diana Wetheread
at Thunder's good-bye party, Unity Church
Mansion, Dallas, Texas*

Catherine and I did sit together and devise a plan we put into action at a later workshop. This is what we did: On the third day of the workshop, I would walk in during a break wearing my blue jeans, denim jacket, cowboy boots, and cowboy hat. It was like Moses parting the Red Sea. The question in the air seemed to be, "What's this motorcycle moll doing here?" I proceeded to ask people for a light for my cigarette and to try to strike up conversations, mostly to no avail. After the break, the participants went back behind closed doors. Fifteen minutes into Catherine's presentation, I entered the room. You could almost read the thought forms in the room: "Oh, my God, they've let her in." Catherine then said, "I would like to introduce you to a friend of mine who is dressed quite appropriately for her job, which is Alcohol and Drug Specialist for the Dallas Intertribal Center. Dressed in her jeans and denim jacket, she ministers to her clients in the inner city of Dallas." I then made my own presentation, confronting the group on their judgments of me.

Then I slipped into the next room and put on an Evan Picone suit and silk blouse. A crew worked on my make-up and hair. Approximately twenty minutes later, I reappeared in the lecture hall. This time the unspoken thoughts were completely different: "Who's *this* woman?" Catherine introduced me again by name. She said that I worked with prominent Dallas corporations seeking funds for the Dallas Intertribal Center. She added, "She is appropriately dressed for the job she does." Jaws dropped and people almost fell off their chairs; they couldn't believe that the two women were the same.

Catherine and I became very good friends. The pain of our first meeting was transformed into a beautiful teaching. The workshop helped me change my beliefs about life and prosperity. What I learned from them has become a part of my walk, keeping me in integrity and in the Universal Flow. I will always be thankful to Tom and Catherine Adelstein for the changes they helped make in my life. They used the proceeds from their workshops to buy a large mansion, which they donated to the Dallas Unity Church. This is only one example of their generosity.

In 1990, after I had been on the road some nine years, the Spirit led me to purchase the land that became the Thunder-Horse Ranch. Tom Adelstein held two Prosperity Workshops, raising $7,000 to help save our Ranch. In 1991, Catherine held a Prosperity Workshop Reunion and invited me as a speaker. It was wonderful to see everyone again. We left with a major donation for the Ranch, lots of hugs and "strokes," and a van full of roses. I am so grateful for the generosity of these two individuals in my life.

The Creator also provided me with a complete series of Rolfing sessions by Chuck Lustfield, a rolfer from Dallas. After each of the ten sessions, his wife Barbara gave me a massage. I grew over two inches in height and released a lot of the old memories that were binding my body. I'm so grateful to these two people.

The next gift of healing was from Dr. Virgil Chrane. He has perfected a chiropractic alignment process, The Alphabiotic System, that was developed by his father. The process is taught only by Dr. Chrane and is widely used throughout the world. For the last ten years, he has gifted to me these alignments that seem to turn the power back on in my brain. They have been incredibly beneficial to me in my work.

I really don't know the technical nature of the Alphabiotic System, but once, after completing a Vision Quest at Lake Whitney, Texas, I found myself grouchy, hateful, and full of paranoid thoughts. I went to Dr. Chrane, and he found that one of my legs was three inches shorter than the other. He said that this condition is common to psychics and spiritual people who use the right side of their brains. He cracked my neck three or four times, and I felt the negativity blow out of the back of my head. Instantly, I was in love with the world again. Colors were brighter and things tasted better.

As I've passed through Dallas over the years on the road, Dr. Chrane has always seen me, either at the office or at home, no matter what time it was, always free of charge. He, his son Michael and friend, Barbara Sheridan, have always offered their Alphabiotic Center for whatever ceremonies or teachings or classes I've wanted to share in Dallas. Very precious people in the Universe.

Chira Morgan entered my life approximately a year after I went on the road. For over eight years, she has gifted me with colonics and vitamin therapy, all at her own cost. She is a beautiful Indian sister whose love and patience have helped detoxify my mind as well as my colon. Thank you, Chira.

With the help of these people and others, I began to gather new energy and to reclaim the parts of myself I had denied for so long. I moved from struggling and living life as a victim to living in faith and taking responsibility for my life. I thank all of my teachers, therapists, doctors, and all the other beautiful people for their love and sharing of life-changing techniques.

Remembering the prayer I made on Galveston Island for healing to come in my life, I wish to thank the Creator and all those who heard that prayer and helped me to physically and emotionally regain health.

Chira Morgan, Tina Emerson and Thunder on the land in North Central Texas

"Tell them how your house used to be a road house in Dallas with lots of Indian people coming through."
Grandmother Grace Spotted Eagle

12

ELDERS & DALLAS

Part of my prayer for healing had been a vow to follow the spiritual ways taught by my Elders. During that next year, 1982, I had the opportunity to spend a lot of time with my Elders, some of whom I knew already, and some who came into my life for the first time.

Leonard Crow Dog

One of those Elders was Leonard, who came to Dallas to perform a *yuwipi* ceremony at Shirley Barclay's house.

A *yuwipi* (also called a House Ceremony) takes place in a darkened room. The leader of this ceremony is wrapped in a quilt and tied up with leather thongs in sometimes as many as a hundred knots. During the ceremony, the Spirit comes into the room and unties the knots and returns the leather thongs to the leader in a very tight ball. It is a healing ceremony.

Leonard, the Warriors, and I arrived at Shirley Barclay's home. Leonard needed hundreds of tobacco ties for the ceremony. We didn't have any red cloth, so the men wearing red shirts donated them for the ties. Leonard, some of the warriors, and I made the hundreds of tobacco ties. Then the ceremony began.

Leonard was wrapped in his Star Quilt and laid in the middle of the room with the ties all around him. During the ceremony, blue lightning ran up and down the walls. A lightning bolt cracked in the middle of the room, visible to everyone there. The spirit of Crazy Horse rode in and smacked a man whom perhaps the Spirit found out of integrity.

Leonard had me hold the Sacred Pipe, which meant I was in an honoring stance, kneeling or squatting for well over three hours. Every time I felt my body hurt or the Pipe became very heavy, Spirit lights would run up and down the Pipe stem and brush my face, giving me renewed strength not to let that Pipe go down.

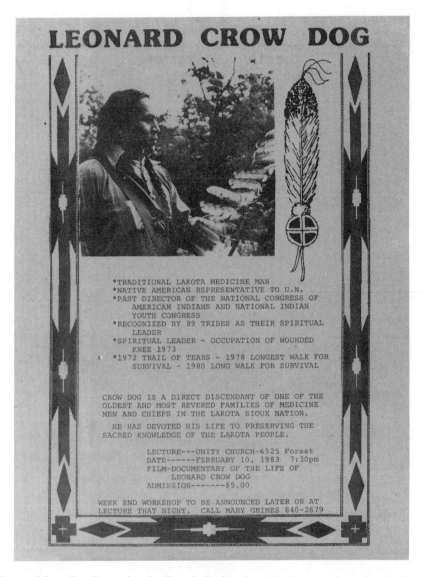

Leonard Crow Dog Poster done by Thunder back in the 1980s for a visit he made to Dallas

Many of the forty or fifty people in that room received healing. An Eagle head on the altar came alive and flew around the room. An owl hooted. I saw the styes fall off an old woman's eyes. When the lights came on at the end of the ceremony, we saw the Spirit had untied the 100 knots and wrapped the ties all together in a tight little baseball-like bundle. It was a good ceremony.

My Lesson Called Judgement

On the way home after the ceremony, Leonard wanted to stop at a bar. Judgment came up in me, but I had to surrender, for it's my feeling that if I have chosen a teacher, I have no right whatsoever to judge him. So into the bar we went — Leonard, several Warriors, and me.

Drinks were ordered. Judgment arose again. Leonard leaned over and said, "Thunder, hey, in a few minutes there's gonna be an Indian girl come out on that runway." I realized then that we were in a strip joint. He said, "I want you to go up and take her off the runway." I was full of judgment by then. I looked up and said to God, "Please notice I am drinking a Coke."

Sure enough, out walked a beautiful Indian girl with no clothes on. Whatever my judgments, I do what my Elders tell me to, for I've learned they always say and do things for specific reasons. I scrambled up onto the runway and tackled her. By then, she had seen Leonard, who was like the Pope of her people. She fought me like crazy, both to get away from me and for her very life and integrity — and she was much taller than I was.

Somehow I got her to the side of the runway. The Warriors put their jackets around her and brought her to Leonard. He took her face into his hands. He didn't talk about what she looked like or what she was doing, but he told her that he wanted to come by and see her, that she was loved on the reservation, and that her family was worried about her. He said he had heard she was using cocaine and gave her some ideas about how to stop. He let her know that she was loved and needed on the planet and respected for whatever she was doing to take care of her children. In the course of this conversation, I saw this woman transform from an emotional wreck into a proud Indian woman, all the while sitting naked under Warrior jackets.

Two weeks later, she came to the Dallas Intertribal Center for counselling, started a typing course, and began to change her life. I

Tlakaelel

learned that the child she was trying to support was autistic. If I had stayed stuck in my judgments, I would never have seen that beautiful lesson and transformation.

Tlakaelel

I had the good fortune to meet Tlakaelel, a *Teopizkeh*, or Sun Priest, from Mexico City. Many times I have heard him introduced as an Aztec Sun Priest, but *Aztec* is a name given to some Mexican people by the Spanish, in the same way *Sioux* is a name given to the Lakota people by the French. *Aztec* is probably a corruption of *Itzachitlatlan*, The Land of the Red Giants of Atlan. Atlan refers to Atlantis. Steve Schoff, a photographer and friend, and one of Tlakaelel's interpreters, recalls Tlakaelel explaining that this reference to Atlantis scared the Spanish, so *Atlan* became *Aztlan*, and then *Aztec*.

The first time I saw Tlakaelel, I saw in his eyes the message of the Universe. He seemed to see into my soul. He was stern and a little scary, but when he looked at me and my son, he smiled in a way that just opened my heart. His interpreter at that time, J.J. Reyna, and I were friends, so later when Tlakaelel needed a place to stay, he stayed in our home. I also traveled with him a few times.

Tlakaelel came through Dallas in 1982, trying to raise support for a spiritual school, Kalpulli Koakaklo. His plan was to build self-sufficient communities around Kalpulli, which would function as their spiritual center. As he outlined the social structure he had in mind, his plan seemed very well defined and clear, based entirely on his belief that man is a conscious and rational being with the inherent knowledge that his energy influences and is influenced by and intertwined with everything in the universe. Tlakaelel felt that, in living a simple life, giving and taking care to have what is necessary for the physical body and for the mind, the spiritual aspect of man can expand without limit. With this wider vision, man can best live on this Earth, truly acknowledging that we are all brothers and sisters who must live in peace and mutual respect. By maintaining the ecological balance in nature on all of its different levels, the vegetable, animal, and mineral worlds can have true communication.

On his first trip through, Tlakaelel brought his son, Akasha; two students, Cristino and Topili; and an interpreter, J. J. Reyna. The weeks we spent together were very special and very sacred. I helped set up lectures for them to give at the Intertribal Center.

I spent a lot of time with those four Mexican people who could not speak to me in a language that I could understand. Working with so many Lakotas under similar conditions, I had developed my own sign language. One night, two ladies arrived at our apartment. They wanted a blessing from Tlakaelel. J.J., the interpreter, was not there, so I tried to convey what they wanted to Tlakaelel by putting my hands together and bowing my head. His black eyes snapped and he stood up and left the room. I didn't know what I'd done wrong. Soon J.J. returned and I explained what had happened. He went to find out what had upset Tlakaelel, and soon came out laughing. He said, "Thunder, when you asked Tlakaelel if he would do a blessing for these women, he thought you were asking him to marry them, and that just isn't done in his country." The ladies got their blessing and, from then on, no matter where he was, if Tlakaelel got bored, he would put his hands together and bow his head, and we would all burst out laughing.

Later, Tlakaelel met with Uncle Leonard, and these two men, Spiritual Leaders from the South and the North, got along magnificently. It was a very powerful experience to hear them talking about ceremonies.

As Tlakaelel was leaving, he wrote out a note that I could use to gain entrance to the sacred Dance of the Sun in Mexico. Although I have been in Mexico, I have never Sundanced there, but I know it is a great honor to have been asked.

After 1982, I Sundanced often with Cristino and Topili. In 1983, I was privileged to meet Tlakaelel again, with all of his beautiful people, at

Tlakaelel leading Dancers to enter Sundance circle in Mexico

Crow Dog's Paradise. One of the people journeying with him was a lady from Mexico City by the name of Xilonem, meaning "Sweet Corn." Years later I would meet Xilonem again and do ceremony with her in Mexico City. Her son, Alejandro, and another friend, Denhi, whom I later adopted as my daughter, were all a part of this wonderful Mexican connection.

Tlakaelel, a hard-looking but soft-hearted man, won over many hearts and made many friends in Dallas. He would talk until all hours of the night, telling Creation stories, so proud of his people, so proud of his way to pray. His chest showed the scarring of many Sundances. You could see from his walk that he was a strong leader among all men, not only his own people.

The Mandate of Huey Tlahtoani Kuauhtemoktzin

The Mexican people in the City of Mexico-Tenochtitlan, cultural capital of the Confederation of Anahuak, had been under seige by the Spanish invaders for months. There no longer remained either food or drinkable water. There were no more weapons.

All of the warriors had given their all, fighting a long time without sleep. The situation was desperate, and the people could not continue the resistance much longer.

Kuauhtemoktzin, Maximum Spokesman for the Supreme Council of Anahuak, addressed the people. His mandate was delivered on the eve of a great change. With this change, the evolution of an ancient indigenous culture would be interrupted for 500 years. His message has served these many generations as a blueprint for indigenous survival. Instructing the citizens of this flourishing culture to preserve their heritage by passing it down to their descendants, Kuauhtemoktzin must have envisioned fully that they were to live in oppression, in spiritual darkness, for generations. How must he have felt? This message is one of the great testaments of individual courage, and of the courage of indigenous people. Half a millenium later, this message has endured, and the people with it. They are here watching the dawn. Many thanks go to Steve Schoff, who helped obtain this piece for this book, even calling Tlakealel in Mexico to make sure its translation was correct.

The message, delivered again by Tlakaelel, is nearly 500 years old and was passed down through his family by Oral Tradition for seventeen generations. Many years after his first Dallas visit, I saw it printed in the pages of *Itzmolini Xochitl*, a newsletter of the Kalpulli Koakolko, USA, in Boston. With his permission, I share it here:

Nauitlamatl
The Message of Cuauhtemoc

The message of Kuauhtemoktzin, delivered on August 13, 1521, has been passed down through the Oral Tradition in the family of Tlakaelel for seventeen Generations.

For the guardians of all time, for men of the future. Our Sun has gone. Our sun has gone and left us in darkness. We know that it will rise again. Once again it will come to illuminate us. It will be with us in the mansion of death. We will reunite valiantly. We must shield and hide away all those things in our hearts that we know are the treasures. We will destroy the temples, our places of meditation, our houses of song and dance, our ball courts, our schools for our children, our universities. We will close the doors and leave the streets deserted. We will stay hidden until our Sun comes out. Our homes will become our temples, they will become our meditation places, they will become our houses of song and dance, our ceremonial ball courts, our schools, our universities. We will wait until our new Sun comes. Parents are obliged to teach the culture, the man with his sons, the woman with her daughters, and they will tell the children of their children of their children what our beloved culture has done. They will pass on the lamp of our destiny and our traditions which our ancestors, with love, have given to us. Do not forget to tell your children or their children, with proper respect. Tell them how it was . . . how it will be . . . how we will rise again . . . how to gain strength and how our culture will fulfill its great destiny on Mother Earth.

So much time, 500 years. Tlakaelel told me that prophecy had predicted that the time of spiritual darkness would begin with the arrival of the Europeans. Then the world would plunge into materialism. Imbalance would threaten the planet. But after 500 years, the Condor of the South would meet the Eagle of the North, signalling the return of light to the planet and the dawn of a golden era.

We live in the time of this prophecy's fulfillment. Maestro Tlakaelel of Mexico came to the United States, and he and Leonard Crow Dog of South Dakota did a ceremony about this prophecy at a Sundance at Crow Dog Paradise, in South Dakota. Tlakaelel brought many Mexican people to dance in our Sundance. I was there and privileged to see and hear the tellings. They told us Sundancers that the ceremony was the culmination of the prophecy, that the time would come of Peace Talking, tellings of the old, and reunification of the native peoples in order to help the Earth and her inhabitants.

At the ceremony, Grandpa Henry Crow Dog, Leonard's father, talked about a vision he had had of tepees lining up from South Dakota all the way to Mexico. He knew from this vision that someday Tlakaelel would come to South Dakota and the energies of the Northern and Southern indigenous peoples would be unified.

Ten years after that ceremony, those same two Elders, came to our Thunder-Horse Ranch here in Texas. Leonard did a ceremonial blessing of this land even before it was ours, in 1989, and Tlakaelel did ceremony here after Wolf Song II, in 1992.

When Tlakaelel first spoke in Dallas, a business executive challenged his teachings. Tlakaelel told the man, through his interpreter, to hug a tree and send a telepathic message to his mother to call him at 7:00. Although the man he-hawed the whole exercise, he left the gathering a little bit early to get home, just in case. Exactly at 7:00, the call came.

The man later gifted Tlakaelel with a contribution, and Tlakaelel went shopping and got presents and lots of food to share with our family. He also got money together to send back to his wife, whom he always talked about with so much love. My life was truly blessed by meeting this man. I loved his heart, his singing, and his dancing.

In 1987, in the middle of winter, surrounded by ice and snow, on our way to a Mexican restaurant in Chicago to have dinner with my adopted daughter, Denhi, there was a horrible noise and the brakes on our van failed completely. We managed to pull over, park, and walk the remaining few blocks to the restaurant. With hardly any money and faced with major auto repairs, we were all a little depressed. Denhi was running late, and as we all sat around the table, discussing our plight, I received a great big hug from behind. There stood Cristino, Topili, and two other male Mexican Sundancers I had danced with at Crow Dog's Paradise. Then in came Alejandro and Julio. Finally, Denhi arrived. She was as surprised as we were that in a matter of ten minutes, it just "happened" that I should be surrounded by seven Mexican Sundancers. We laughed and joked, shared stories, and every three minutes someone spoke the words, "The car, it is no problem."

Very soon we were at the garage of another brother Sundancer which, by some coincidence, was a mere half-block from where our car had broken down. All the Sundancers pushed while I guided the car through the streets of Chicago. By then, I didn't care if the car got fixed or not, it was just so good to see my friends again. But the car was fixed — probably a $300-400 job — in about an hour, for absolutely no charge. All these people were devotees of Tlakaelel.

They all stayed with us while the van was being fixed. It was about twenty below zero outside, and the garage was not very well insulated, so I had to laugh when one of my road crew observed, "It's kind of hot in here, isn't it?" It must have been all that loving energy from the Sun in their hearts. They all chipped in and gave us some money, and we set off again down the road with happy tummies, happy hearts, and a happy car.

Tlakaelel is a great man, a wonderful role model of a Peace Elder. With the dark black eyes that only Medicine Men possess, he can look into your soul and, with just a smile, turn your life around.

Rolling Thunder

In 1982, I received a call from my friend Catherine Adelstein to set up a meeting with Dr. Donald Curtis, minister of the Unity Church in Dallas, regarding Rolling Thunder. (Later in our relationship, Rolling Thunder would allow me to call him R.T.) She asked me to help them with R.T.'s upcoming lecture, for they had not really had that much experience with Native people. I quickly said yes, for I had heard and seen Rolling Thunder once in Chicago, and found him so inspiring that I had written to him at his camp, Meta Tantay, in Nevada.

I received a call from Meta Tantay three days later. Long lists of facts and details started flowing over the phone lines: arrival dates, dietary requirements and a grocery list that cost over $250, and instructions as to how to care for him and how to buy food that is fresh and alive. Since he would be honoring our home, I hung up the phone terrified that I might not do things right.

Wonder and the kids cleaned the house from top to bottom. I made arrangements for television, radio, and newspaper interviews. The day for R.T.'s arrival was at hand. We all went to the airport to start a new page in our lives.

Imagine the blackest eyes that peer into your soul and see its journey from past to future; a man who, if he becomes angry, can create a thunder-lightning-wind storm with a word; a sharp, shrewd intellect that walks in balance with Nature and All That Is; a man who can pick up a rattlesnake and learn its story; a man who has personal knowledge of and relationship with 2,200 plants. This is Rolling Thunder.

Rolling Thunder with fan

"Rolling Thunder," means *song to the gods* or *walking with the Truth*. Rolling Thunder is a Native American of the Cherokee tribe. For over thirty-six years, he made his living by working for the railroad as a brakeman. He has appeared with and maintains a close relationship with the Grateful Dead music group and, in the fall of 1975, he toured the continent with The Rolling Thunder Review, which included Bob Dylan. During 1972 and 1973, he helped make the film, *Billy Jack*, as well as its sequel in 1975, *The Trial of Billy Jack*. Today you can still find Billy Jack trucks parked at Meta Tantay. Actually, R.T. *is* Billy Jack, or so some say.

Rolling Thunder Stepped Off the Plane

He was truly "bigger than life." We recognized each other's spirits right away. He said we had walked together many times before. "This time," he said, "I get to be the Teacher," and he laughed. Mike Thor and Ksab, R.T.'s son-in-law, had come along. They cooked for R.T. All of us stayed up the first night until 4:00 a.m. listening to R.T.'s stories.

R.T. would say, "All pollution comes out of the minds of man. Therefore, the cleansing of the Earth must start with the cleansing of our minds. We'll have to clean up our own Spirits before we can clean up our land. To heal is to live in harmony with all life. If people don't change their ways quickly, then there will be great upheaval. I've had Visions of the coming planetary cleansing. We are told that cleansing in the past involved either fire or water but this time, it will involve *both* fire and water."

R.T. told us about ancient prophecies that predicted that, just before the next world war breaks out, a third of the sky will light up red when the moon rises, and that the sun may reverse its course, rising in the West and setting in the East. R.T. talked about a first-ever medicine man counsel in Oklahoma, where a very old board with Indian writing on it was brought out. The writing said that the Spirit of Brotherhood will be born among Native peoples here, in this land, and then spread around the world. R.T. talked about the circle of life, continuity of life and Indian nations. The circle is found everywhere in the natural world. The very atoms in our bodies are composed of concentric circles orbiting a spherical nucleus. The Earth is round. He told me if you beam a beam of light out into space for billions of miles, it will eventually arc back around in a circle to its starting point. The circle connects all.

My sons Rich and John began training with Mike Thor to be Warriors for R.T. Richard had spent a lot of time on the road with Leonard and learned a lot. Mike and R.T. were very impressed with his style and mannerisms, or actually the lack of them.

I was overwhelmed by the time we finally got to bed. I had to work the next day and the kids had school, and we all woke the next morning cross-eyed.

At the Indian Center, there was much hubbub and a lot of controversy about R.T. and the plan for his visit. That did not make for a nice peaceful day, to say the least.

I arrived home to learn how the day had gone for R.T. The interview at Channel 11 was great. The interview with a leading Dallas newspaper, however, was a disaster. The interviewer seemed to dislike R.T. from the moment they met. She said he was a fake and a phony because she had heard some Indian had said so. An Indian at the Cherokee Native American Cultural Center had been rude and belligerent. R.T.

was furious. It was like the wrath of God had appeared in our living room. Of course, I felt completely responsible for R.T.'s pain right then, and R.T. agreed that everything was all my fault.

We had dinner that night at a very fancy restaurant in Dallas with my friends Tom Baker and Walter Covert. R.T. sat there, thoughtfully puffing away on his corncob pipe filled with Five Brothers tobacco. He said he didn't get involved in politics, but he would like to see a law based on the old medicine way that the chiefs and medicine people couldn't eat until all the other people were fed.

At home that night, we had another story telling session till 4:00 the next morning . . .

Next Day's Schedule

Again I woke up feeling as though I had been beaten up. At the office, everyone had negative opinions to share about R.T. I asked Rick Lucero, Director of the Dallas Intertribal Center, if we should cancel R.T.'s visit. He said, "Heck no. At least the people are alive and moving." I told Rick that I would be honest with R.T. and that he ultimately should be the one to make the decision about whether or not to cancel the visit.

Later that day, we went to "ghostbust" an empty mansion nearby belonging to some wealthy people. R.T. talked with a small crying spirit child, helped to reconcile its difficulties, and then helped it to pass to the other side. The wealthy folks asked R.T. and the rest of us not to mention what had happened — "You know, what would everyone think?" R.T. just laughed and said, "Don't worry. We won't tell anyone we cleaned up your shit for you."

R.T. became instantly attuned to each situation. A true warrior is always alert and ready for action, in the "now" at every moment, flowing with the people.

At home, again stories until 4:00 a.m. Feeling the power of his energy and medicine, we asked when he first knew he could heal. R.T. answered, "All I can say is that I woke up one morning, and this force was with me for the first time. I'd been doctored — in my sleep — the night before by a Sun god and his helpers, and when I awoke I knew something was different. I felt this great power within me. But I had to learn to *live* with the tremendous force, to watch every thought or emotion I had, twenty-four hours a day. Since the force is so strong, you see, it has a great potential for misuse, and it could really hurt someone if it were employed in a negative or destructive way." He added to my kids, "Your mother, here, is a tremendous healer. She also has power." This was pretty shocking to hear. I looked at him and he smiled.

I didn't have to worry about waking up that morning, because we never went to bed. We did Sun Rise ceremony at a park in Oak Cliff, leaving the house about 4:00 a.m. to be there before the sun rose. It was so very wonderful to stand with R.T. in a circle before dawn, singing and praying as he has done most of his life. We walked around the park at sunrise, identifying all the plants at breakneck speed, for I had to go to work, and everyone else had appointments.

That evening, some "brilliant" person brought R.T. that day's newspaper, dated January 27, 1983, with a headline that read, "Who Was That Medicine Man? Rolling Thunder Travels Under a Cloud of Mystery." The article quoted a number of people who said things like, "Rolling who?" and "I've never heard of him." It was a very negative story. I prayed hard for my life while he exploded.

All of a sudden, R.T. calmed down, breathed, took my hand, and told me not to worry. Everything would be all right.

When I got up the next morning, I noticed that Snakey, my precious snake stick, was gone from my altar. The night before, I had prayed at the altar, and the stick had been there then. I had been the last one to go to bed. No one had come in our bedroom. Where was it? I asked Wonder, the kids, Ksab, and Mike, and no one knew anything about it.

Then R.T. came out for breakfast. He looked at me with a twinkle in his eye, held up Snakey, and asked casually, "Did you lose something?" I answered, "I guess Snakey got lonely last night." I immediately offered it to him as a gift, but he said, "No, it wishes to come back and be your staff of Life." He passed me the staff and we held it together for what seemed like hours, but was probably only about ten minutes. It felt like 474 currents of raw energy ran between us. He said, "I have given you a shot of energy, an initiation. You are now a Thunder person, a Warrior for Peace, a Clan Mother of Warriors of Truth." I said something about not being able to set up a very good lecture. R.T. just smiled and said, "You just wait, Thunder Warrior, and see what happens."

I went off with Mike Thor and Johnny to do last-minute organizing. I was the go-between for those folks who wanted to talk to R.T. alone, before or after the lecture. There were gifts and letters to be presented and amazing people who wanted to express their gratitude for having received healing. There was a lady who had danced with the Dallas Ballet with a badly injured leg, a person who said he was an old friend, and two Indians from Oklahoma, Randy No Name and a man Randy introduced to me as one of his Elders, Fred Wahapapah. The moment I looked into Fred's eyes, I knew I was seeing another old friend. All these folks Spirit told me were okay to see R.T. He healed the lady's leg, was glad to see his old friend, and asked Randy No Name and Fred Wahapapah to sit on stage with him. An Indian woman asked R.T. for money to get home, and he gave it to her.

Close to 2,000 folks showed up to see R.T. in the church which that morning had looked so big and empty. The Chapel was completely filled with people, so some sat in other rooms watching video monitors, and others sat outside, where speakers had been set up. Indians were given free admission and priority treatment. I was busier than a cat covering poopoo when Mike ran up and said that R.T. wanted to see me. R.T. wanted me to introduce him. In front of all of those people? I begged him to reconsider. He said, "The Spirits talk to and through you. Do it." I did, and it was a success. The Spirit talked good! The workshop went the same way.

On Saturday night, one of my Lakota brothers, one who had said especially bad things about R.T., called to say he had been arrested for drinking and needed $600 to get out of jail. R.T. gave it to him.

Sunday we rested — much as we could, with R.T. around. He had been given some gifts from a witch who had been a friend many years, always denying her involvement in the willful form of Spiritual endeavor. But the energy on the gifts was very negative. Recently, she finally acknowledged that she has always been a witch; but R.T. had that one pegged all along.

Monday was the day scheduled for the talk at the Indian Center. R.T. still wanted to keep the commitment. I was scared. As we walked through the Center, we could feel the negativity. People showed up, but some came only to argue. After his talk, R.T. said to me, "I came here today to show you what you work in everyday. Your light is a magnet attracting people who want to attack it. You need to be out there sharing with the people your knowledge and wisdom." R.T. had sacrificed to prove a point to me. I will always be grateful.

That night, he said I needed medicine. J.J. Reyna and I were sent on a treasure hunt for just the right ingredients. R.T. made a medicine for protection. He said I was a great woman with a job and a mission and that I was wasting my energies on one-on-one communication when I could affect many more people. He talked about my marriage and the stress I was under and blessed me. I was deeply honored.

The next day, as we took R.T. and crew to their plane, it began to Thunder at the Dallas International Airport — Rolling Thunder. There was bright sunshine on one side of the airport and thunder, lightning, and rain on the other. I cried as I stood between Sun and rain and the Eagle went up into the clouds. As the plane disappeared, a huge thunderbolt appeared in the sky and the rain poured down to cleanse Dallas of the smog in men's minds.

Yes, our lives had been changed. Before R.T. had left, he named Wonder and honored my children, John Crazy Horse, and J.J. Reyna. He had paid all the grocery bills and other expenses and given money to Fred and Randy to get back to Oklahoma.

Ron Williams, R.T.'s psychic consultant, stayed, parked at our apartment house, and saw clients from his R.V. Ron is of Choctaw ancestry. He has traveled all over with R.T., and R.T. says he is about 90 percent accurate in his readings. He has an international reputation and has foreseen plane crashes, health problems for John Wayne, Ronald Reagan, and Pope John Paul II, many of the ups and downs of precious metals, world economic developments, earthquakes, weather changes, and my divorce. He told me he kept seeing a silver chain break. At a time when I wanted desperately to save the marriage, Ron helped me clear up some confusion.

A couple of weeks passed and R.T. called. He said he was going to be in Houston, Texas, and wished for us to meet him there.

Fred Wahapapah visited from Oklahoma again. He stayed a couple of nights and told us of his Sundance plans for the year. He teasingly offered to be my guide, if I needed to Sundance that year. I tried to change the subject, but Wonder kept going on about how Leonard had told me I needed to Dance. I felt like choking him. I told Fred about R.T.'s call, and he said, "Hey, let's all go."

Rolling Thunder with Thunder, Horse, Sparky and Charlotte Dann from Nevada

So Fred, Wonder and I went down to Houston, arriving about five minutes late for R.T's talk at the huge Cullen Auditorium at the University of Houston campus. As we walked in, Mike Thor came running down and said, "Thunder, R.T. is waiting for you to introduce him." I went directly on stage to introduce this great man to 1,000 folks eyeing me in my blue jeans and Thunder t-shirt. I was honored, but also worried I would embarrass R.T. by not being dressed properly in the Indian way. Sure enough, he scolded me afterwards. Since then, I've always remembered to put my skirt on in the car.

The next night, Ron was to be on a radio show with Gary Wayne, another psychic, at the Houston Rodeo. I went with Ron, while Wonder and Fred stayed to take care of R.T. There wasn't much time to get acquainted with Gary, and I really don't know if he noticed me or not, but when he started taking requests from the crowd, I asked for a reading. He said, "I see two sides of you. I see one side that can be very comical, and another that is very serious. It seems that you know how to fit your mood to the people you're with. You know when to be quiet, but you also can talk a lot. You'll probably have a revelation this year, a very deep inside revelation. The healing work is very strong with you and you need to practice it. If you don't practice it, you may feel sort of sick and stagnated and not know why. You'll be with friends or talking with people, but you'll just feel empty inside. People may say, 'Come live with us for awhile,' not because you won't have a home, but because they want your energy or your support — not financial support but just the support of your being and the energy that you generate. I feel that you are going to open up a center that will be involved in consciousness raising. It will be very successful and will get a lot of attention, even though it may not be all that much different in appearance than other places. People will come there to find more completeness. Your marriage needs more work, more flexibility. The minute he puts controls on you or you put controls on him, it's fireworks. I see you involved with a lady from South Dakota who will help you. You're either going to write a book or record a lot of notes, but these notes will have significance in an orderly form."

The revelation Gary saw was Sundance Walk, which we began in May. I have stayed with lots of folks in their homes, and I have opened a center on the land. The marriage dissolved due to control issues. The lady from South Dakota was Grace Spotted Eagle. And now, as you can see, I have written a book.

We returned home and again R.T. talked into the night.

The next morning, just after dawn, R.T. woke me and then Mike Thor. We both ran after him (he walks so fast), and soon found ourselves in the middle of a golf green. Black clouds were rolling our way. R.T. said a tornado or hurricane was coming, and we had to stop it. He gave each of us an Eagle feather. Then he took out his Sacred Eagle Wing and started yelling and chanting. I was very nervous with my small Eagle feather, doing — I hoped — as instructed, holding position and praying for the clouds to break up. As R.T. walked around the golf green and continued to yell and chant, the clouds began to break up. I'll never forget him standing there with his arms out to the Universe, and the Universe responding.

R.T. and I remain close to his day. I honor him so. He has helped many, many people, especially me.

Rolling Thunder

It was so very dark. I was in pain from what Grandma had said to me, and my head was aching. She continued to speak as Sparky gave her a cup of coffee. Her hand held Sparky's for a moment and Sparky smiled sweetly at her. It was a great moment for them, but for me it was very painful, thinking it might be Sparky's last chance to hold Grandma's hand. I dropped my head, even though she could not have seen my eyes clearly, and brushed away a tear. Still looking at Sparky, she said, "Tell them about how you got the message to go to the Dance that first year." I just kept writing and crying.

Grandmother Grace Spotted Eagle

13

THE CALL TO THE DANCE

In spring 1983, my secretary at the Dallas Intertribal Center came into my office to say that Leonard Crow Dog was on the phone. She was pretty excited. I got on the phone and said, "Hey, Uncle, what's happening?" He said, "Niece, I have been thinking. I remember your heart attack and how the Creator brought you back, and I also remember it's time for you to Sundance."

As you can imagine, I wasn't exactly thrilled to hear this. "Well, Uncle, I have a problem with Dancing this year." I told him all my problems with the job and all the great things we had done through Alcohol Programs. I shared with him that my heart was invested in helping the Indian people of Dallas. Silence met me from the other end of the phone. I said that I didn't have anything to wear to the Sundance and besides, I didn't even know how to do the Sundance. "Uh-huh," said Uncle Leonard, as he proceeded to give me about five pages of instructions of what I needed to do to prepare. He said that he would be sending up the Pipe, and he gave me an unbelievable list of things for the Dance that I would have to bring together. Not only was I in resistance, but I really didn't see how I could find the resources to make it all happen.

I hung up the phone still trying to think of ways out, feeling how much I honored Leonard, but how afraid I was — no, terrified. My doctors had told me after the heart attack that I shouldn't even go into a Sweat Lodge, and here we were talking about the Sundance. I had seen the Dance in South Dakota, and my memory was of strong young warriors performing an incredible feat of endurance. I couldn't see myself in that picture at all.

An hour later my secretary came in and announced, "Rolling Thunder is on the phone!"

By now the Indian Center was in great excitement — first Leonard Crow Dog, and next Rolling Thunder.

Now at seventy-eight years of age, Rolling Thunder still goes out *every* morning to pray for the Planet. He builds a little fire, sings his song, and prays to dispel negativity. Even when he was very sick, he had some people carry him out so as not to miss a day's prayers.

I breathed and smiled to myself that this was just a friendly call to see how I was doing, for Rolling Thunder didn't Sundance or have a Pipe — that wasn't his way. It felt good to hear him say, "*Osiyo* ("Hello" in Cherokee), Thunder Woman." He told me that he had been out praying that morning and had had a vision, and he thought he'd better call me and tell me what the Spirit had said. Now my breathing stopped and I froze. Rolling Thunder said that, in that early Nevada morning, the Spirit had told him that I should Sundance that year. "Uh huh, R.T., thank you. I think I got that," I said. He added, "Well, I guess, Thunder Woman, you will be going to the great Sundance this year. If you need anything or if there is anything that I can help you with, just give me a call. Please pray for me at the Sundance!" I hung up the phone and just sat there for a moment. I thought, "Something is happening here."

Then the next call came in. This time it was Wallace Black Elk. By now the secretary was beside herself, and everybody at the Center was thinking that major earth changes were about to happen, or maybe an ancient prophecy was about to manifest.

Now, this call had me worried me even before I picked it up, for Grandpa was a Sundance Chief; but my rational mind said it would just be too much of a coincidence. I picked up the phone, and right away Grandpa said, "Daughter, uh, Grandpa Spirit, like that, tells me you're going to Sundance this year. So, uh, you'll need medicine to wear and you need to come by Colorado before you go to South Dakota." Then Grandma Grace took the phone and went on and on about what I needed to do and about how she'd like to make the Sundance dress, or at least sew some stitches on it. I said that it was good to hear their voices, but that I was not sure I was going to Dance this year. Grandma shot back, "Thunder, didn't you hear Wallace? He said you are going to Dance!" I hung up the phone and told my secretary to cancel some of my appointments, for I had to leave the office for a little while.

You have to understand, dear Readers, that my Elders don't hang around a lot together, and they certainly don't call each other up on the phone to discuss my spiritual life. For this to have happened all in one day was nothing short of a miracle.

I was completely overwhelmed. As I mentioned before, I was a specialist on alcohol and drug abuse at the Center, but after these three phone calls, I decided to go out and get drunk. I left the center, took myself to a bar, and sat down. I ordered a double shot of Jack Daniels but before I could take a good gulp, a big Indian brother came over and said, "I can't believe it, Thunder! Here you go around telling us all this stuff about getting sober, taking responsibility, and changing our lives, and here you are about to take a drink!"

I looked at him for a long hard moment. This guy was six-foot-five inches and one mean "mother," as he called himself. I had worked with him for a long time, helping him get sober and then, sadly, watching as he would get drunk again. His whole family were clients. Many Friday nights, I had found him at this very bar. I never went in to drink myself (at this writing, I have been drug- and alcohol-free for fifteen years), but I would try to rescue his pay check. I would leave him just so much from the check and hand the rest to his wife waiting outside. The wife would come to the Center and ask me to do this for her and when I looked out the window and saw her six children in the car, I couldn't refuse. When he drank, he was a mean guy.

I looked into his eyes and he looked into mine. He said, "Hey, you have saved my butt many times. Now I want to help you." As he watched, I just poured my drink on the floor, kicked back my chair, and started to stomp out. For a moment, I thought we might fight, but then I smiled and said, "Thank you." He smiled back and said, "Hey Thunder, whatever it is, it can't be that bad. Don't give it up yet." We hugged. I went out to my car, cried, composed myself, and went back to work.

Back at the office, Herman was waiting to see me, and he was in very bad shape. Herman lived in a cardboard box under the Dallas freeway. It was pretty obvious that he'd recently been in a fight, for he had a gash on his hand and it was developing gangrene. He would not see anyone else but me for help and, quite frankly, no one else wanted to see him. As we sat down in my office to examine his very dirty hand, all of a sudden, his usually unclear way of talking changed. My head jerked up, and I saw that Herman had a light around him. Herman had life in his dull eyes and though I really can't explain it, Herman was glowing. He began to speak eloquently about my soul's purpose on the planet and how I had to Sundance to save my life, to express gratitude for my life, to become a spiritual person who would be of much help to many people. I said to myself, "Is this Herman?" I just sat there and stared at him, for I realized that at that moment, it was not Herman, but the Spirit that was talking. Then, as suddenly as it started, it stopped. I watched as the slouch and dull eyes returned, and Herman took on again the appearance of a beaten man, a victim of himself and society.

I quickly asked him if he remembered what he had just said to me. He just looked at me and said, "I hurt, please help me." I took him back to the clinic to see a doctor. As I was leaving the room, I turned back to look at him again. Herman looked up and winked at me, then returned his attention to the doctor. I left shaking my head.

Back in my little office, as I was thinking over the events of the day, my secretary came in to say I had another call, from an old teacher in Indiana. She told me, "I was watching the Hawk this morning and, as the Hawk flew, it told me that you were going to Sundance." I just said, "Ooookaaaay."

I sat at my desk and stared at a big poster of Leonard Crow Dog. The poster says "We are still here," meaning that the Indian people are still alive and still needing help in this world today. I smiled, breathed, and wrote out my resignation.

> *Success is not a destination —*
> *it's a journey. True success can*
> *be measured by how much creativity*
> *you can express when you're feeling low.*

The above is a note I wrote to myself before I walked into the director's office at the Center. The director was a really special human being, and he and I had a good relationship. As I shared my resignation with him, he was visibly irritated and shocked. While at the Dallas Intertribal Center, I had helped to save the alcohol program and raise over $38,000 — all in all, not a bad track record. I had been a controversial person at times, but there always had been support from the director and sometimes from the board and a lot of other wonderful folks. Our meeting was bittersweet. After I told him my plan, he took me out to dinner and shared his feelings about his own spiritual life. I will always truly honor this man and the beautiful people at the Dallas Intertribal Center.

Then I went home to face my family with the decision I had already made without first counseling with them. We talked a long time about what would happen. Not all Sundancers give up their jobs and dedicate their lives to walking a spiritual path "on the road," but part of the prophecy of my after-death experience had been that when I started Sundancing, I would let go completely of the "Today World as I knew it." I would gift my life in service to the Universe, no longer just to a nine-to-five job or the traditional demands of everyday life.

My husband, who at the time was receiving unemployment insurance, agreed to the plan immediately; but my children were shocked, scared, upset, and really angry. They felt that I was abandoning them. As Beth said, "Mother, *children* run away, not mothers." We talked late into the night, and I took the next day off from work to finish the conversation. I was saddened that my husband did want to go — he and I were not getting along — and that my children did not. I shared my fears about leaving them and their making it on their own. After much, much sharing, we began to make plans and to explore what money and options were available to make it all work.

Richard decided that he wanted to stay in Dallas and suggested that his brother and sister live with him. He would find another place since our apartment at the time was too expensive to keep. He was nineteen, had been out of school for several years, and had a pretty good job, so he could provide a space for all the children to be together. Beth, who was seventeen, was also already out of school and working, so my only concerns about schooling were centered on John Eric, who was only fifteen.

We found a house in the area and put down a security deposit. Richard would rent out two of the bedrooms to family friends to help pay the rent. Johnny would spend the summer with his grandparents in Indianapolis.

As if Universally scheduled, Fred Wahapapah showed up the next evening. When he heard about my decision to go on the road, he laughed and offered again his services as a guide. Things were starting to fit together. I offered the kids whatever they needed from my belongings and started to give away or sell everything else. We held a gigantic yard sale. Fred told me approximately how much money I would need for a year with him on the road, paying my equal share of gas, mileage, and food.

I went back to work to tie up loose ends so the next person could take over my job with ease. My last day at the Center was to be May 10, 1983.

One day, I visited Bob and Lucy Hooks, two of the most beautiful people I was lucky enough to know in Dallas. Bob was of Iroquois descent and Lucy was European. Many of my lunch hours while working at the Center had been spent with these two, watching them create incredible masterpieces from little beads and string. They ran the American Indian Tepee House in Dallas, where a lot of the American Indian people brought their crafts to sell on consignment. Often, if a craftsperson's family was in crisis, Bob would buy the items himself. Their house was just like a museum. Everywhere you looked there were beaded earrings, pipe bags, and exquisite ceremonial clothes. Bob was quite a storyteller, too. Often I would be late returning from lunch only because I couldn't tear myself away from one of Bob's magnificent stories.

On this visit, I shared with them my decision to go on the road and to Sundance. Off-handedly, Bob asked me what I would be needing. I told him the list was long and that I just didn't have the money to get everything. He told me to go get my list from the car and let him look at it. We went on drinking coffee and smoking cigarettes, and finally I did go get the list. He and Lucy looked it over, and he told me where I could get all the things I needed.

Every so often during our conversation, Bob would wander off to another part of the house and put something into a bag. As I was leaving, he and Lucy handed me the bag, and in it were most of the ceremonial items that I needed to dance the Sundance. If I had paid for them, they would have cost several hundred dollars. I was overwhelmed. Bob just waved his hand and said, "All we ask is that you come back here and visit us every time you come through Dallas. Some day you'll have the money you need to pay for these things, I'm just not worried about it. You have to dance for the people so that the people might live."

Later that year, I did go back to see the Hooks with some money to start repaying my bill. Bob just laughed and said, "It's all paid off!" It seems that whenever anyone who knew me came in to make a purchase, if he felt they might have a little extra money, he'd tell them about my bill, and how, knowing me, I wouldn't rest until it was paid off. So would they pay something on it? He would always add, "It's not right for an Indian person to pay for the things that they need to Sundance. All the things they need should come as gifts of the Universe."

For a while, every time I visited the Hooks and really admired something there, the item would be handed to me in a sack on my way out the door. After I had been Sundancing a while, I finally caught on and made sure that I kept my admiration to myself. Some visits later, they told me sorrowfully that they were frustrated, something must be wrong with their work, as I never seemed to like anything any more. Bob said, "Since you won't tell us what you like, I'm just going to have to give you this really expensive piece. Now, I'm a poor man, and that would hurt my budget, so you should tell us what you really would like." Every year, for all the Dances, they have made sure that I've had the things that I've needed. In return, all they have asked is that I pray for their family and all the people. Thanks, Bob and Lucy.

We were scheduled to leave on May 11th. We somehow got the kids moved into their new place and stayed for about a week with our friend Dee. Dee made my Sundance dress that year and Dorothy, one of the Center board members, made my Dancing shawl.

The Center gave me a goodbye party, and one of my favorite board members, Ada, gave me a beautiful Dancing belt she had handmade. At that party, I received another very special gift.

One of my clients at the Center was a full-blood Indian woman who had been a $1000-a-day heroin addict. She was a street person, a tough cookie, who had made her money from prostitution and stealing. I'd been working with her in recovery for a long time, during which she had gotten pregnant and given birth to a little girl. The child was born with a weak immune system which, along with the stress from heroin withdrawal, caused her to die within two hours after her birth. I held her in my arms as she gasped her last breath. I'll never forget the pain I felt that day and the prayers I made for that baby and her mother. As a client, the mother had done a tremendous job of getting off heroin, learning social skills, and moving towards being a responsible person in society. She was still pretty tough though, and I trusted her just about as far as I could throw her, which wasn't far, because she was one big girl.

A week before I left the Indian center, she walked into my office and asked for my blue jean jacket. The jacket was one of the few things that would be going with me. I asked her what the hell she wanted it for. She said, "None of your business. I'll get it back to you the day of your goodbye party." We stood for a few moments looking at each other. Finally, I picked up the jacket, tossed it over to her, and told her I would track her down if she didn't get it back to me.

Well, the jacket came back. She brought it to the party and threw it at me, saying, "If you share as much love and patience with those people on the Road as you've given me, it's gotta change the world." It was probably the only time we got close to saying we loved each other.

On the back of my jacket, the young woman had drawn an elaborate medicine wheel, three feathers, and a snake with its head in the Sun and my headband around it, representing my staff Snakey and the headband my mother had left with me in the crib. The three feathers represented my children. Since then, many patches have been added all over the jacket from the different places I've worked in and loved, such as the Catskill Mountains in New York; the Cherokee Council Grounds at Red Clay, Tennessee; Tucson, Arizona, where I had a vision; and Etowah Mounds, Georgia, where I had another vision. There is a patch from the Indiana Deer Hunters Association, given to me by my father. There is a patch shaped like an arrowhead with a sword and three lightning bolts, which means Thunder, Truth. Rolling Thunder gave me this patch and has one like it on his jacket, too. There is also has a patch from the Indianapolis Motor Speedway, where I witnessed fourteen of the greatest spectacles in racing, the Kentucky Buffalo Park patch, where my Buffalo Girl Skull comes from, and patches from New Mexico, South Dakota, the Pan Am games, Yin and Yang, and Pepsi Cola. On one shoulder there is a patch of a flying white horse right next to my "Halley's Comet, Coming Soon to a Sky near You" patch, and patches from Rudi's Big Indian Center, the Rocky Mountains, Oregon, New York, Colorado, Lake Whitney, and Galveston Island. On the other shoulder is a pyramid and a patch from the Grateful Dead that says "Gratefully Dedicated." These patches were sewn on by people all across this country, many by Grandma Grace.

The jacket goes with me everywhere. For a long time, it was the only coat I owned. It is the only piece of medicine, except the Pipe, that has traveled with me every day I've been on the road. When that beautiful young woman in recovery gifted me with her drawing on the back of my blue jean jacket, it was like the beginning of a chronicle of my spiritual path.

We had another going away party at Dorothy's house. Everyone wrote prayers on pieces of paper to burn in the Sweat Lodge fire. In the Sweat Lodge, I was presented with the Sacred Pipe that had been sent by Leonard Crow Dog for me. The pipe came with instructions from Leonard that if I met a Medicine Elder before getting to Crow Dog's Paradise, I should ask that Elder to bless it. If not, Leonard would do it himself when I got to the Sundance. I was also instructed to get to Leonard's early, so that I could Vision Quest.

The Prosperity Workshop people gave me a party, too, as did my group at Shirley Barclay's. The whole thing moved so very fast; before I knew it, we were *on the road.*

As we pulled out of Dallas, heading towards Minnesota and eventually Crow Dog's Paradise, it felt like my heart was being wrenched from my body at leaving my kids. I shall never forget their faces. As I look back, this truly was the roughest thing I ever did in my whole life. I was terrified for them and filled with guilt at what I was doing to them. At that moment, I just wanted to call it all off and stay there with them.

"Talk about going to the Sundance, especially that first year. Whenever a person is on a spiritual pilgrimage, all kinds of things happen. Now, those are pretty special trips aren't they?"

Grandmother Grace Spotted Eagle

14

THE ROAD TO THE DANCE

With Wonder driving our little blue Mercury Zephyr car that I had named Blue Star, he, Fred Wahapapah, and I headed north from Dallas.

Our first stop was at the home of Crystal Bill, a friend of Shirley Barclay's who then lived in Royal, Arkansas. He is a phenomenally brilliant man who has created photographic masterpieces of light and color using lasers and crystals. He gifted us with a whole bushel basket of crystals he had dug up himself to be used as gifts at the Sundance. This man, whose heart is so generous, gave us a basket of crystals to gift to the Sundancers each year for five years straight, until he moved to New York and we lost contact. These crystal gifts were always loved by all the Elders and Dancers who received them.

We visited relatives all along the route until we got to Indianapolis. Fred and I made a speech attended by several hundred people at Indiana University, my old alma mater. We spoke other places as well, usually of the things that I was used to speaking about: Yellow Thunder Camp and Leonard Peltier. With prodding from Fred, I gradually began to talk about myself. This was new and scary. I found myself in a quandary as to what to do with the money I received as a stipend for these talks. This was the first time I ever received any money from a lecture, as this was the first time I was representing myself, and not a specific cause.

I called Leonard Crow Dog for advice. Should I send the money to the Black Hills Alliance? Should I send it to the Leonard Peltier Fund? I told the truth, and that was that I really needed it myself. He said, "You keep half of the money, and the other half split between the other two places. Send it to them, explaining that you are now sharing with the people as a part of your spiritual commitment, and that you will no longer be someone they can call on to make lectures solely on their behalf." Out of a desire to be particularly clear in my integrity, I split the stipend as advised and wrote a letter saying that from then on I would have to decline being a spokesperson for their specific causes, because I would be sharing from my own personal experiences walking a spiritual path. Then I needed to make a clear delineation about it; yet almost every time I have spoken to the people, I have shared papers and materials about Yellow Thunder Camp and/or Leonard Peltier.

In Indianapolis, there was a huge gathering at which I introduced Fred to the Indianapolis Indian group. They held a Sweat Lodge that night. An old friend, Jeff Hale (Two Feathers), ran the Lodge, and I gifted him with tobacco and asked him to bless the Pipe that had been sent by Leonard. A tear ran down his cheek as he said he would be honored and proud to do so. It was a beautiful ceremony that night, and everyone seemed very happy.

Fred and I went to two prisons in the area at which he was permitted to talk to the male prisoners and I was permitted to talk to the females. The response was great. Next we took Fred to the sixty-third running of the Indianapolis 500-mile race. You really can't show someone around Indianapolis without hitting the Indy 500! Then we all went to my old friend John Macri's and spoke to his Reality Group.

While I was in Indianapolis, an opportunity arose to make use of the lessons I received in the Prosperity Workshop when I heard that one of my Indian brothers had been jailed for raping a woman. Having known this brother for years, I found the charge against him very hard to believe, so I went to visit his lawyer. The lawyer was clearly apathetic to his client, perhaps because he was being paid by the state. He seemed to have no plan for defending him in court. He asked me to be a character witness. At the time I was dressed in my blue jeans and blue jean jacket. I felt that it was because of the way I was dressed that he wanted me to be there; my appearance would be detrimental to my friend and would make for a quick and easy case for the lawyer.

I went home, dug my Evan Picone suit out of my duffle bag, put on my silk shirt, had my hair done, borrowed some make-up and a burgundy briefcase, and showed up in court the next day. Since I knew the court system very well, I decided to go into the judge's office to check the court docket. There I found the judge, the defending attorney, and the state attorney making a deal to send my friend away.

Fred and daughter & Thunder and Margo in Dallas, Texas, on the land with children

Because I looked like another attorney, they didn't bother to stop talking. After a few moments, the judge looked up and asked me who I was representing. I smiled and said that I would be discussing my friend's case at a news conference in fifteen minutes unless he was given a fair chance to prove his innocence of the rape charges. I proceeded to list all the reasons why he could not have done it.

In about an hour, court convened. My friend was brought before the judge and, after a fair trial, was found not guilty. One week later the actual rapist was caught. Had I not stayed to finish the Prosperity Workshop so long ago, I probably wouldn't have realized the importance of dressing appropriately for the role you are going to play in this dance of life. Choosing to surrender my feelings so long ago had just saved my brother from going to the penitentiary.

We hit the road again, this time heading towards Leonard's for my Vision Quest. I was very excited because my youngest son, John Eric, was going with us. My heart felt good that he was with us. Fred had gone on ahead, so now it was Wonder, Johnny, and me in Blue Star, making the trip to destiny. The car was packed full with lots and lots of gifts for Leonard and his family.

Our first stop was in Minneapolis, Minnesota, where we stayed with Fred's daughter and grandson. I spoke at the alcohol rehab house. We also visited the American Indian Survival School, where the old Indian ways of awareness and living in relationship to Mother Earth are taught.

Fred, Wonder, and Thunder all working on the van at Pat Pederson's home in Wisconsin

Wisconsin was our next stop, where we met a lady friend of Fred's. Then the true challenge of the road began, the part where Creator redirects what you think is your course. The car broke down. We had to spend a lot of money and a lot of time to fix it, and I missed the time when I was supposed to be at Bear Butte, South Dakota, or at Crow Dog's Paradise in Rosebud, South Dakota, doing my Vision Quest.

I kept calling Leonard, but I couldn't get through to him. I didn't know what to do. Fred said that he knew a really wonderful medicine person at the Lac Courte Oreilles Indian Reservation, an Ojibwa Reservation, in Hayward, Wisconsin. I could go out on my blanket — Vision Quest — there. Since I had Visioned before in the Lakota way, I was pretty well prepared with the things I needed. I didn't have time to deal with the fear that comes up around Vision Quest, because everything was happening so fast.

The reservation was beautiful in June. The trees were all a brilliant green; it was green everywhere. After being in Texas so long, it was great to see so much green.

It was after dark before we pulled up to the place where we were told the medicine man would be. I walked up to the fire, and there beside it sat Philip Martin, the spiritual man. I was wearing my regular attire for those days — my blue jeans, cowboy boots, and blue jean jacket. He didn't pay any attention to me at all, while Fred, a man with five million friends, proceeded to laugh and talk with all the people there. Finally, after about two hours, Philip Martin noticed me and my family. He looked at me and said, "So, you want to Vision Quest." "Yes, sir," I said. "Well," he answered flatly, "you're staying at our house tonight, so we'll talk later on. Are you prepared to go out in the morning?" I said, "Yes, sir." Since I had already gifted him with tobacco when we began talking, I took out a pack of cigarettes and offered him one. He said he didn't smoke that brand. I found out later that he did, but it seemed really clear that he didn't like me very much.

At Philip's house we unpacked our stuff. Philip said that we ought to go to bed early because we'd be up at 5:00 in the morning. It was a hard night to go to sleep.

True to his word, he awakened us at 4:30, and he was in full irritating mode. We proceeded to the ceremonial grounds near his home on the reservation, where a man named Hank had been working, probably all night long, building a huge pyre of wood about six feet tall completely covered with cedar. Cedar is sometimes put on the Vision Quest fire for purification of the thoughts and the visions coming from the Spirit world to you. At the base of the pyre, there were about forty big rocks that would be heated for the Sweat Lodge. I stood and prayed at the fire for a long time, getting ready to make my journey to the Spirit world. It was wonderful having my husband and my young son John with me. I thought about everything — my life so far, my kids, the planet.

Philip was pushing my buttons at every opportunity. He asked, "Did you think to bring some prayer ties?" I said, "Yes, sir." "How many?" "Six hundred and six," I answered, proud of myself for having prepared properly in the way I knew. "Good," he said, "I need twenty." I tried not to be irritated, even though I became the laughing stock of all the Indian people who showed up in those early morning hours. They hung the tobacco ties around the Sweat Lodge area like they were decorating Christmas trees, laughing and pointing at me all the while.

At the goodbye party given by the Prosperity Workshop, Catherine had gifted me a $80 ceramic manicure. For the first time in my life, my nails were long and beautiful. Phillip looked at them and said, "Are they real? Are they yours?" When I said no, he said, "We go into the Sacred Sweat Lodge with just what the creator has given us at birth. Get rid of them." After an hour with a hammer, my nails were back to natural bloody stubs. I was furious — and hurt. But I have never had ceramic nails again and for over a year, my natural nails did not look

Philip Martin   Fred

right. Besides all my other irritations with Philip, I was especially irked that whenever he talked to me, he would mumble in low tones, while he would talk in normal tones and usually in Ojibwa to everyone else. I never really understood anything he was saying to me, so I would have to ask questions and then be told how stupid I was and that I should open my ears.

The night before, we had talked about a place called Spirit Lake where I might quest, where most of the Ojibwa people quested. With all my fear and apprehension, I was calmed by the idea of sitting on this old, ancestral, traditional site for the Vision of the Universe to unfold to my seeking eyes.

As we were starting the Lodge, I walked up to Philip with my little duffle bag packed so I could be taken up to Spirit Lake right afterwards. Then he told me I would be Visioning in the Sweat Lodge. All my Lakota-trained ego flared up. How dare this man! Didn't he know I'd Vision Quested before, and with Leonard Crow Dog? And now he was going to treat me like a baby and keep me in the Sweat Lodge? I was roiling with anger inside.

The Lodge began, and the rocks were brought in and placed in the pit, representing the womb of Mother Earth. The water was brought in and the door was shut. Philip sang a song, Fred sang a song, and then Philip started to pray. He said his name in Ojibwa and then in English. "*Kitschy Manitou* [Great Spirit], This is Rolling Thunder, coming to pray to you today and plead for the vision and the safety of this girl child." So his name, too, was Rolling Thunder, the same as my honored teacher from Carlin, Nevada. The Sweat Lodge was wonderful.

After a very long Sweat, I was taken out of the Lodge. I was not allowed to look at anyone: this is how you stay in your ceremonial internal space and maintain the integrity of your Vision. I dressed as Philip's helpers put down a Buffalo Robe and all of my sacred things. I was taken back into the Lodge and remained there about two days.

Most of those two days were spent with off-and-on bouts of anger: "How can I get a vision here in the Sweat Lodge? This is so stupid. I could have been visioning at Bear Butte, watching the Eagles, and here I am in this Lodge with this stupid man outside watching after me." On and on I went, being mad, never really getting comfortable, and never praying with the Pipe. In other words, I wasn't being grateful for the opportunity to be on Vision Quest.

By the middle of the second day I was pretty calm, and I was beginning to get hungry. I had been crying a lot that morning and the anger somehow had broken. I was still not having a great time, but I was no longer having a horrible time. I decided to have a cigarette.

The Vision of a Spiritual Camp

As I lit the lighter, I saw before me four bare-chested male spirits, all different ages. I put out the flame, and then sat in complete silence for perhaps an hour as my mind screamed, "Oh, my God, there are spirits in here!"

Then I heard my young son Johnny yelling about a bear. I heard everyone start screaming and running and, once again, I became furious. My mind said, "Look, they're trying to scare me. They just don't know I am too smart for that. They're not going to scare me." Then I heard a huge growl, and the Lodge shook, and I heard scraping sounds outside. I thought, "I'm getting tired of this. Now look what they're doing!"

That's when one of the spirits started to talk. "They are not childish; you are. We've been here for a long time, and you have never once acknowledged our presence, offered us sacreds, or thanked us for coming. You are very ungrateful for this sacred space that you have been put in." In a moment, I was a flurry of movement, lighting the sage and cedar and sweet grass, throwing tobacco all over, and praying non-stop. There was one thing about being in the Sweat Lodge: the

*Thunder's VQ fire taken before the quest,
just as the fire was getting ready to be lit, Lac
Courte Oreilles Indian Reservation, Wis.*

spirits were pretty close, and there really wasn't anywhere to go, because they were blocking the door.

They talked for hours. They gave me much information, some of which I cannot share at this time, but one piece that I can.

It was the vision of a camp, a Spiritual University, which now exists as the Thunder-Horse Ranch. The spirits said that I would walk on the road for a certain number of years, being educated in the traditional Native American sense of the word. Then I would start developing Spiritual Universities around the country. Among others, there would be one in Texas, one in Indiana, and one in the East. The first Spiritual University would teach survival skills. The second would be a spiritual retreat. These places would be like oases in the desert where people could come and receive a drink of spirituality to help their lives work better. Through the formation of these centers, many people would gain healing and education about all ways of praying and about traditional ceremonies with which to renew themselves. Each site would be deemed sacred ceremonial land. These camps would be for the people, for the cultures of all four races, a home for the Spirit that walks with me, and sacred land on which to reconstruct the family of man — a family that is guided by the Spirit not Today World.

The spirits talked for a long time about my purpose on the planet and some of the things that I needed to achieve in my life. They also taught me that the definition of the word "grateful" was breathing, laughing, and enjoying what the Universe had given me — life itself. Being grateful for every breath and every moment is a key to being happy and at peace. The spirits said many times that I was not living in gratefulness. I apologized profusely for my stupidity and ungratefulness, and that was the only time that they really smiled. They said that they always would be around any time I needed their help.

They then told me the signs by which I would know it was time to complete my journey on the road and start looking for a piece of land where my roots could grow downward and the Spirit could grow outward. They told me that I was a bridge between the White world and the Indian world, and that one of the things I would teach others was respect, respect going from one world to another, respect going both ways.

As they were getting ready to leave, they critiqued my clothes. They didn't like the bib overalls I had on and told me that I should wear skirts and Indian dresses. They told me to develop beauty, and to be proud of who I was as a woman, for other women would see this and also become proud. Recently, when Leonard Crow Dog said, "What I've seen you do many times in your life, Thunder, is create peace and beauty out of chaos," I could almost see those four spirits smiling that I was doing what they told me to do.

I think the spirits must have talked all night, although in a dark Sweat Lodge there is no reference for measuring linear time or space. As I was saying my goodbyes, tears rolled down my cheeks, for I had truly experienced a Vision.

Almost immediately, the flap to the Sweat Lodge opened, and in popped Philip Martin. "So, you had a vision, did you? The Spirits came. And *Maqua* came [*Maqua* is the Ojibwa word for Bear]. So now, today, on your third day of the journey, you're going to go to Spirit Lake. Come outside and prepare," he said.

I crawled out of the Sweat Lodge and, as I stood up, I noticed the top of my overalls was unhooked, so my pants were starting to slip off. Being in an altered state, I couldn't quite grasp what was wrong, so Philip came over and started to help me with my overalls — but both metal fasteners had been twisted and tied in a knot. John Eric still carries one of these messages from the Spirit world in his medicine bag.

I was taken to a spot that had been prepared for me at Spirit Lake. As we approached a clearing in the woods on the Lake, a huge Eagle flew overhead. All the Indians took this as a sign that my vision was complete and right away started praying out loud. I spent the next night and day offering my gratefulness to the Spirit and planning my new wardrobe. When they came to get me on the fourth day, I hated to leave. The spot was beautiful. I felt safe and totally at peace for one of the first times in my life. Isn't it ironic that this way of praying can create safety in the middle of strange woods, when, in Today World living, we have to fight, and we never ever feel completely safe, but are always looking out for what is coming at us? On the blanket, I could be excited about the arrival of a raccoon or a butterfly, because I was on a Spirit journey. I was immersed in the Spirit world with no time and space, safe and grateful to be traveling through eons of Spirit/ Ceremony time.

Philip and his helpers took me back to the ceremonial area. I saw that on the Sweat Lodge and nearby trees there were claw marks of a huge black bear. I indeed had had a visitation from *Maqua*, the Bear. Philip later said that the Bear had given me his blessing and shared his power with me.

We then went to Philip's house where we talked. Philip interpreted my experience and told me that I had truly had a vision. He congratulated me. Then I was allowed to shower and put on a brand new dress that had been made for me by the local women. I felt important for maybe the first time in my life.

The Indian people had cooked a huge dinner, brought gifts, and were laughing and happy that I had received a Vision for my life. I was overjoyed to see my husband and son again. They showed me the claw marks on our car, Blue Star. Wonder had jumped into the car to escape the huge, over-a-thousand-pound bear, who had actually tried to open the door of the car: there were claw marks right at the door handle. Later, on the road, I would often rub my fingers over these marks, remembering how the bear had blessed me — and Wonder as well!

We stayed with Philip for about a week. I gave a talk at the local alcohol program facility and at the school on the reservation. We met Bob, the director of the reservation radio station, and his wife Gail. Gail, one of the radio personalities, took the dean of girls from the reservation school and me out to the woods to tape several hours of programming about women and their roles in Today World and in the Indian world. Then I helped the dean develop a self-image workshop for all the girls at the school.

Philip and I were fast becoming friends. I loved to cook for him, because he lived alone and didn't cook good meals for himself. The number of pizza boxes around the house was unbelievable. The days flew by and I never knew what might happen next. One morning, I opened the freezer and found what I thought was a roast. When I unwrapped it, it turned out to be a huge bear paw. Then a knock at the door announced a local Indian man who brought in an owl for me to take apart. Being part Cheyenne, I was not thrilled to do this, since the owl is rather a taboo to Cheyenne people. To top things off, Philip asked me if I would run some ceremonies for some of the local women. He explained that it could get a little sticky, however, for an outside Indian person, especially a half-breed, to run a ceremony there on the Reservation, so I would have to go through an initiation and a naming ceremony.

I countered with, "I really do not know how to run any ceremonies. I would be happy to talk to people, to share my experiences, but I have no authority to run any ceremony. I've never been told that I could do that." He smiled and said, "Well, we'll talk about it."

That night, as I was fixing supper, Johnny was hanging out with the local teenagers, and my husband was hanging out with the men folks, Philip came in and said, "Put dinner on hold. There's a Midewiwin Elder coming tonight, and we're going to do ceremony." The Midewiwin, I'd been told, is a secret powerful medicine society formed primarily among woodland Indian tribes. Most of the time, even their name was whispered. Generally, you just didn't talk about them.

It was a great honor to be invited to this ceremony. When we arrived, the ceremonial fire was burning brightly, and many Indian people, some of whom were very old, were sitting around it. We all got ready to go into the Lodge. The last person to enter was a very old, old man. He had a translator with him. The ceremony started. I was soon to understand the Lodge was my naming ceremony. The old man and Philip Martin gifted me my Ojibwa name identical to the name gifted me by Leonard Crow Dog. Perhaps Philip knew my name already, yet I couldn't remember ever having told him.

I was told that I was going through a high initiation and that then I would be worthy to do ceremony on the Ojibwa reservation. I froze with fear, because I didn't know and didn't have permission to do any ceremony. Then I heard a very loud, stern, clear voice say, "The Creator, and this medicine man, have now given you permission to run a Sweat Lodge ceremony here on this reservation." I was honored and grateful.

Afterwards we had a great feast and heard many stories of the Ojibwa people and how they gathered the wild rice, their sacred ceremonial dish. It was a wonderful night.

The next night, and every night thereafter until we left, I ran lodges for the women. In the Lakota way, tobacco is offered many times to the Spirit working through the leader of a ceremony on a person's behalf; but these women gifted food and handicrafts, and most brought their children. There was always a huge feast after the ceremony. Philip loved it because, in his words, "Ever since you've come I've eaten a great meal every day."

Our time at the Lac Courte Oreilles Reservation was ending much too quickly. We had to get back to Indianapolis, then on to Dallas to get ready for Sundance. Every morning I'd been at his place, I had come out to find Philip sitting at the table, looking out the window. Every morning I had asked him what he was doing. Every morning he had answered, "Watching the trees grow." That last morning, before we headed out, I asked Philip, "Tell me, Philip, why do you always watch the trees grow?" He replied, "Trees are lucky; they're not like people. They know their original instructions, and they can just grow. Now, take a person, if they were a tree, they would have a heck of a strange-looking trunk, because every time a person changed their mind, they'd be off growing in a different direction. Could you imagine what they'd look like?"

By then, Philip wanted me and my husband to move to the reservation, take over the ceremonial grounds, and help him out. He had Sweat Lodges going all the time, with all kinds of people, not only Indians, coming for the ceremony. He would laugh and say, "All these people, why, they used to be just old drunks. Take me, for instance, I was on skid row for twenty-six years." Then he would get serious, very serious, and ask me to come back to live someday, for who would take care of his people—the renegades, he called them. I really loved and still love that group of people: Hank, who did the fires; Bob, who loved to eat and laugh; Chicken Coop Pat; and Farmer Pat. I miss them sometimes when I get a whiff of pine trees. Philip was a great man with a lot of compassion. As it turned out, I would get to Sundance with him for two years at the Mt. Hood Sundance. I danced behind him when he broke from the Tree of Life in his first dance. Later, several others and I Sundanced for him and prayed for his spirit when he passed on to the Spirit world. But first, we shared many more visits and lots of laughter together. Thank you, Fred, for bringing so many wonderful memories into my life.

Back we went to Indianapolis, driving Blue Star to drop off Johnny, who was going to go back to Dallas with John Crazy Horse. As we let him off at John Crazy Horse's, he said, "If the rest of the road is like that last visit, you're going to be really tired out by the time you get back home, Mom . . . I love you." This turned out to be all too true. Being on the road was and is hard, but I love the people that I meet.

We left our car, Blue Star, with friends and joined Fred in his VW van, and off we drove to Oklahoma. We visited and stayed with Fred's mother and stepfather, really beautiful people, in Shawnee. We were lucky enough to get there in time to go to the Potawatami Homecoming Pow Wow and then to Philip Deer's "Youth and Elder Conference," where I saw many old friends — Clyde Bellecourt, Vernon Bellecourt, and the singer Floyd Westerman. I also got to see John Trudell, a poet, resistance leader, and a man with a huge heart. There were all kinds of other wonderful people there from Guatemala, Africa, Tibet — from all over. Vernon Bellecourt asked me to act as recording secretary for a lot of the conference. It was a good time, and many world issues were brought to the fore.

At this gathering, some members of the Masai, a tribe of warriors from Africa, enacted the old traditional way the warriors geared up for battle. They formed a double line, one line as the aggressors and the other as the defenders. They growled and made horrible noises and faces at each other to try to scare each other and build up their adrenalin and life force for battle. Then we all got up and did it as well. It was fascinating.

From Shawnee, Oklahoma we traveled back to Dallas to visit the kids. I was given desk space at the Dallas Metaphysical Center where, after Sundancing, I was scheduled to return as a consultant the next winter. We stayed in Dallas about ten days. While I was there, my kids threw a birthday party to celebrate my thirty-ninth birthday, and I got to see a lot of my friends. Johnny had returned by then with John Crazy Horse. Richard seemed to be getting along fine, and Beth had decided to move to Indianapolis with her boyfriend Charles. Beth and Charlie headed out with us to Minnesota to get Fred's Sundance stuff and then back to Indianapolis to meet Charlie's mother and family.

Finally, we left Indianapolis. We went back to see our friends at the Lac Courte Oreilles Reservation, then on to Yellow Thunder camp, Rose Bud, Rapid City, Bear Butte, and finally Mt. Hood, Oregon, for the first Sundance.

Our original intention was to attend four different Sundances that year, but our route radically changed when the van once again broke down, this time in Oregon, causing about a week's down time and my not making it to Leonard Crow Dog's. I tried to reach Leonard, but couldn't. Once we were on the move again, he could not reach me either. I was heartbroken, yet we had to keep pushing on. I was beginning to learn the rules of the Road.

Life on the Road

I want to share a little bit now about what it's like being on the road. I am a very responsible, work-oriented individual. At first, being on the road was very hard. I immediately took on the feminine role of doing all the cooking and laundry, keeping the van clean, and trying my best to keep everything organized. When we were guests at other people's homes, I cooked and cleaned there. Then we would ride for several days at a time, not knowing where we were going to be sleeping or when we would be eating.

When you're cooped up in a van, you can't be arguing with each other, because the energies of an argument will make everyone sick and also, believe it or not, cause mechanical problems or an accident. Gone were the luxuries of my own refrigerator to keep my special foods, a nice warm bath at the end of the day, watching a favorite TV show, or reading the newspaper over coffee in the morning. It some-how isn't the same to get your coffee and read, say, the *San Francisco Gazette*, when you don't know the history of the city, the ongoing stories, or whatever happened when the case got solved — *and* you're barrelling down the road at sixty miles an hour enroute to some other place with some other news. It was just as well, since my Elders had advised me not to read newspapers, watch TV, or listen to the radio, so that I would become attuned to the Earth and begin to hear her talking to me.

But some of those luxuries were hard to give up. During the nine years I was on the road, Christmas time was always the hardest — not having anywhere to put up a Christmas tree or enough money to buy presents for my kids. I loved to give presents, especially to my kids. Many people over the years helped me get Christmas presents together for them. I want to thank all the people in the United States who put up Christmas lights, because all their lights became beacons of joy for me. I loved the lights, but sometimes they made me cry, for I did not have a home in which to have Christmas. Over the years, I always went back to the children and usually cooked them Christmas dinner. Every Christmas, doing a ceremony or sacred Sweat Lodge, I remember those people who helped this "road person" have a wonderful Christmas for her children. Even though my schedule was never my own, I managed not to miss a Thanksgiving or Christmas with my family, and there was always lots of joy and laughter, and also, somehow, there were presents under the trees at my kids' homes. I want to thank all the people who open up their homes to people on the road and treat them in a good way.

It is so lonesome at times on the road. When you're dependent on other people's hospitality, it's easy to feel you have overstayed your welcome and that your presence is creating a strain. I am always mindful of this feeling and try always to leave places better than I found them. This is not to say that bringing in the Spirit is not sometimes needed to help along change and forward movement in the spiritual sense. Grandma used to say, "Thunder, when you are on the road, in giving up your home, all homes become your own. Treat the homes as if they were your home. Always leave beauty." We spend a lot of time cleaning up before leaving a space. Many is the time, after a ceremony in a strange town, that it hurts to see people leaving. They leave feeling good, healed, and ready to go back to their homes to share the energy with their families. Standing in the dark, picking up trash and cleaning up whoever's ceremonial area we were in, I felt lonely. Knowing I didn't have any place to go that night was really hard. Those were the times that I had to work on my gratefulness.

Before leaving a ceremonial ground, if I had any extra money, I would buy a rose bush and plant it somewhere. I never really knew why, but I always knew that I might never be back to this place; and it seemed important to leave it a little better than I found it. Then I heard a story about the Dalai Lama. When he and his people were forced to leave their ancestral homes in Tibet, they planted flowers all along their escape route. They knew that they might not ever have the opportunity to see those flowers bloom, but they also knew that other people would see them and experience beauty along the path.

Why did the Elders have me go on the road, following the Pipe? I believe the answer to this question is that in this way I would expand my vision by attuning myself to the flow of the Universe and to the fact that everything I see at any time is a part of my world. With that understanding, I can no longer overlook or deny the people who are hungry, troubled, or needing help. Everyone is a part of me.

I was wherever I needed to be at any given time, per the Spirit, with enhanced opportunities for service to the people of this planet. There was the accident on the side of the road when Spirit worked through me to stop the bleeding of a child who otherwise might have bled to death before the ambulance arrived. Then there was the accident that left a lady's eye hanging out. I pressed the eye back into its socket and covered it with a Garfield bandaid. Later, I heard her eyesight had been saved in this way. Garfield bandaids are my favorites.

To be in this kind of service, a person has to be taken out of the little box they feel they can control and flung into the world that they cannot control. Responsibility, yes; firm scheduling, no. Every time I tried to assert my own will and control a situation, chaos erupted. Every time I listened to Spirit, healing occurred.

Impeccable timing was always the standard. Once, after getting gas at a filling station, none of the road crew would get back in the car. I looked at the store clock and counted off six minutes while they kept me waiting. I soon learned that, six minutes down the road, a tanker had rolled over eight cars on the freeway and caused a thirty-car pile up. Of course, we were there to help — but only because the Spirit kept us from being one of the cars that was rolled on. Coincidence? I don't think so.

Another time, the Spirit told me to pull over. I really didn't want to, but I did anyway, while everybody in the car complained. I told them to look out the window at the hawk, and by the time they realized there wasn't a hawk, I knew it was time to move on. Soon we came upon a bus that had veered over the median into what would have been our lane of traffic, killing several people. It obviously had not been our time to go, but it was our time to help out at the accident site.

In 1985, my road crew consisted of one delightful Cherokee girl named Sparky Shooting Star. She and I traveled many miles and months together. One night, coming out of Arkansas, we stopped at a 7-11, which happens to be the most wonderful store in the world. It was about 3:00 or 4:00 in the morning, and I needed a Pepsi. As I was getting out of the car and walking into the store, the Spirit told me that there was about to be a robbery and the young girl at the counter was about to get shot and killed.

As I opened the door, sure enough there was a girl at the counter, and all around her body was the look of death. I immediately asked the Spirit, "What am I to do?" No answer. Grandma used to say that Spirit always seems to feel you've got what it takes to handle the situation and, if you just act, it will turn out okay. I didn't have to wait long. In a few short seconds, two very scruffy men walked in. It was real clear that one of them had a gun in his pocket.

There was no time to think about what to do, so I walked right up to the two men and said, "Spirit tells me you're going to rob this place, and you're going to kill this young girl, and you just can't do that." The men, already a little more nervous than your regular 7-11 customers, totally freaked out. At that point they decided to shoot me. I said, "What good would that do?" and suggested I might come back to haunt them.

Sparky had not been informed about these latest of Spirit offerings. Suddenly I saw two cans of 10W40 motor oil fly into the air from the other side of the aisle. Sparky ran quickly down to the far end of the aisle, stood there in disbelief, then started waving frantically at me to stop my course of action.

Obviously, the girl at the counter was very interested in the conversation that was going on. I proceeded to tell the men to take what they needed, get their gas, and leave this girl with her life. Now, it's really interesting that often when people are magnetizing disaster to themselves, they get very upset when some short little fat lady disrupts the flow. The girl screamed over the counter to me, "You can't do that! I'd have to pay for this stuff!" It was too much for the robbers, so they left.

I went over to the counter to the girl. It was soon very clear why she did not want to live. Her mother had died earlier that spring, leaving her to take care of five children, and that very morning her sister had run off after a disagreement about house chores. Of course she wasn't making much money where she was working, so life had just become too big a burden. In the course of talking with her for about a half hour, I guess I heard her say twenty times, "I want to die." We kept talking to her, and at last she began to smile. That smile meant a lot to me right then.

At that moment, the two guys came back. It seems that they had gone down the road and realized that they needed to rob this store after all, because there weren't that many on the way to Memphis, and who was I, anyway. Suddenly it all seemed pretty funny. I started laughing and making funny remarks, I don't know why, because this time I was sure they had come back to shoot me. I told them all about Karma and how, if they shot the girl, they'd have to atone for it in this lifetime or in another. I added, "And look at her, now she doesn't even want to die." And she said, "No, I don't." They told us they had to do something, so they were just going to take the gas. I said go ahead. This time the girl only laughed and said, "Yes, please take what you need. Please don't kill us." She mumbled that she would handle it somehow. We didn't have much money with us that trip. The gas came to about fifteen dollars, so I gave her half of that, and we were on our way. Many times I have prayed for this young girl. I hope that her life is better today. It's funny how people's faces seem to come up from time to time and flip through your mind.

The road may seem very romantic to some people. To a mother of three, a wife who had always been used to taking care of her family, her job, and her world, the road was a very different place. I soon found out what Swami Rama meant when he later told me, "The world is a hologram, an illusion. To enhance your illusion and to break down its confines, you must get out and experience new pieces of the puzzle."

On the road I've learned how people can draw misfortune to their lives in the way of accidents or other things that hurt them. I have met single mothers, alone and in poverty, taking care of their children without any help and doing very well. I have also met very miserable millionaires. Circumstances do not determine whether we are happy, but our attitudes do.

A car that would not run suddenly ran as good as new after a healing from a single Eagle Feather. It continued to run until we got to the place where Spirit wanted us to be, and then someone was there who knew how to fix it. My whole view of car mechanics is, when you put the key in, if the car starts, it's a good day, and, if it doesn't, it's time to pray.

On the road, I found that there was always a purpose behind our breakdowns. When the van wouldn't run, I would clean it and put my life back into order. When that was done, usually the expertise, the right car part, or the money to buy it would magically appear from someone stopping to help us. And the people who stopped to help us usually received a healing from the Spirit during their service. In the Universe, it's give and receive; the great circle always goes around. On the road, you take a leap of faith and let Spirit run your life completely. It's a level of trust we rarely learn growing up, but it hasn't let me down yet. Sometimes it's scary, but it works. When you live by your intuition and Spirit, ruled by your heart, that *is* the flow of the Universe.

By now, I have traveled thousands and thousands of miles by car or van across these United States. I have traveled by boat, train, car and airplane to Mexico, Yucatan, Australia, Hawaii, Egypt, Switzerland, France, Italy, India and England. Wherever I have gone, I have found that people are the same. Most wish to be loving and kind and, if given the chance, will be so. I have experienced some pretty scary things, like what happened at the 7-11, but my faith is strong that all will turn out all right for the Universe! I love the road and I am glad to have had the opportunity to have learned by being on the road. Everytime we leave the gates of Thunder-Horse Ranch, I sing *On the Road Again.*

Thunder Shield with Snake

"Tell them about your first Sundance in Oregon. Remember when you said you saw yourself as a little girl?" Grandma said. I answered, "Yes." By now it was too dark to see the paper in front of me. She said, "Let's let everyone know that Martin High Bear is a good guy."

15

DANCING THE SUNDANCE

The state of Oregon is incredibly majestic. We drove through towering trees, past the waterfalls of the White River, toward the base of Mount Hood. I had heard that the Sundance camp is located there because of the Indian belief that Mount Hood is connected to Mount St. Helens, and that it may be the next volcano to blow up if prayers are not made by the Native people.

Passing through the Tygh Valley, Fred took us to Ms. Piggy's Restaurant. Over the years I grew to love this place, and it became a traditional, necessary stop. But this was my first trip there and I could only think about how awful the food was and how angry the people were at us for coming in. We stopped again in Wamic, a town with one store, the only store anywhere near the Sundance grounds. Then we went on into the Mount Hood National Forest.

Driving through the tall pines, it got wilder and wilder. I saw the eagles flying. Drawn on the paved road was a buffalo skull and an arrow and the words, "That Way." From then on, our only guides were little pieces of red material hung on trees. I could hardly breathe, I was so excited. Fred just looked at me and laughed. I really was getting to enjoy Fred. He had a wonderful way of laughing. "Well, we are almost there," he said as he reached over and took hold of my hand. My husband mumbled something in the back seat about not knowing why I was scared, but as I looked over my shoulder at him, I saw he was scared also. I just smiled.

We finally arrived at the gate and two of the meanest-looking warriors, later to be two of my best friends, approached the car.

These warriors had the power to say "Stay" or "Leave." Their job was to search the car for any drugs, alcohol, cameras, tape recorders, or weapons. Luckily they knew Fred, so they didn't rip the car apart. They passed Fred a sheet of paper and asked, "How many Sundancers

Martin High Bear   *Brave Buffalo*

in the car?" Fred said, "Two." I caught my breath. Fred signed the sheet
and handed it back to the warriors. They passed it to me. I didn't know
whether to sign it or not. I was terrified I was going to insult them if
I signed it. Fred whispered under his breath, "Sign that damn thing!"
They both leaned in my window. I popped a couple of packs of
cigarettes out the window and we all laughed. As we were waved on
through, Fred said, "Isn't that why you came here?" I said, "I think I'm
going to throw up."

We set up our camp. The people from Lac Courte Oreilles Indian
Reservation and the medicine man Philip Martin had also come to
dance, and they joined Wonder, Fred, and me. We made a little circle.
The Sundance Chief and Medicine Elders visited and asked each camp
the number of Sundancers. If the answer was none, they would walk
on. But Fred kept saying three, and I kept hiding in my tent. They saw
Fred and they saw Philip, but where was number three?

There are four days of cleansing and purification before the dance.
All Dancers go though a series of Sweat Lodges to purify themselves
to enter the Mystery Circle. Male and female Sundancers sweat in
separate Lodges. We had arrived at the grounds late, well into the
second day of purification, so we had to pray hard to catch up.

Fred went off to the men's Sweat as I approached the women's. I just
stood there as people looked over me, under me, and to either side, but
never at me. Finally I mumbled, "I think I might be Sundancing," as
vaguely as possible.

I was taken into the Lodge and it was a hard sweat. The Head Woman Dancer running the Lodge, a full-blood Hoopa from California, was rough on us. Nobody seemed to like me. In fact, I was sure everybody hated me.

After this wonderful get-together, I dragged myself back to my tent. Fred, social butterfly that he was, was happy as a lark. I thought I was dying and nobody cared. This was not a great balance of male/female energy.

First thing the next morning, all the Sundancers had to ask permission to dance. We went to see the Medicine Man, Martin High Bear. I was deathly ill and frozen with fear. I had awakened that morning thinking, "What in the hell am I doing? I'm not a full-blood Indian. It's all a mistake!"

I loaded the Pipe Uncle had sent me. I sure missed him right then. I sat for a long time praying, thinking of Leonard and his parents, Grandpa Henry and Grandma Mary, and tears came to my eyes. Why had the Universe been so cruel to me to not let me dance at Crow Dog's Paradise? I wondered, cried, reflected, and then, running out of things to do, I finally got up and slowly carried the Pipe to Grandfather Martin's tepee, where I was to ask to dance. It all felt so different from what I had expected. Leonard and his family were not there, my friends were not there. I sure missed Crow Dog's Paradise and the comfort of knowing — anything at all. As I walked toward the tepee, I thought about what I would say. I knew that I was supposed to present my gifts and ask to be a Sundancer and for permission to die. Forget about the Sundance — I was sure this experience alone would kill me.

Hope was but a foot away. An Indian man walked by me, very angry, though I could see major sadness under the anger. A very cordial Indian woman spat at me and explained, "He has been told that he cannot dance. Many today will be told they can't dance." Then she smiled ever so sweetly, making sure I caught the drift of her communication.

My heart leapt for joy. As popular as I was there, there was no way that they would let me dance.

In front of the tepee there was a line of people waiting to go in to the Elders and a line of people coming out. As I waited in the line going in, I heard loud words like, "You're a white man. You can't dance!" I knew I didn't look full-blood. This would be a piece of cake.

A very rough-looking warrior pulled the flap of the tepee aside and growled at me with teeth that could snap a head off. "Do you want to talk with Martin?" "Yes, sir," I said. "Well, get in here, you are holding up the line." I walked into the tepee clutching the Pipe and my gifts. There sat Martin High Bear, a slight man, almost small. He smiled and reached out his hand. I started to give him the Pipe, but he laughed with an easy smile and motioned for my hand. Shaking my hand, he had me sit down, and then went around the circle of people and introduced them. There was a man known as Papasan Eastman, whom we would later call Brave Buffalo. He was a very imposing Elder surrounded by light. There were also a number of other older women and men whose names I later could not remember.

They all turned to Martin, and Grandfather Martin looked at me. Speechless, I presented the Pipe to him, and he took it. I laid out my gifts and finally held out some tobacco. We held it together, and he asked, "Why do you want to Sundance?" I started to stutter. All sorts of stupid things popped out of my mouth. I said I was not sure I had enough Indian background, I didn't think I was worthy enough, and I was sorry if I had embarrassed him in any way by even coming here today. He smiled with eyes which held the Universe, and said, "Yes, Leonard and Wallace both told me about you." My heart sank. "You're from Leonard's family. You have died and come back, and now you need to dance to thank the Creator." All the Indian people just nodded their heads and looked at the ground.

The script was not going as I had thought it would. I tried to convince them that I didn't really belong there, but they ignored me. Grandfather Martin reached down and lit the Pipe from Leonard, smoked it, and passed it around the circle. I sat in front of him, waiting. He looked at everyone and they seemed to communicate silently. He handed the Pipe back to me and said, "Be in the compound at ten o'clock tonight. It's an honor to have you here. You have been accepted by your peers. You shall dance your year and see if you are worthy enough to become a Sundancer."

I held back the tears until I got out of the tepee. Then I cried harder than any of the people who had been denied permission. The Indian people outside all tried to console me because they thought I'd been rejected. "It's okay," they told me. "Not everyone is meant to be a

Sundancer. It's an Indian tradition, not White." I was crying so hard I couldn't tell them I had been accepted.

I entered our camp, still sobbing. Wonder and Fred both jumped up. Philip Martin ran and grabbed me and said, "What happened? Were you refused?" I choked out that Martin had said to be in the compound at ten o'clock. Fred started jumping around and yelling, "You made it, you made it!" Then he turned around and asked, "Why are you crying?" I answered, "Because I made it!"

Philip Martin and I worked all day making sage crowns, bracelets, and anklets. If we fell in the Sundance, we would be carried out by those sage rings, since the Helpers could not touch our bodies. The rings were wrapped in cloth for reinforcement, so as to be able to support our full body weight if need be.

Many tests came up that day. The Sundance energies had caused one woman, a born-again Christian, to go crazy. She came toward Philip and me with an open Bible. I knew I couldn't handle it, so I jumped up and ran inside my tent; but Philip did not get away. She read to him from the Bible about how awful pagan dances shouldn't happen. She read on and on, until poor Philip exploded and I rolled out of the tent laughing. After she left, we used sage to clean up the area of the anger energy. By then we were both laughing. At dinner that night, every-body talked about how rough this Dance was going to be. The more they talked, the more I couldn't eat. I want to say right here and now that this was the last time I ever missed a meal before a Sundance. All through the four days of the Dance when I couldn't eat anything I kept remembering that last plate of food I could have had.

The camp grew quiet and the seriousness of the ceremony could be felt everywhere. At 9:45 p.m., I opened the last can of Pepsi I would see for four days and started to eat a chocolate bar. Wonder and Farmer Pat from Lac Courte Oreilles Reservation helped me carry my things as I walked behind Fred and Philip Martin into the compound.

As the only half-breed, I wasn't the most popular person there, so I had to sleep outside the women's tepee on the ground. It was pretty cold and I was scared. I stayed awake all night long, feeling totally abandoned.

At 4:00 a.m., I heard for the first time the announcement that will stay in my memory forever: "Good Morning America, this is the Anpo Sundance. Are all you Sundancers ready? Good Morning America and

Good Morning Sundancers!" By 4:30 a.m., we were in the Sweat Lodge, praying. By 5:00, we were in the tepee getting dressed. Notice, at last a space had been created for me there. I put on the dress Dee had made and Grandma had stitched, the shawl from Dorothy, Medicine from Grandpa Wallace, and my sage crown and bracelets. Then I went outside and threw up.

We began to line up. As a new Dancer, I was placed at the end of the line. The tears started to roll and were not to stop for two days. I wasn't crying *for* anything; it was more a deep crying of genetic remembrance. Then we heard the Entrance Song.

As we walked from the Sweat Lodge compound toward the entrance to the Great Mystery Circle through the East Gate as the Entrance Song was sung, I was no longer Mary Grimes; I was someone who had done this life after life after life. I sang the song and even knew the meaning of its words. I could feel the power as we neared the East Gate of the Great Mystery Arbor. I knew then that I would never be the same again.

We entered the East Gate and saluted all the Directions. By then, I felt I had been in the Sundance forever and that the Spirit realm had reopened for me.

As we lined up for the first dance of the first round, I saw my first Vision. It was a vision within a vision. I saw myself at about age three, sitting in a swing. As that little girl, I looked up because the swing was screeching, and I saw a vision of Indian Dancers dancing the Sundance. I was three years old, waiting for a social worker to come and take me away. I lived in a series of foster homes back then. I remembered that time vividly. I realized the Elders had come to me that day because I was being taken away from my Grandma. I did not want to go and I was scared. I didn't recall where I was taken or which social worker it was who picked me up, but I did remember very clearly sitting in that swing, being scared, and listening to the rusty squeak.

Here I was some thirty-five years later, and the squeak of the swing was the call of the Eagle Bone whistles, but I had transcended time and space to step into that vision. Could I at age three have been comforted by the fact that some day I would be a Sundancer? Had the Sundance spirits gone to the little three-year-old to comfort her in her fears?

We danced our first round to each of the Four Directions and the Tree of Life. The rhythm was hypnotic, powerful, primal. We gave our Pipes to the Medicine Elders. All the Dancers' Pipes were set on a huge

Thunder's first vision, a vision within a vision

altar, lined up side by side on a bed of sacred sage. Then we went under the shade arbor in the West to rest.

This was a timeless place. The arbor and Mystery Circle looked as they had probably looked for 2000 years. The great ceremony of the Native American people had survived all that time in the face of terrible odds and oppression. I felt so proud and so humbled. Inside the Mystery Circle the spirits came to be with us. As I danced, my Ancestors crowded around me.

The Circle is surrounded by a sacred barrier of sage. Only the Dancers, Medicine People, and the Helpers may enter. In the center stands the Tree of Life, selected and cut down in an ancient ceremonial way. The tree is brought to the circle on the shoulders of the Dancers, who often carry it for miles. No branch may touch the ground, or a new tree must be found and brought in. The tree is raised and set in place on a wave of sacred song and prayer. The concentrated energy of everyone there in honoring this tree is indescribable. Cloth prayer bouquets of many colors fly from its branches, lifting the prayers of the Dancers to the Creator. It is a vision of phenomenal beauty.

The brothers attach ropes of woven horsehair or hemp to the tree of life. At various times during the Dance, those Dancers who have made a commitment to pray in the way of piercing the skin lie down next to the tree, one by one, to be pierced through the flesh of the chest by the

Medicine Man. A special song of prayer to the Great Mystery for pity and compassion is sung over and over as this is done. Skewers are placed through these wounds and attached to the ropes hanging from the tree. All through the Dance, but especially at this time, sacrifice is made for the well-being of family, friends, and all the people. The Dancers pray for healings for the sick and help for those in trouble, and they pray in thanksgiving for the gifts of Spirit that have already been received. As they pray and sacrifice, their pain and suffering are transformed to the joy and ecstasy of union with the Creator. The men dance connected to the tree by these horsehair ropes until their visions come. At this time they break away, pulling the skewers through their flesh in offering to the Creator. The Elders say that men pierce at the Sundance because, unlike women, they cannot go through the suffering and sacrifice of childbirth. They must sacrifice in this way to connect with both the Mother and Father principles of Universal energy.

There was an arbor of cedar boughs adjoining the Mystery Circle at Mt. Hood. Around the circle there were between two and three thousand people supporting our Dance. I sat with Fred, Philip, and many other wonderful people in the rest arbor. I lay on the Pendleton blanket that Leonard had wrapped around me a week before my heart attack. Everyone teased me because I had such an expensive blanket. I was given the nickname Dallas. By then I felt so loved and so lucky to be in this sacred space. Many still did not like me, but in spite of that I felt loved.

On the second round of the first day Philip Martin decided to pierce. I had told him I would be there to support him. I went to my Head Woman Dancer (the woman in charge of female dancers) and asked how to do that. She told me that I had to swing out of the circle of Dancers, run all the way around saluting each direction, and come in behind him. I felt caught between wanting to support Philip and fearing to do something wrong. Because he was the oldest man in the dance, and it was a special request, Philip prepared to be pierced and then to break immediately from the Tree of Life. When he was in position to break, I couldn't wait any longer. I left the line of women in what I prayed was the right way, ran completely around the arbor and came up behind him. As I danced behind Philip, I fanned him with my fan. I watched as he prayed and smiled at the Sun, almost hypnotized. I saw him finish saying his prayers and start the movement of breaking from the Tree of Life. It seemed that the pain and ecstacy of the breaking was absolutely all-encompassing. I did not know just how I would take seeing a man pull wooden skewers out of his chest. Would I faint at the sight of blood? But when the time came, instead of being a horrible ordeal, it was one of the truest expressions of love. The Indian comes to the Dance with all that he has, his Pipe and his body, and he gives them to the Creator. So simple, yet so profound. As I returned to the circle, I felt that I was just beginning to understand the Sundance.

During the first two days of the Dance, I felt every physical pain. There were only split seconds of time when I was transported elsewhere, when the drum became my heart and the Universe was with me. I kept smelling my own body and feeling my pain. The temperature in Oregon stayed around 120 degrees.

There was a Buffalo Dancer in the Dance, wearing a full buffalo headdress and robe. If the energy of the Dancers got low, he took a sage pot and danced around the circle of the spectators. If a woman among them was on her Moon or if someone there had bad thoughts, the sage smoke billowed toward them. The warriors then came and took that person away. We always felt better and had more energy afterward.

The third day of the Sundance is called the Day of Tests. By then, my mouth was so dry that it felt like reptile scales inside. My lips were cracked and bleeding and my face was chapped. It felt like the top of my head had been burned off. Every part of my body hurt. I actually felt my liver and other organs jump in my body.

It was on this day that I experienced a reoccurrence of the heart attack. I had severe chest pains and I couldn't breathe. I fell down and struggled to get back up. Brave Buffalo came over and did medicine on me. He kept saying, "You have to trust the Great Spirit. You cannot do this alone." Then I fell down again. I just couldn't go on. There was dirt in my mouth. I have never felt so helpless, hopeless, hurting, and weak. I was sure I was going to die.

I remember crying out in desperate prayer for the Great Spirit to help me. All of a sudden, my energy changed. It was as if I had been transported to a totally different reality. It felt like the very first day of the Dance and I got up and danced stronger than ever before. I had learned the meaning of surrender, that there is a force that will answer when called upon, and knew I would never again be alone.

I still had not been able to look directly at the Sun. One of the Helpers took his Eagle Fan and put it under my chin, jerking my head straight up. The Helpers yelled, "You're Sundancers. Don't look at the earth. Be proud of the Sun!" As I looked at the Sun my eyes burned, and it was hard. All of a sudden, a blue haze covered the Sun. I kept looking intently and then I was taken from this place to another, through the Sun to another Sun. There I was told many things. The Spirit of the Sun behind the Sun told me that we are all the same soul; we just have different bodies, different hair, different looks. We all come here to teach, but mostly we come to learn. Learning how to get along with each other, learning compassion is the key. Suddenly I was heavy again. As I came back from the vision, I landed on Earth very hard. I don't know how long I was gone, but I returned to a different round of the Dance.

Then a Spirit visited me and danced with me for a while. He said that my life would be totally changed. He gave me an Eagle feather. I opened my physical hand and there it was. Just then, Martin High Bear, the Medicine Man, appeared before me and said, "It is good."

On and on we danced. During the nights, we tried to sleep. The third night was the hardest, for there was lots of crying, lots of aching, lots of pain; but there were also Sundance visions in our dreams. During the day, many Elders, including Chief Matthew King and Grandfather Fools Crow, came to talk as the Sundancers rested in the arbor between rounds. The Elders spoke to us about the legends, about the old ways, about what we as Sundancers had to do and to pray for.

An old lady asked me to wear her shawl for a round. She needed a prayer for her family. I put on the shawl and went out to dance. During this round my daughter's face came before me. For a second I was standing in a dining room I'd never seen before, and Beth was getting ready to answer the phone. She stopped and looked at me. I said, "I love you." After the Sundance, the first call I made was to my children. Beth recounted the incident perfectly, describing the dining room in exact detail, and asked, "Mother, why weren't you wearing your own shawl?"

During another round of the Dance, I saw both my sons. I visited each one, and, as with Beth, each one knew when the visit had been made. To each one I said, "I love you."

One man joined the spectators with about fifty followers. He set up his little camp near the East Gate, placing huge pyramid crystals in front of his group. Every time the Sundancers danced to that area, he picked up the crystals and pointed them at us. We got weaker every time we passed him. Obviously he was doing something to the Mystery Circle. I was wearing a beaded crystal that Leonard had given me. The Medicine Man asked me if he could use it. I told him I had a bigger one that he was welcome to use, a crystal about seven inches high and five inches in diameter that had been gifted to me as a healing crystal by Crystal Bill. Martin High Bear and Quese, a Mexican Medicine Man, turned it upside down in a bowl of salt water. Immediately, a rainbow appeared over the Sundance arena that everyone could see. As we danced out for the next round, we all felt re-energized.

We watched the man at the East Gate. One by one, all of his followers left him. By the end of the Dance, he was sitting alone. I hope it was a good lesson to him. Unfortunately, several Dancers were injured by the manipulative energy. One broke his nose, one was bitten by a spider, and everybody was weakened. I do not understand why people play games with spiritual energy. Some people want to take it instead of collecting it to use for the healing of others.

Every so often I looked out at the spectators and saw someone I knew who couldn't possibly be in Oregon. Sometimes it was someone I hadn't seen in years. Often it was someone I had had an argument with. I made prayers about them, and the arguments replayed themselves before me. I thought about what I could have said, what would have made a difference, and how I could make it right and repair the friendship. I did not figure out until later what these visions really meant. For about six months after each Dance, I often met up on the road with the person I'd thought I'd seen at the Dance and would be given a second chance to heal the rift. In the Great Mystery Circle, it didn't matter whose fault it was, only that it had happened and needed to be healed.

This lesson has completely changed my life. If I have a disagreement with someone now, I do all I can to resolve things with them in a good way, for I know that otherwise I will relive the problem in the Sundance. The Great Mystery's way is toward healing, and the sooner it is done, the better.

I saw many things at the Dance that will never leave me. A Cheyenne Indian pierced on the first day and remained pierced to the Tree for all four days. At night he sat and played his flute. We fanned him as we danced by him. If the Dancers were acting pitiful, we had him to keep us going, along with the Medicine Men and the Helpers kicking our butts. He was a big man, weighing every bit of 300 pounds. He'd talk about the old people in pain and the children, and tell us to remember what we were dancing for. How could we cry and act pitiful after that?

From that Dance and several other Dances, I have seen that there is a difference in the ways the Lakota and the Cheyenne break from their pierces. The Cheyenne warriors are more flamboyant. They run at full speed and break literally in mid-air. Most of the Cheyenne men had been pierced to the Tree of Life for four days; their wounds were already starting to heal when they broke. I am proud to be part Cheyenne and thankful to that big fellow with the flute who taught me so much about what that means.

There was another man that some Indians called the token white, but that many really loved. He was a good man and a great Dancer. His tepee was painted with Egyptian symbols and a picture of a pharaoh; it stood out in the camp, to say the least. He did things differently from some of the Indians, but he was a warrior when it came time to break. He dragged lots of buffalo skulls from ropes piercing his back, and sometimes he pierced more than once during a Sundance. He had beautiful Sundance skirts. One year, he had a skirt with a picture of the Pleiades sewn on it. His wife was the nurse in camp. She took care of me after I experienced that heart trouble. I'll always be grateful to her for that. They are very wonderful people whom I still see from time to time on the circuit.

One of the Helpers was an identical twin to the man I had an almost-affair with in Dallas. I looked at him and my heart stopped. As he talked to me, that whole situation came back to me. I had ample time in the next four days to fall in love and then out of love with that insane man from my past, and then to put it all back into proper perspective.

A Lakota Helper named Max, whom I had seen at Leonard's, was a master at the game of temptation. The Helpers loved to find out the Dancers' weaknesses. As we came off the field, they'd say things like, "I just had a vision of a seven-foot Pepsi!" or "Potato chips, every-body!" Brave Buffalo used to say, "Here comes the A&W truck." Max would start off describing everything he had had to eat — dinner the night before, breakfast that morning — and then he would pour a cup of coffee right in front of everybody. He had a penguin cooler that made a loud noise when you pushed down the head to pour. Max would shake it until we could hear the ice cubes rattling and exclaim, "Oh good, they haven't melted." If the Dance didn't get you, Max would. Max always left the Dance early, before the Sundancers got out. I think that is the only reason he survived to torment us the next year. In later years, I would hear the Sundancers asking who the Helpers would be, always groaning if Max's name came up. Actually, Max is a really neat guy, with lots of heart and compassion, but I can say that now because at the moment I'm not at the Sundance.

A girl from Arizona had an Eagle feather sewn in her arm for all the Indians in prison. After the Dance, she always gave her beautiful Sundance dress to one of the little Indian girls. She was so very beautiful and full of love.

It was fun in the arbor. Everyone talked about their families, where they'd come from, what their dreams were, and about their work. On the third day, the Medicine Man told me I was dancing the steps that I would walk that whole next year. I would be seeking the lessons of the West, to quiet my mind and to learn introspection.

As each round ended on each of the four days, a certain number of the Dancers' Pipes were brought out and gifted to the spectators or support Dancers to smoke for the people. It was beautiful to see the Dancers line up in the Great Mystery Circle to hand their Pipes to a person that had been praying for them and supporting them in that way. After the Pipes had been smoked, before the next round started, the supporters would hand the Pipes back into the Sundancers.

By the morning of the fourth day, everybody looked bad. The temperature was over 120 degrees, and we still had many Pipes left to smoke.

Since I was last in line on the women's side, my Pipe was the last Pipe to be smoked out. As I presented my Pipe, I was joined by Brave Buffalo, who presented the Sundance Pipe to the people. I finally looked into the eyes of someone other than a Dancer and presented my Pipe to one of the women Elders who had given me permission to Dance. As she took the Pipe, she smiled and nodded her head to me. It felt good. It is always a profound moment for me when I hand my Pipe to someone to smoke and to care for.

After dancing for four full days, it was almost over — or so I thought. Then the Elders, the Medicine People, Grandpa Fools Crow, Matthew

King, and other chiefs of the area began to make speeches. It was the final test, for I didn't know how much longer I could go on. I just kept praying. Hours went by, hours and hours.

I had given flesh, I had seen men pierce and hang from the Tree of Life, and then there were the speeches, but there was nothing in my life that could have prepared me for what happened next. As we made our exit out of the East Gate, two to three thousand people lined up to thank the Dancers, to shake our hands and kiss us. Old women kissed my feet and old men took my hands and cried in them. The Dancers did whatever was needed for healings for all these people who had prayed for us and supported us so beautifully. By the time I got to the end of the line of spectators, I had gifted everything I had to them. They were so grateful, I'll never forget it.

After we got through being thanked, we took our Pipes apart. We went through one more Sweat Lodge and said one last prayer. We got water. An old Medicine Woman gave us each a drink of black tea to remove all the toxins from our bodies. The tea hit my stomach and came right back up. Then *washne* — dried grains, fruit, and meat — was shoved into my mouth to give the body exactly what it needs. And then I took off running.

Wonder was waiting right on the other side of the compound with a Pepsi. I was so happy to see him. A fire truck had been brought in to spray the Dancers down. Just as I got to it, the water ran out. One of the Helpers said, "Don't worry, Dallas." He picked up a huge oil can of water and dumped it on my head.

By then, Philip, Fred, and some other Dancers, Whirlwind, Betty, and Sugar Bear, had caught up to me. More drums of water were dumped over us, and we all just rolled and laughed in the mud. We looked like the Navajo Mud Dancers, but who cared.

Then we could go back to camp and get dressed for the feast of buffalo meat, dog soup, and corn soup. I don't think I've ever eaten so much in my life. There was a big give-away, and all the dancers received gifts. For that moment, everything was perfect and beautiful.

As we said our goodbyes, I realized I wasn't a stranger anymore. All the people from Lac Courte Oreilles Reservation went back East to Green Grass, and we headed out to California. I was full of hopes and dreams for a better marriage and a happier life.

During the Dance, one of the Medicine Men had given me the challenge to learn about women's sexual issues, and the spirits had told me to teach a workshop about women. Grandmother Grace later would call it, "The Rite of the Woman Warrior." She and I devised a ceremony for it.

Laughter, pain, death, rebirth, new energy, and the smell and taste of sage all intermingle at the Sundance with the greatest highs and the greatest lows imaginable on this planet. They say the Sundance is the oldest way of the Indian/Initiate on the North American continent.

First Year, Second Sundance Davis, California (Fred's Brother) Bill Wapahpah's Sundance

The Sundance gates had been opened and light streamed across our trail west. We went next to Bill Wapahpah's Sundance in Davis, California. Bill was an organizer of the American Indian Movement. He had stayed in my home in Indiana, and it was good to see him and his wife again.

There I also saw Mary Jane Wilson, an old friend who had made me a Sundance dress. She planned to get married at the Sundance. I heard news about Dennis Banks and other old friends from the American Indian Movement. Vernon and Clyde Bellecourt were there, and I got to see Clyde pierce from the Tree of Life. We also went to D.Q. University. For years I had raised money for this Native American college, and so I was excited to finally see it.

Because I had already danced my commitment that year, I was allowed to dance only one day. The temperature was over a hundred. The days were dusty and the nights were filled with mosquitos. I danced the last day to help support the Dancers, and that night I got to see my friend Mary Jane get married. I had a really good time.

I met up with a Cheyenne friend who had lived with us for six months in Indianapolis. Unfortunately, instead of being happy to see us, on the first day of the Dance he caused a disturbance. I'd been asked to sing with the drummers, so that morning I had put on a Rolling Thunder shirt. This kid started a ruckus so that the warriors demanded that I take off the shirt. The Medicine Men at this Dance were Vincent Black Feather, Moves Camp, and Bill Wapahpah. Bill was called over.

Sundance tree

I was pulled away from the drummers and several other Elders gathered around. I spoke for what I believed to be right: friendship, respect, and honor of my Elder, Rolling Thunder. I told them that Rolling Thunder had put on many benefits for the college and for the American Indian Movement. After much arguing, they allowed me to go back to the drum, and as a statement in support of this Elder, I wore the shirt all three days while I was at the drum. Later, people came up and thanked me for that.

Still, it hurt that this kid, whom I thought was my old friend, was not happy to see us, especially after the time he'd spent at our house, during which we had to put up with his drinking and take care of his son, while he snuck out one night on a drunken spree with our kids and our brand new Monte Carlo car. The fiasco ended with his totaling the car and putting Beth in the hospital. Finally, I had talked to him about his drinking. He had stayed on a short while after that, and I thought we had parted as friends. Instead, he just looked at us as if we were dogs and called us names. It's amazing to me how Indians love to fight with each other. If they'd just stop fighting among themselves, there wouldn't be a cause they couldn't win.

After the Dance, we went back to Bill's. I will never forget him fixing us sandwiches and chips before we took off down the road. Bill is gone now, but his generosity and love for people will live on forever.

First Year, Third Sundance
Big Mountain

From the Sundance at Davis, we drove down to Hopi/Navaho country. This was the first year of the Big Mountain Sundance. I had worked a lot with some of the Elders in the Big Mountain resistance. They still have much to worry about in saving their land. I was most excited to go to the Dance there.

This was a whole different world. The food was different, the terrain was different. As we approached the camp, a sign said, "Seventeen miles to Big Mountain Encampment"; then underneath, "Seventeen minutes." Actually, it took hours. All the way in, Fred argued with his girlfriend. He got it out of his system by driving the car like a maniac. It was the longest, dirtiest, roughest seventeen miles I've ever seen. We almost ran over the edge of a canyon, and then we hit a stump and tore out the whole transmission. Where we tore out the transmission was where we stopped to camp. As I said, emotion manifests at the Sundance.

We went through security and I signed up as a Sundancer, with more confidence this time. We thought we were late arriving, but actually we were early. Everybody was worried because the Medicine Chief hadn't shown up. Then I found out who the Medicine Chief was — Leonard Crow Dog! The last time I had talked to Leonard was just after he told me to Sundance. As I hadn't made it to his Sundance, I was not sure of my reception, and this made me very nervous.

Mary Jane Wilson told me to run a Sweat Lodge. I told her, "I've only run a few Lodges. I can't run a Sweat Lodge here at the Sundance." She said I was a Sundancer and it was part of my job, so I'd better get used to it.

Then a woman I'll call Sue showed up. She was a well-known speaker on Native American Spirituality all over this country and Europe. She arrived in a huge RV, which Wonder helped her to park. Our paths had crossed before without the most flowing results. This time she quickly managed to alienate most of the camp by announcing that she was going to be a Sundancer and therefore was a very important person. The Indians decided to make her not so important. Somehow, she had insulted some of the Grandmas and other women in the camp, which is not a good move to make — but it seemed that any move she made was wrong. I tried to avoid her, for I felt I had enough problems, and I also tried to avoid talking about her to other women. I just wanted to avoid the negativity.

I ran three or four Lodges for all the people, and then I noticed there was a controversy building around Sue. Ernie Peters had told her she couldn't dance. She was furious. She argued with me and anybody else she could corner. People said she offered money to be allowed to dance, as if this sacred ceremony about life, death, and rebirth, could be bought. If Spirit says you're not ready to dance, no amount of money in the world is going to matter. I watched the whole thing escalate and made prayers.

The group from Lac Courte Oreilles Reservation pulled in. An Indian boy from Indianapolis, Chris Johnson, who had been raised with my kids, was with them. We were all so happy to see each other. Chris looked as though he'd been having a pretty hard time of it. He was sick, and I was worried about him. We got him a tent and brought him into our camp. It was about 1:30 in the morning when I saw a gray van with Texas plates pulling in. It was Uncle Leonard. I hollered at him and he yelled back, "Niece, why did you not come to my Sundance, and now I see you here at Big Mountain Sundance!" He jumped out and I was glad to see that he was laughing. The whole family was with him. I hadn't seen the kids or a bunch of the other people for a while. I told Leonard why I hadn't made it to his Dance and that I'd danced under Martin High Bear. He said, "Come over here and shake my hand. It's good to see you." He asked me how many days I was going to dance, and I was quick to tell him only one. Then he told me that I could assist him with the women Sundancers and sing at the drum, and that I might dance several days, he did not know. I gulped. He said he needed help, for it was his first time here. It was really good seeing Uncle Leonard that way.

He asked me to run a Sweat Lodge from sundown to sunup the next night for about twenty elderly Navajo and Hopi women. I was introduced to two interpreters, a Navajo and a Hopi. I was in awe of these women. We started a little bit late; it was already getting dark. I sang a song to the Sun in keeping with what my teacher had told me about how to start the ceremony at that time. It was hard getting those older ladies moving. Their average age was seventy. There were some as young as thirty-four, some near one hundred. I knew that this was going to be a long night for me.

I was walking with them through a wash in the ravine when I felt a snake. "Why you stop?" the interpreter asked. "Because there's a snake." "Oh, yes, it's right by your foot," she said casually. "Oh shit," I thought. In my pocket was a pouch of tobacco. I eased out the tobacco, made a prayer, and carefully offered the tobacco to the snake. Then I thought I heard the snake tell me that someone in the Lodge would turn away that night from another way of spirituality or religion and return to their own Indian way. I thanked the snake and kept walking. Then the interpreter told me that many times you can't hear the snake's rattles because their tails get burned off in the desert heat.

Finally we got to the Sweat Lodge. I believe none of these Elders had ever been in a Sweat Lodge before. They were used to purifying in another way, in natural hot springs with a blanket over them. It took much talking through interpreters to get the Elders to take their heavy clothes off. Finally, it was agreed that they could all go into the Lodge in their slips. To see all those old women going into the Sweat Lodge was just remarkable. I spent a lot of that night crying, it touched my heart so.

I poured water for that Lodge and explained the truths I'd learned from my Elders about the ceremony. The Lodge is the womb of Mother Earth, and we are reborn inside it. I described how the dome of the lodge is the back of the turtle and the altar is the turtle's head. As we enter the Lodge, so do we enter into the essence of this Turtle Island, the North American continent. The Lodge is a place to pray and release our pain and fear. It is a place of healing and connection to the Creator. The interpreters shared all this with the old women and heard all of them answer me and acknowledge what I was saying. Each old woman prayed, and the prayers were translated and shared with us all. All of the Elders sang songs. It was beautiful.

One of the interpreters suddenly began to cry. She told me she had been a nun for thirty-four years, but that night she vowed to return to her Indian ways. She said a rattlesnake had told her on the way to the Lodge that this was a good time to do so. That sure was one busy snake.

By the time the morning star had risen, the Sweat was finished. I came out of the Lodge and a fireman brought me a bucket of water. First I offered the water to all the old women, but they all refrained from drinking out of respect for the Sundancers, so I didn't drink either. Then the fireman told me Leonard had said I could have that bucket of water to wash my body, which I did gratefully. Hidden in a grove of trees, I watched the stars and made prayers for all the dancers.

I returned to the Sweat Lodge area and, as I was preparing to put my Pipe away, I looked up and saw Leonard coming out of the night. "Uncle," I said, "you look like a vision." He said, "I am." We both laughed. We sat by the fire and talked. He told me the peyote meeting was still going on, but he had come back to hear the old women praying and singing. He had been listening for a very long time, and it made him feel so good.

Then he studied me and said, "You know what's the matter with you?" I said, "Nooooo." "You can't see well enough," he answered. "People can still fool you." He proceeded to put a finger on my third eye and turn my brain to soup. He told me to look off in the distance. I could see a snake under a bush twenty miles away. He worked with my third eye as if he were working a dial, until I could see the Elders and all kinds of colors. Then he patted me on the back and said, "Well good, Niece, now you can see better." Then he promptly left. Of course, at that point I couldn't see anything. I stumbled all the way back to my tent. There I collapsed, buzzing with energy, and tried to go to sleep.

At daybreak, about twenty minutes later, just as I'd fallen asleep, Leonard and Gary woke me up to run the Sundance women's Sweat. I fell out of the tent in a red silk nightgown that Catherine Adelstein had given me as a goodbye present from Dallas. Of course, I became the brunt of their jokes for days.

I took off, third eye blaring, to run the Sweat. As I walked up toward the Lodge, a young man sitting by the fire said, "She's a white woman. She can't run Sweat Lodges in this Sundancer compound."

This kid was a Sundancer who had hung from the Tree of Life, and he was really honored in those parts. But I was not going to just walk away when Uncle had told me to do something. I just held my Pipe, sat down on a little hill, and had the fireman go get Leonard. Leonard tore that guy a new hindend. He said, "She's probably more Indian than you ever thought about being. If I'm going to be Medicine Chief, she's going to run that Lodge. She's my family. She's my relation. She's going to run that Lodge." Leonard told him to apologize to me. He didn't, and I certainly didn't say anything.

It was a great Lodge with good-hearted women. We prayed together and then they went out to start the Dance. Leonard told me to get dressed, he wanted me to sing at the drum. It was time to start the Dance and the singers hadn't shown up yet. I was still relatively new to all this and I didn't know all the songs, but Leonard, his wife, Gary, and I sang the Sundance Entrance Song as the Dancers approached the East Gate. Then Leonard ran around, got himself dressed in his full bonnet, and brought the Dancers in. It was a grand entrance. To me, there is no other Sundance Chief like Leonard Crow Dog.

Every once in a while Leonard ran over to help us sing. Thank God, before the morning was over, the singers showed up and we were relieved of that duty. It was a pretty busy day doing all that was needed to help support Uncle and still take care of some of the older women.

Leonard did healings that night. Hundreds of old people were brought in, some in wheelchairs. Leonard brought lightning to the Tree of Life, and an Eagle formed in the sky over the East Gate. He worked on all those people with a hot coal in his mouth. As he breathed through the coal the sparks flew out. It was incredible to watch.

As he was going from person to person, I decided to jump in line and get a healing too. When he got to me, through the hot coal in his mouth, he said, "What are you doing here?" "I'm sorry, Uncle Leonard!" I said. He started to choke as I jumped out of the healing line. I prayed really hard that he would not swallow that coal.

After this phenomenal night of ceremony was over, we all walked through the arbor. Leonard said, "Give me a cigarette." Rules are you can't smoke cigarettes in the arbor, but since Leonard was having one, his wife and I had one too. Then a lady from the camp came up and proceeded to tell Leonard to put out his cigarette. Leonard said, "Don't you know who I am? I'm Leonard Crow Dog, I run this thing!" She faded into the night.

Leonard turned to his wife and said, "Did you see that? I brought lightning to the Tree of Life, I brought an Eagle to the East Gate." His wife said, "No, Leonard, I didn't. You broke my glasses last week." For

Thunder and Mary Jane Wilson at Wolf Song III, in Australia, 1993

the life of me I could not understand how anyone, even if they were blind, could have missed that flash of lightning.

Late that night, some Tibetan monks came, and Leonard asked me to run a Lodge for some of them. I didn't have an interpreter and they seemed to chant all the time. They didn't know what I was saying and I didn't know what they were saying, so we took drums into the Sweat Lodge and took turns singing songs.

I finally got to bed about 3:00 a.m., only to be awakened again at 5:00. The day before, Sue had offered me tobacco to take her to meet Leonard. I really didn't want to do that, but I did. I had to sit there while the Elders ripped her apart for having announced she was going to be assistant Sundance Chief in Europe. I felt sorry for her. Leonard said that if she could go through the women's Sweat and the women said okay, then she could Sundance. I was there with Mary Jane, and I sure did hope he would tell Mary Jane to run that Sweat Lodge, but he said, "Okay, in the morning, Niece, you run the Lodge."

The women tore Sue apart for the second time. They voted her out, citing her insults and violations. Even though I did not vote, Sue seemed to blame it all on me. After she screamed at me, I held her for a half hour while she cried. I really did feel sorry for her. The sad truth is that I feel that she brought most of her sorrow on herself and that she had approached everything in too aggressive a way. I was sad when I had to tell Leonard what the women had decided. "Fate is Fate, Niece." he said. I left wondering about Fate and why there had to be so many judgments in Fate's name.

Then Leonard reappeared. "Come on in the Dance today, I want you to help me out," he said. I ran around at breakneck speed to get ready. It was the first round, and the men were already piercing. Leonard had me fan the men so that I might see the piercing close up. Somehow, I'd thus far avoided that. I prayed, "Oh Tunkashila! Please don't let me faint." I fanned man after man.

The Computer Story

After the Dancers had entered the Mystery Circle, Leonard took me to the Tree of Life, put me on my knees, and had me make a special prayer and ceremony for the restoration of my life. He sang a song, and again I saw the Vision of the Elders smiling at me. It was beautiful.

I had a wonderful Vision come to me of what I call "the Computer." A long time ago, before we came down to Earth, we were all up in Heaven. This was the Soul Bank. In the Soul Bank, everything was peaceful and wonderful, there were no problems, and everyone knew that they were a part of God, that all souls were equal, and that all was just one flow of the Universe.

Then one day a Big Guy came up to Heaven and asked for volunteers to go down to Earth to help out, since Earth was getting itself into so much trouble with negative thinking, pollution, wars, and so forth. We all said, "EARTH? Nuh-uh, no way! You go down there, you get stuck in your emotions and attached to physical stuff, and you lose track of the fact that you're a Master. Forget it!"

But the Big Guy was patient and loving, and also a pretty good salesperson. He talked about opportunities to grow and learn, to make a difference, to help lots of people, and maybe to get Earth back on the right track. By the time he was done talking, we were all ready to go.

We ran over to a big computer center where we could punch in our choice of opportunities for growth and service. When my turn came, I punched in the big stuff: "abandoned by mother at three weeks old," "half breed," "father wanted a boy," etc. Everyone punched the buttons that looked to them like the best opportunities, and then we all zipped down to Earth. The first thing that happened to me on arrival was that I forgot how to breathe, someone slapped me, and I cried.

Wouldn't you know it? We all got stuck in our emotions and physical addictions and forgot that we were Masters. We even forgot that we forgot. We forgot that we all had been equal up there as souls and began judging each other relentlessly. We forgot that we *chose* the opportunities for growth in our lives, we denied responsibility, and we began to think of ourselves as victims.

So what are we doing here now? We're remembering. It's time to put all the emotional stuff aside, let go of judgment and fear, and start being who we really are. We all *are* Masters.

During this vision, I was taken again through the Sun to the Sun behind, and, again, I passed out on the field and had to be dragged off. At least that night I didn't have to run the Sweat; Mary Jane did. She laughed at me for passing out on the field, but I knew she was happy that I'd had a vision. I was happy I'd had a vision; at first I had thought I was dying.

The next day, as I was helping the Dance, I noticed from inside the Sundance Arbor that one of the Navajo women Elders was leaving. I had met a lot of the women involved in the Hopi/Navajo Land Resistance since I had been at Big Mountain, and one of the greatest of them was this Navajo Elder, seventy-eight-year-old Virginia Smith. I had sat with her in the Sweat Lodge and poured water. She had told me about how the government came and took her sheep, and that all she knew about was her sheep. So she got her gun and shot at the government people. She showed me the picture of her with her gun and Navajo basket in *Newsweek*. The government agents hit her and knocked her into a gully, and then they put her in jail; but she still kept going. She took me to her home. Her whole life had been spent in a twenty-mile area where she walked everyday in heavy clothing, tending her sheep. She was a real heroine to me. I felt privileged to meet this woman and proud of her and her spirit.

When I saw that she was leaving the Dance, I got one of the guards at the gate of the Arbor to hand her out my shell Sundance belt. Those old grandmas like shells, and I could see that she was happy. She smiled and waved thanks. Uncle saw her smiling, too. He waved at her and said, "That is why we are here, for the old people and the children."

Then I asked the fireman to look for a piece of rope to wrap around me and hold my shawl. Sue saw this from the supporter side of the Dance and took off her belt and sent it in to me. It was a great gesture. I think witnessing the beauty and sacrifice of the Dance had helped her work through her anger and disappointment. She may not have made it into the Dance, but her belt did.

Mid-afternoon, I came on my Moon and had to be taken out of the Dance. Mary Jane was there to support me and assure me that I hadn't done anything wrong. I stayed around our camp. Mary Jane brought me a plate of feast food. What an honor that this great woman, who traveled all over the world for Indian causes, still thought of me.

My Moon lasted just that one afternoon, but I waited my twenty-four hours. When I knew I was clear, I came back into the camp again. Leonard said he didn't think it had really been my moon, but some more clearing from my operation. He also said that he wanted Wonder and me to go to a ceremony of the Tibetans and the Hopi and Navajo Elders blessing the blue corn they later would pass out to the Dancers. Those Tibetans were happy to see me. It was a wonderful ceremony.

Then we went with Leonard, his wife, and the family to see the Sacred Tablets of the Elders. On this land, there were pieces of ancient pottery everywhere. I asked Uncle if people ever could take those pieces of pottery. He said no, they were sacred and should be left right where they were. I felt so blessed and grateful just to be there.

We returned to camp and I went to check the progress on the car. Soon Uncle also came by to survey the progress. Then a group of women came by looking for him and asking for somebody to help with the birth of a baby. Uncle waved at me and I volunteered.

The other women and I drove for quite a while. Then the car stopped in the middle of nowhere. We all got out and went into a hogan where a beautiful Indian woman was in labor. I assisted the Elder who was delivering the baby and listened to her songs. Soon the child was born. Standing there washing my hands, I heard the old woman saying the baby was angry. In the old days, she said, if the baby was born angry, they might have thought about sending it back to the Spirit World, because it would never be happy its whole life. At the time, I couldn't understand that way of thinking, but since then, I have met many angry people in my travels who have caused me to recall the Elder's words: "Some people just do not want to give up their anger, and the people did not want anger to fill the villages." Later, I told Leonard and his wife what the old women had said. Leonard said that in no way could this old custom be judged by Today World standards.

Leonard and family were getting ready to go. He offered me some money to fix our car which, of course, we didn't accept. I hated to see them leave, but I felt full and happy. He made me vow that I would be at Crow Dog's Paradise the next year. I told him I would make sure I was. Back at our camp, I found that someone had already fixed the car.

There's something about Sundance goodbyes; you know they are never for long. Whether or not you see a person again in this life, they are a part of you you'll never forget. I said goodbye to Mary Jane, who had helped me so much, as she left with her new husband.

There are so many other wonderful ones that I've met at the Sundance, like Grandfather David Menonga. He was about 100 years old. He was brought in by a Helper who also carried a box that held a huge necklace of herkimer diamonds. The Helper opened the box and put the necklace on the old man as he watched and prayed for the ceremony. He talked to the Sundancers as we rested in the arbor. One night after ceremony, he and Leonard called me over. He told me that I was different from all the rest because my job was to blend both worlds. He gave me a pair of earrings made from the same herkimers as his necklace. They were little hearts. I still have them today.

I was down at the kitchen just before we left, saying goodbye to all the people. The beautiful Navajo and Hopi women kept coming up and giving me food. They remembered me from the Sweat Lodge. Suddenly, up came the man whom Leonard had yelled at for telling me I couldn't run a Sweat Lodge. At the end of the Dance, I had seen Leonard gift him with something very special. Leonard loves sticks. Before a Dance, he'd find a stick the size of a staff. He'd work on it all the way through the Dance, adding feathers and pretty stones. At the end of the ceremony, he'd present this staff to the warrior who had pierced and broken in a good way. That year Leonard gave his stick to this man. He had been pulled up into the Tree of Life and had danced perfectly in the air, just as if he were standing on Earth. And when it was time, somehow he threw his body to a horizontal position and broke free.

I turned around and just looked at him, and he said, "I'm sorry, damn you," and walked away. I turned around to the corn soup in my hand and said, "Thank you, Tunkashila. That's as close as he can get." He didn't do it for me or himself, but to honor Leonard Crow Dog, one of the greatest Native Americans to walk this continent. I honor him that he did it.

I went back to our camp. We decided that Chris Johnson would travel with us on the road for a while. There was no room in our car, so he would to go back to Lac Courte Oreilles Reservation and wait for us there. Fred was ready to roll, calling out, "Load them up and move them out!" As we drove off, Leonard and his wife came by one more time. As we were already driving away, Leonard began to reel off all the things he needed me to do in the Universe. I hung out of the car, catching about as many as I could and laughing at how lucky I was to know this man and be in his family.

First Year Blues

These are some of my remembrances from my first year of the Sundance. I have many more years under my belt now. I have found the Dance part is always good; it is the living in the real world afterwards that really gets to you, living each day as a sensitive person who cares and loves, while other people are in pain, old folks go hungry, etc. I can be a saint in the ceremony, but afterwards I can be the opposite. How to bring the Spirit of the ceremony into everyday life is the big challenge.

After my first year of dancing, I was filled with many emotions. Sometimes I felt like there was a fire running through my body from head to foot, ripping up old things for me to look at.

After one Dance, I went into a store to find myself terrified of the store; the loud noises, the different colors, and the energies — and the smells were overwhelming. I was buying some bologna and bread when two ladies got into an argument over who was first in the check-out line. I just dropped everything and ran out.

Fred was a big help that first year. He, Wonder, and I stayed together for a while. Then he left us at Shirley Barclay's home in Dallas for the winter. It was hard leaving him and seeing him leave. We separated after some arguments, some crying, but with a lot of respect for each other. He is still one of the most wonderful men in the Universe to me. I have seen him since, and we have had other journeys and adventures — but that is another story for another time. I honor all that he has done in my life.

"Well, there are just a few more things I want talked about. Let's see . . . . Oh, yes, how about that workshop that we did together, 'Rite of the Woman Warrior.' How about me telling you to be a teacher and about all those women and children ceremonies I had you start doing. Now, that ought to make a pretty good book. Make sure you make me look good!"

Grandma put down her coffee cup, put out her last cigarette (remember, she stopped smoking), and we hugged. "When you going to get this done — next week?"

I watched as she walked over to hug everyone at the camp, looking everyone in the eyes and saying something to each of them that was important for their lives. She got into Sparky Shooting Star's car, our eyes met one last time, and then she was gone.

16

JUST A FEW MORE THINGS TO SAY
AND THEN IT IS ALL OVER CHAPTER

Rite of the Woman Warrior Workshop
Right After Year One Sundance

I came out of the first year of Sundance with the mission of leading a workshop on woman's sexual issues. I went to Colorado right after the Dance, and Grandma and I sat down at her kitchen table to make up a program with exercises, wisdom that needed to be shared, and a ceremony. Then I called up my good friend and sister, Dr. Elizabeth Gaines (Twinky), in Indianapolis and asked her to set it up. She agreed, and the workshop was on its way. I gathered the information and materials I needed for the ceremony from Grandma and left for Indy.

On the day of the workshop, I walked into John Macri's restaurant, where we were meeting, and was shocked that of approximately 160 people gathered, over 100 were men. "What happened?" I asked Twinky. She said, "It was advertised just as you dictated it to me, and I really don't know." She and I quickly revised the workshop. During the sharing that day, we found that many men were scared of women's energy and wanted to know about Women Warriors.

I shared the experience and wisdom that was given to me by Grandma and other Grandmothers. It was mostly about women sitting in circle together and learning to support each other. I found on the road that many of my biggest challenges were presented by women.

I presented that workshop many times around the country that year, and I was amazed that there were always more men attending than women, and that those men were always interested in the women's ceremony. My big question was, where were the *women*?

I used to watch as people would gather in the name of a ceremony, but with a personal game plan of finding a "beautiful woman" or a "beautiful hunk." This inspired me to create my "Sex and Spirituality" talk that I share when issues of sexuality come up. Boiled down, it is my belief that Sexual energy and Spiritual energy are the same energy — Creation/Spirit/Higher Self — but at different vibrations. A ceremony is not a good place to make relationships of an intimate nature, for the lower vibration energy should be kept separate from the higher vibration energy. Sexual energy, which is connected to the root chakra (Earth), is lower in vibration than Spirituality (Sky), which is connected to the heart and upper chakras. When I work with people, I only work from the heart chakra and up. I have seen many a sister go through the whole program — many of them as my own clients at a battered women's shelter — leave the center, enter into a relationship right away, and find themselves bringing in the same old kind of energies of abuse, because they are afraid to walk in their own power and spirituality. They choose not to internalize within themselves all the lessons and wisdom that they heard shared, but to seek it in an outward reflection.

I have worked at Neuro-Linguistic Programming gatherings, where I've found that matching a person walking through their fears with ceremony made a complete picture of wholeness for them to heal by. Most of these gatherings were wonderfully run, with good rules, regulations, and boundaries set to enable people to go through the program and re-emerge as childlike. This was wonderful learning for people. On the other side of fear, I have watched people find an energy — some call it ecstasy — that I see more as old, trapped energy breaking through to a new freedom.

I was always excited in the earlier days of those NLP camps to be called upon to offer a ceremony to help ground the energy. It was like the Sundance: after four days and nights of making major breakthroughs, we would ground the energy in ceremony and thank the Spirit for its help. But at some of the camps, people used the energy for sexual contact, instead of ceremony. At one camp in California, I arrived to find all the people naked and having a party throwing water-filled balloons. I was very embarrassed and could not stay, for I had come to do a ceremony. I went to a nearby motel and came back only when everyone had their clothes on and there were no more balloons.

Only a handful showed up for the ceremony. We prayed prayers for safety at a nearby nuclear plant. I held up the Pipe to offer it to the Great Mystery and the ground rumbled. When we returned to the camp house, we learned that there had been an earthquake and that the nuclear plant had been closed down. Coincidence? I don't think so. The Spirit is powerful and prayers do make a difference.

A Story About Energy Cords

The Old Ones say that when we are born, we not only have a umbilical cord attached to our mothers, we also have a silver cord still attached to the Universe/Planet we originally came from. When I first heard this, I began to wonder about these cords.

I have since learned that humans have energy cords between themselves. Mothers and babies are corded, fathers and babies are corded, husbands and wives are corded, lovers are corded, etc., and this seems normal. But we can also be corded to strangers, situations, memories, and any other energies out there in the world. We are each born with an energy system that is unique, and management of that system is important. We must learn how to live in our own bodies and find out about our own energies.

More than once as we traveled across this land talking and working with folks, Grandmother Grace Spotted Eagle said to me, "Look at that guy. He is sexually cording those swooning females. Don't do that as a teacher. If a person uses sexual energies to cord to others, then that is a life force violation, because they will return to him just for that feeling and not the message that he is sharing."

I asked her just what she meant.

"You have sight, Stupid," she said. "Look at that man, just around the unmentionable area [root chakra], and what do you see?"

I looked at the male teacher, at the area Grandma mentioned, and I was shocked to see fiery red lines, like red spider web threads. Grandma said these were called cords. These red spider webs seemed to be floating loose, and then, all of a sudden, zap, they would connect to the same exact area on many of the lecture participants.

"I can see it, Grandma. Why is he doing this?" I asked.

"Well, I am not sure he knows what he is doing, but what did you notice most about the recipients of the cords from him?" Grandma said.

"Well, they were very interested."

"More like they are panting for him. Instead of teaching from the heart, he is teaching from the sexual organs." She grunted.

"A teacher must be responsible to the people/students. A teacher should feed the people, not suck their energy or attach them to him/herself by that life cord. Now, that guy is a pretty shallow teacher. He might be popular for a short time, but soon his students will break those cords, or he will break them himself when he has gotten what he needs. Then he will have to go out and do the same thing all over again."

I have spent many years watching, working for awareness, and learning major disciplines to make sure that, when I am sharing with people, it is from the heart chakra up, and not the heart chakra down.

Spirit also has shared with me that others can and will try to attach to my energy. I have found that many people seek a teacher so they can reside under that teacher's umbrella of protection and life force, so they won't have to use their own energies to learn in life. This stops the gifts that the Spirit has for their own growth. Early in my Walk, I learned ways of cutting energy cords with others — but always with love.

I have found that ceremonies do this naturally. There is nothing like a Sweat Lodge to purify the mind, heart, and body of all toxins — and I feel that a codependent cord is a toxin. I feel that it is good to cut the cords from beings trying to use the energies of others to energize themselves. Being responsible for building my own inner and outer energy fields and giving my energy back to the Earth Mother with love keeps my energy clear.

So many today say, "Please love me," and then cord you so that they're literally draining your sacred life force. You can still love them without making them dependant on your energy, or making yourself dependent on theirs.

Children's Rites of Passage Ceremonies

Grandma was very interested in and loved the children.

*Nancy Moore and son, Jason, on the land at Thunder Horse Ranch,
meeting Leonard Crow Dog*

"Vision Quest, Vision Quest, all these adults want to do Vision
Quest. It is the children that should be questing for a Vision for
humanity. Today World's children don't get the benefit of being given
permission to be a man or a woman, like in the old days," Grace said.

She and I talked to other Grandmas, who told us of old ceremonies
for the children, and we worked out a system. I am happy now that
every spring we do Children's Rites of Passage. I have seen these
ceremonies have some really remarkable effects on hardened street
kids and kids that are starting on drugs. One child stopped drugs when
he started making his prayer ties, and then stayed clean all through
high school. Last time I talked with him, he still was doing fine.

Here at the Ranch, the children have marvelous leaders, like Horse,
David Corrado, Nancy Moore, Sparky Shooting Star, Sandy Collins,
and Tina Emerson, who lead them through their lessons. Horse and
David work with the boys, and Nancy, Sparky, Sandy, and Tina work
with the girls. The kids are brought into either all-male or all-female
tepees and are given old lessons of time-honored ways of becoming a
man or a woman. With those lessons, they prepare for their Vision
Quest. Right before they leave for the Vision Quest ceremony, during
which they go to the hill for one to four days, we have a cord-cutting
ceremony. In the ceremony, the child is literally tied to his or her father
and/or mother with a golden cord. If a parent is not there, then a
surrogate is provided for them if they wish. The parent(s) give permis-

Thunder and group of children at Rites of Passage — Vision Quest led by Visiting Elder Buck Ghost Horse and Thunder on Thunder Horse Ranch

sion for the child to go and learn of being a man or woman and to seek a Vision from the Great Mystery. It is a pretty emotional ceremony. I don't care how hardened the kids or the parents are, usually there is not a dry eye in the place. The child is released from being a little boy or girl.

One year, we had a sixty-seven-year-old grandmother that took part in the ceremony. Last year, at Thunder Horse Ranch, a twenty-four year old movie star, seven adult women, and thirteen children with their parents participated. A whole family came to deal with a father who had abused and molested his child. The father was facing criminal charges and had gone into therapy. I allowed the father to come onto the land and take part in the cord cutting ceremony of his sixteen-year-old daughter, in which she said, "I am now becoming a woman and you cannot take advantage of me any longer. I do not hate you, but I do blame you for all that has happened to me. I thank you for giving me my freedom and now wish to go on to become a woman. Perhaps someday I will become a woman who is free of fear and abuse." She ended her tear-filled statement by choking out the words, "I love you, Daddy." We were all crying along with her, for the movie star and the seven adult women present, including myself, had been abused.

Immediately after the cord was cut, and the sixteen-year-old girl took the hand of the beautiful movie star and ran out the door to the Sweat Lodge, the whole room gasped for breath and broke up in tears. I asked the father to leave, with a friend for support, and I encouraged him to go right to a prearranged counseling session where he could express himself. When he left, I returned to the tent where the ceremony had taken place. It was very quiet, and I said, "The father is gone." The whole room broke out clapping. What a healing for all. The family is doing better now, with everyone in counseling.

Then comes the Vision Quest. Usually the parents will have gotten their child a new outfit. When the child is either without parents or without means, Horse and I will always buy them a t-shirt or something so that they have a new piece of clothing to reflect their new self. Upon returning from the Quest, they again go through the Sweat Lodge and then dress in their new clothes and make ready for their return to the whole group. Then we have a party with lots of food and surprises. One year, Nancy Moore rented carrier pigeons that took off as the children came into view. Another year, we had fireworks. Everyone on the land gathers at the door of the tent to welcome the children. Pouches are prepared for the boys and baskets for the girls, in which all the people place gifts. Guest Elders, like Buck Ghost Horse, Luciano Perez, and Grandmother Kitty, to name a few from just one year, have come to work with the children at this ceremony. I remember one group in which the boys carried staffs that they had made on their own and new pouches that Horse had hand-crafted for them, and the girls carried beautiful baskets that Nancy Moore and Lisa Fahl-Stafford had made and filled with feathers, stones, and other pretty things. The boys were straight and tall and very Warrior-like and the girls were very beautiful, strong, and proud. I cried the whole walk from the Sweat Lodge to the tent. This is my very favorite gathering and ceremony, and again, thanks go to Grandma Grace for helping me to put it all together.

"Tell Them That I Have Told You To Be a Teacher"

Grandma used to say: "Thunder, you are a teacher!"
"A teacher of what?" I used to say.
She would say, "A teacher of what you need to know."

"That's easy," I would answer, "for you say I am pretty stupid." We both would laugh. Today, I always laugh when I tell a group of people that I am here tonight to teach them what I need to know. The looks on their faces are precious. I have taught about love (sure did not know about that), I have taught about sexual issues (sure did not know about that, either), and I have taught about how to get along with others (another one that I did not know). Yep, I sure have had and still have a lot to teach.

Then one day Grandma said, "You should take students." I looked at her stupidly. "Let's see, Grandma, I am walking and teaching what I need to know, following the Pipe, and making my bed every morning. What kind of students do you think I should get?"

"Smart ones!" she said.

I could not help but see the ad in the paper: "Woman, walking and teaching what she needs to know, does not know where she is going, and specializes in making her bed each morning, needs student." I just laughed. But I could not laugh long for, as usual, when Grandma said something should happen, it did. Everywhere I went from then on, someone would walk up and ask to be my student.

Students have been the most beautiful reflections of myself possible. In the beginning, it was mostly women that joined me on the road. So of course, one day Grandma said, "Why do you have only women with you?"

"Well," I said, "didn't you tell me to have only women students?"

"No, ninny, if you just teach women, then where is the opposite reflection of yourself? Where is the balance of male and female?"

"Well, what can I teach a man?" I sure did not want to share that I did not trust myself with a man in the teacher/student relationship.

"Well, you could teach him about intuition, creativity, and joy!" she snapped. "Remember, you don't have to have a sexual relationship with a man, you can be just his teacher."

I fidgeted in the chair and wanted the conversation to end. "I am on the road, and I am being celibate, and I don't want any temptations on my walk as a teacher."

"Hogwash," she looked me right in the eyes. "There are two kinds of people on this planet, male and female, and you are supposed to reach out and teach both. Now, next time you come through, have a male Warrior with you."

Somehow I did, and I have had some very wonderful reflections of my male side in Warriors who have traveled on the road with me. Not once have I had a sexual relationship with one of my Warriors — well, except one, Jeffrey "White Horse" Hubbell, and then only when we first had quit the teacher/student relationship and taken a break from each other. Grandma did it again and showed me that I could teach what I needed to know, even about males and females, sex and spirituality. I have chosen not to pursue spiritual power through sexual relationships with any of my teachers or students.

I have learned a lot from those that have called me Teacher. There are always places inside me where the wounded child will appear to remind me that I have not fully healed.

Recently I was talking with my friend/former student/editor of this very book, Augusta Ogden, who is also a Tarot Card Reader. Augusta and I have been together for about seven years. I asked her to read the cards around one of those still unhealed issues. I asked this question about those that have called me teacher and that I have called students: "Why is it sometimes painful when we separate or disconnect, or when aspects of the relationship change?" From Augusta's reading and from a talk with Horse, an answer came to me. I call it *Fear of Flying*.

Grandma told me a long time ago, "Many will come and ask for your help, but you see them in a higher way than they see themselves. You see the beauty and they see the everyday self. So, Daughter, you have to be careful. Don't get caught in your view or rob them of theirs!"

It took me a long time to understand that some people choose to define themselves by their pain, rather than by their higher selves. Some people will only allow themselves to see their own limitations, not the endless possibilities Spirit offers them in their lives. They say they want to transform their lives, they ask you to be their teacher; but it seems that right at the gate of transformation, they back off. They say, "No, I can't do that," or "You're asking too much from me," or "It's too hard." That sort of response to a request or suggestion from one of my Elders was never an option for me. I was taught by Grandma and my other Elders that, in choosing a teacher, I would be undertaking service to the Spirit. By being in service and in complete surrender to the Spirit, I have been blessed by insights beyond anything I could have imagined.

What does it mean to be in service? A lot of you have monetary and other conditions you place on your service. My uncle would call to tell me that there were 700 Indians on their way into town and I should find a place for them to stay and food for them to eat; he'd see me in two days. So that's what I did. I had no conditions on what I would do or not do. My teachers didn't allow them.

Grandma Twylah asked me to bring twenty-six blankets to her for Wolf Song I, a gathering of indigenous Elders at her home on the Cattaraugus Reservation in upstate New York. I said I would mail them. She told me no, I had to bring them. First, I had to get twenty-six blankets. Then, because the car was broken down at the ranch, I had to rent a vehicle. When I finally arrived, she pulled me into a circle of the Elders. I thought she was making a mistake. Then she got up to the microphone and said, "I want to introduce the next Peace Elder, Mary Thunder. Next year, Wolf Song II is going to be on her land in Texas."

Somehow we put together all that it took for Wolf Song II, and I did not even think about how I could not do it. One day, when I got a call that five Aboriginals and five Columbians wanted airline tickets to come to the gathering, I called in a panic, "Now Grandma Twylah, I am crazy. This whole Wolf Song thing is making me crazy. I want you to pray for me." She laughed and said, "No, Thunder Girl, I won't pray for you. The problem with you is that you are not grateful enough. Go out there and make a prayer for gratefulness."

I went out to the Quan Yen garden and I made a prayer of gratefulness for the Elders from Bogota and from Australia that wanted to come. Their airfares would cost about $10,000 and I had no money, but I just kept forcing myself to say thank you for the opportunity to have Columbians and Aboriginals here at Thunder Horse Ranch for Wolf Song II. Going back to the house, I felt better, believe it or not, and even could visualize the Elders coming through the front gate. As I got into the house, the phone rang and a friend said, "I have some airline mileage, and I want to offer to help pay for the Elders to come from Colombia." Except for one five-thousand dollar grant, Wolf Song II was funded only by wonderful human beings from all over who wished to gather for Peace and support Grandmother Twylah's vision.

That's how it works. You have to give it a chance. I could have just as easily said, "Well Grandma, God bless your heart, I can't do it"; but I wasn't trained that way. Whatever I was asked to do, I did. In this Today World, if someone comes to us and asks us to do something, we say we can't, our schedule is too full. I was taught that whatever is in front of you is service; every situation is karma. It's what you do with it that creates karma or not. Causeless karma is how I try to live.

I have had some amazing students; they all know more than I do. So what makes me their teacher? Maybe just that I have learned to reinforce just how much they themselves are teachers. A long time ago, one of the first predictions about my work was that I would be a teacher of the teachers. I feel that this is very true.

One time Grandma Grace said to me, "See that woman over there. Her life source is her pain. If Grandpa were to heal her before she is ready to let the pain go, she might die. Healers, they got to be careful about this. Many people that receive healings get mad at the healer because they were very comfortable with their "old" pain and they just don't know what to do with themselves without it."

We have to be willing to let go of our pain — old addictions, excess emotions, worry, anger, resentments, low self esteem, and all the "I Can'ts." Every attachment to pain in our lives is like a knot that ties us to a particular place or time. The more knots we have, the less able we are to fly. A good teacher can show a student how to be light enough to fly, but if a student is unwilling to untie those knots or release that pain, then a teacher who tells them they can fly will just make them angry.

All the ones I have looked to as teachers are still in my life. When I am with Leonard Crow Dog and my stuff begins to come up, I just breathe and ask him what to do about it. It never occurs to me to blame him. If fact, I am always grateful to him for helping me see one more piece of myself that is not working in the Universal Order. Leonard says that each one of us is the Great Mystery, in that we can't see ourselves to know what is keeping us from our most spiritual essence. We need teachers to bring out that essence and show it to us. I am glad Leonard Crow Dog is in my life to do that.

What we need in the world today is more Elders — not more people trying to be teachers, but more Elders to pray for us.

What keeps some people from being good teachers today? I feel that they don't want to move their own stuff. They want the glory of being a teacher, but they don't know how to sacrifice for their students. I knew a lady who had twenty-two students, all running around and getting her this and getting her that. I asked her, "What are you teaching these people?" "I'm teaching them to respect me," she said.

"What else?" I said. She replied: "Right now, that's it." People need to learn how to live, how to get along with each other, how to love.

Grandma once said, "Thunder, you are going to have some of the most magnificent Warriors on the planet."

"Now, Grandma, tell me why I'm going to have such fabulous Warriors."

"Why? Because in the old days, the Warrior women taught the Warriors," she said.

"What did they teach them?" I wanted to know.

"They taught them intuition. They taught them how to be invisible. They taught them to move with the energy and to move the energy through their bodies in any situation, so that none of it would get blocked and create a place of illness or suffering. They taught them to support and they taught them to nurture."

She went on, "How can you teach someone? You can teach only by example. You have to be in awareness of the energy you put out. Whatever energy you put out into the Universe is your responsibility. Remember, Thunder, you have to clean up your messes," she smiled.

I have since come to feel as my truth that a teacher is the reflection of the student's higher self. As a student, you must listen to what a teacher has to say, even if it is difficult, for a *good* teacher is dedicated to helping students be all that they can be. And when the gates of your dream open and you have learned to allow yourself to fly, you may see your teacher's face before you, smiling.

MI TAKAYE OYACIN!
CIKSUYA CANNA 'SNA CANTEMAWA'STE YELO
Whenever I remember you my heart is happy!

Grandma Grace talking to sisters

"Check you out later, Thunder."

17

✷ ✷ ✷

CHECK YOU OUT LATER, GRANDMA

It was late fall, 1985, and pretty cold in Michigan. My road crew and I were at the Upland Hills Ecological Center, where I had joined Grandma and Grandpa at a gathering. I was scheduled to teach a workshop, give a lecture, and help out with the Sweat Lodge. It was good to be with them again.

When I came out of the Sweat Lodge, I was shaking and my teeth were chattering. I complained that I felt like a popcicle. Grandma said, "Shut up or you will be one," and laughed. I looked at this little bitty lady out in the cold and thought about how many times she and Grandpa had done ceremony for the people in all parts of the country. Later that night, her legs ached and I rubbed them. The question came into my mind: "Why do they do it? They get so tired, and for virtually no money at all." Grandma popped her head up and said, "The people have to live, and you and me and Grandpa have to keep going to help them. Otherwise, the people will go on hurting each other, never learning love, and what will be left for our children? People have to learn love for the rocks, love for the green, love for the sky and sun, love for the creepy-crawlies (insects and reptiles), and love for everything Tunkashila created." She could always read my thoughts, so I had to watch over them or a drum stick on the head might meet a bad one. The Elders have their own way of "Brain Re-programming."

I was always terrified to speak to the people in front of Grandma and Grandpa. When I knew I would be giving a lecture at this gathering, I conveniently set up an interview at the same time for both of them in another room. I found out later that Grandma had told the interviewer, "I can't talk to you now. My daughter is speaking, and I have to go help her out."

I was right in the middle of a phenomenal flow, and in they walked. My voice stuck in my throat and my heart stopped, remembering all

First row: Dennis Graham (Grandma and Grandpa's adopted son), Grandpa Wallace, Grandmother Grace, Thunder; Second row: Sparky Shooting Star and Jim Wolf Yoxall at the Upland Hills Ecological Center, Oxford, Michigan 1985

the years when I'd thought my name was "Shut Up." They sat down, and I knew I had to do something. I asked Grandma if there was anything she wanted to say. She said, "Nope, came to hear you talk." So I asked Grandpa. Same response. There was nothing to do but to breathe and start talking. After a few minutes, some sisters in the corner created a distraction. Grandma got up, pointed her drumstick at them, and said, "Shut up. This is my daughter talking and what she has to say is very important. You'd better listen. Grandpa and I are very proud of her. Besides, I taught her everything she knows." That was a pretty memorable gathering in many ways, for it was there that I first met Jeff White Horse Hubbell (Horse), who is now my husband. At that gathering, I taught the female half of a workshop dealing with male/ female balance. I asked the members of the group to say in one word what signified the feminine to them. When it was Horse's turn, he said, "Hair. Your hair." I felt myself blushing. Grandma turned to me and said, "That young man needs to go on the road with you. I like him." By the end of the gathering, he had decided to leave his hometown and join our road crew.

Over the next two years, Horse and I fell in love and became half-sides. Remembering the gleam in Grandma's eyes, I should have known something like that might happen. Many beautiful people came to travel with us on the road. Throughout it all, Grandma and Grandpa helped and advised — and made sure I got lots of lessons I'd never forget.

The Last Dance With Grandma, 1987

It was a special Sundance that year, my thirteenth in my five years on the circuit, and the first time I would dance under Wallace Black Elk. I had danced under other traditional leaders, such as Leonard Crow Dog, Frank Fools Crow, Martin High Bear, and Brave Buffalo. I had danced in South Dakota, California, Arizona, and at Big Mountain, and I finished my four-year commitment at the Mount Hood, Oregon, Sundance in 1986. To be dancing under my spiritual father's supervision was like coming home. But it would be the last time I'd see Grandma and Grandpa together.

I had not danced at Grandpa's until then for a reason. I had other commitments to finish up first. Right before Sundance season that year, I got an urgent call from Grandma asking me to come to their place because there was trouble brewing. She was worried about Grandpa and that Leonard might get involved. (There was a rumor that Wallace and Leonard Crow Dog did not see eye to eye and that Leonard was going to shut down Wallace's Dance.) Grandma also wanted me to come and head up the women, because they were just not being as respectful as they could be, she said. I just laughed to myself, "Well, self, sounds like Grandma wants me there this year, so I had better go."

I tried to call Leonard to find out what was really happening, but I could not reach him. I had the dress material that Grandma had given me made into a beautiful Sundance dress. Her mother had given that fabric to her for the Dance, but at her mother's memorial, Grandma had

Horse

given it to me to have it made up into a Sundance dress. She asked that I wear that dress and dance for her, for she was too sick and old to dance herself anymore. It only made sense to wear the dress this year at Grandpa's. It was very beautiful — rose-colored with embroidered roses and sixty yards of ribbon, handmade by my sister-in-law Jan Ross, Denise Stroup, Lois Metcalf, and Kathleen Koerner. My thanks to all of them for their beautiful work. Yes, this was the year Grandma had talked about for many years, the year I would dance for her.

After a crazy mixed-up road trip, I arrived late. The Dance had started at sunrise, and I came in about 7:00 am. The guards were waiting for me. When I arrived at the gate, they ushered me right in.

Grandpa came out to the Sundancer's compound and said, "You are a Sundancer, so sweat yourself in and get in here right away."

After finishing the sweat ceremony, I called for the fire man to open the door. As it opened, I saw an old arch enemy standing there. She looked at me with anger in her eyes and said, "I am the Head Woman Dancer and you will do as I say." Well, that will do for hello, I thought. I had the feeling that she would make sure I had a wonderful time. Now, Leonard had never shown up so I never had to play intercessor for that drama but I was in major confusion, after being asked to come, to be treated this way.

As I walked into the arbor, I saw a lot of Indian guys and gals whom I had danced with at other places. One of the Canadian men ran over and hugged me, and said to all, "This is Thunder, and she should go to the front of the line." The white female Head Dancer said, "This is Thunder, and I am in charge, and she will go to the back of the line." So I went to the back of the line with two little girls. One of them turned around and said, "Remember, the last shall go first. That's what my mom says the Bible says." That little girl was beautiful and her attitude was great throughout the Dance, but I can't say the same for myself. The Head Woman Dancer kept pushing me and telling me where to go. People asked what was going on, and I shrugged and said, "I don't know, but I guess I must have made her mad."

When the Dance was over for that day, I went into the woman's tepee, and she told me, "You will sleep there," which happened to be right beside her. Only she had a thick bed of sage and blankets and I had a hole beside the open edge of the tepee in the coldness of Oregon nights. I kept asking myself, What needs to be done here? Should I talk with her, or not? I'd look at her and decide I better not. I did not have even a blanket, for I had left everything to rush into the Dance. I supposed that Horse was still setting up camp and had forgotten to bring me my things, so I just went and sat by the fire. Grandpa came out of his tepee and sat with me a long time, and then he, a couple of others, and I went back into the tepee and talked the whole night. That night I met Lakota Elder Charles Chipps, who would later become my close friend and adopted brother. It was also that night that Grandpa told me to write a book.

The next day was more of the same with Miss Shaggy Hair. I found myself wanting to trip her in the Dance arena. I had to stop myself from punching her in the face. It did seem I had gotten myself into an attitude about this lady. This was the time of the Harmonic Convergence. Why was I so inharmonic, especially in this sacred Dance? I just wanted to keep my peace and see what my part was in the grand scene that was developing.

I was more and more concerned about Grandma. She had not come down as yet. People said that she was really sick. I decided that I had better stop the attitude and start praying as I was supposed to.

On the third night, Grandpa got us all up and we danced to the Moon and Stars. It was dark and cold that night, the night before the Harmonic Convergence. Suddenly, the stars began to move. I thought it was just my eyesight going wild from fatigue, but then I realized that the stars were truly blinking and moving. Then into our view came a Space Ship. It hovered on the horizon and then flew our way to hover over the Sundance Mystery Circle. It felt like rain was coming down on us. The men blew their whistles and the dancers screamed and sang to the ship. Yes, this is truth, and it took place right before the Morning Star on Harmonic Convergence Morning. Horse was there support dancing for me in the dark, and he said that the arena just kind of disappeared. He could tell that something was over it, for the sky was blacked out. The ship left, and Grandpa had us keep dancing right into day four without rest. It was an almost unbelievable and very wonderful night.

Grandma was very sick, but because of the love and support from Sparky and Horse, she finally made it to the Sundance arena for our last round. She sat slumped over, her little body in obvious pain, but she still came down to pray for us. I was crying, but it made me dance harder, with more prayers of gratitude for her being in my life, more prayers for her healing. All the Sundancers felt better when they saw Grandma.

She looked up and saw the dress, and she smiled. She said, "That is my daughter Thunder, and that is my mother's material that she gave to me to Sundance in. Thunder is Sundancing for me." I heard her words all the way across the Sundance arena. I was so proud of her and that I had come.

In the prayer she gave in Lakota, I heard my name several times. I really cried then.

Soon the Dance was over, and our beloved family sat together — Sharon, David, Dennis, Horse, Sparky (Jan Hunt) Shooting Star, Nancy Moore, Butch Henningan, Mike Hull, Diane Ross, and a few students from all over the country — at Grandma and Grandpa's tent. Grandma was hurting so bad, so I asked Diane if she would give her a massage. After the massage, Grandma rejoined us, and we sat together into the night. Grandma leaned over and told me that she had to talk to me. She said, "I am not going to be here long." I took that to mean they were going to be leaving soon. We had so much fun that night, singing, laughing, and telling stories. A day or two after Sundance, my moontime came, and I needed to leave the Sundance ground. Native Americans recognize a woman's menses as her cleansing time; a time for her to connect to Mother Earth, rather than Father Sky. It is a totally different, though very honored, ceremony, and the two energies clash when mixed. I stayed in my camp while Horse and Sparky did last-minute things. I spent the whole day feeling sad that I would not see Grandma and Grandpa again before leaving the West Coast. Grandpa was not sure he wanted Grandma to come down to say goodbye, because he wanted to keep the energies clear.

The van was all packed and we were getting ready to drive out when Grandma appeared. She sat down and we talked for over five hours, through our last sunset together in the physical world. We talked about everything and said our goodbyes. She talked about how people hurt each other in this world. Sometimes people would hurt Grandpa, but Grandpa is a Pipeholder, and because he loves the people so much, he has to take it. Always be humble to the people, she said. Grandpa turns the other cheek and goes on. She told me about how Grandpa has walked the path since he was a little boy, always taking little bitty steps, always working for the people. One day, Spirit recognized him as a Chosen One, and then he could hear the Spirit talk to him. From then on, as long as he has walked in a good way, the Spirit has talked to him to help the people.

When we were done talking, Grandma got in Sparky's car. She told me that when she passed, she did not want me spending a lot of money to come to Colorado, because she knew I did not have it. Tears welled up again, but thank goodness she could not see them. She said she would always be with me to help me out and to keep me strong for the people. She wanted me to dance the following year for her at the Sundance. She asked me not to forget to write words about her in a book, so the people would know how much she loved them. She took my chubby face in her hands and scrunched it together as she'd always done, and said, "Stay just the way you are." The car started and drove a little way, then she stopped and called me over again. She said, "Thunder, you are one of those Chosen Ones, too." Our last words to each other were, "Check you out later."

"We never know what loneliness is until we have lost our mother and our father, and know we just can't do it as good as they did. But because of their love and wisdom, we sure will try . . . "

Leonard Crow Dog

October 10, 1987 found me in New York State visiting my dear friend, Tsultrim Allione, a former Tibetan nun who now teaches Tibetan practices. It was a wonderful visit. Tsultrim is a person I have so much love for. I always learn a lot and really can relax and enjoy myself when we are together. But this visit, in the early morning hours, I started feeling uneasy. Grandma's face came to mind. I tried to call her at home that morning, but I couldn't reach her. A call came through to Tsultrim. The monks and lamas from the newly formed Institute for the Dalai Lama were planning a protest at the United Nations. She, her friend David, Horse, and I were instantly in the van on the way to New York City.

New York City scares me. It's so busy. That day, I felt irritation rising as we headed through the traffic. We were deposited across from the U.N., where monks and lamas were gathered with their bells, chants, and incredible long horns. I was transfixed for a moment. Soon a lama recognized Tsultrim and invited us to join his group. The prayers started. The protest was to call attention to Chinese people killing Tibetans.

It was then that the tears started, and I could not get Grandma out of my mind. It had been just a couple of days since I had last talked to her on the phone, but I just kept thinking about her and her speech to the U.N., and how she was so proud. I kept saying to her, "Grandma, I'm here at the U.N. today. I remember your speech. I love you." I prayed for Tibetans. I prayed for Grandma. My stomach and my nerves were bothering me. I was irritated and strangely sad.

Later that night, Horse and I had a horrible argument. I felt that we could not stay in Tsultrim's home, because she was a Spiritual Master, and I did not want to pollute her space with our negativity. I still could not get through to Grandma. We slept in the van, with Horse at one end and me at the other. During the night we both experienced a horrible thunder and lightning storm shaking the van. In the morning we got up, and somehow we loved each other again. At breakfast, we said to Tsultrim and Sparky, "Boy, that storm was something, wasn't it?" They looked at us blankly, then at each other. Tsultrim said, "Thunder, it did not rain last night." Horse and I took everyone out to look at the van. The ground around it was soaked and rain drops covered the van. Tsultrim gently took my arm and led me in a circle, looking everywhere. Everywhere else it was as dry as the proverbial dog's bone. We all laughed, ate a good breakfast, and then left for our next appointed stop.

Whenever I am on the East Coast, I always visit Grandma Twylah Nitsch, Elder of the Seneca Indian Teaching Lodge. Her Indian name is Yehwehnode; it means "She Whose Voice Rides on the Wind." This beautiful Elder has taught me so much about a part of my heritage. We had a full day's trip to get across the state to the Cattaraugus Indian Reservation. We had left Tsultrim's house later than we had planned, and I felt in a hurry to get to Grandma Twylah's. Horse and I got into another argument, and I began to feel as if all my nerves were frayed. I insisted that we stop at a store, because I had a strong impulse to bring Grandma Twylah some flowers. No store on that long road seemed to have any flowers. I felt irritated that it was taking so long to get there, but I had to stop over and over again to look for flowers. Finally, as we neared the reservation, I saw a field full of wildflowers. We pulled over, and Horse and I got out to pick some. My heart ached so strongly. Horse looked at me and came over and held me. We stood there for a long time, surrounded by flowers and made up. Once we had picked a large bouquet, all the arguments, obstacles, and delays of the trip fell away and soon we arrived at Cattaraugus.

Grandma Twylah Nitsch ran out the door to meet us. She had a worried, sad look on her face. I handed her the flowers. She took the flowers in one hand and me in the other. "Sit down, little girl." Her eyes said it all. "Grandma's gone. There have been about forty calls here trying to let you know." She held me as I cried, then gave me a slip of paper with a number at which to reach Grandpa. I called and asked what I needed to do. He told me details of a ceremony he wanted me to perform. I told him how much I loved him and that I was sorry for him and would pray for him. He told me at what time her stomach started hemorrhaging (while I was at the U.N.) and when she had passed to Spirit World (the thunder and lightning storm). Grandpa said, "Don't come to Colorado. You know how Grandma wanted it. Go and do the ceremony for her."

Grandma Twylah fed us and prayed with us, and helped me so much. I will always be grateful. She wanted us to stay the night with her, but I needed to keep moving. As we drove through the night, my mind returned to the flowers, the flowers that were always my gift to

Sparky, Thunder and Grandma Grace

Grandma Grace when I'd come to see her, the flowers that she would always bawl me out for, but always hope I'd bring, the flowers that represented to her the beauty of all people, all the races of humans.

And I thought about that day's long journey and the overwhelming need to arrive at the door with some flowers in my hand. Was it Grandma Grace's spirit trying to tell me to continue to honor the Elders in my life? Was it a gift from her to me, to tell me not to despair, to tell me she loved me, to say goodbye?

I had never brought flowers to Grandma Twylah before, and, of course, I almost always had brought them to Grandma Grace. And then, among the first words Grandma Twylah spoke to me were, "I am your new Grandma." She reminded me that the way the Universe works, there's never a loss where there isn't a gain. There's never emptiness that can't be refilled. There's never aloneness in full awareness of the present moment. My precious mother was gone, but replaced by an equally precious grandmother.

Shortly after that, on our next trip East, my son Richard Earl, Horse, and I were initiated into the Seneca Indian Teaching Lodge. Grandma Twylah said that, since we had no home base, we had become its first traveling representatives.

In Memorium
Check You Out Later, Grandma

Four days after her passing, on October 15, 1987, I planted a white pine tree at the Upland Hills Ecological Center in Michigan. The tree was a symbol of the Iroquois Nation's White Roots of Peace Tree planted generations ago. Grandma had toured the country for years speaking with the White Roots of Peace group. The tree was also a symbol of my love for Grandma Grace Spotted Eagle, my adopted mother.

We prepared the ground about noon, Colorado time, just as my Spiritual father, Wallace Black Elk, was doing ceremony for Grandma Grace, his beloved partner of so many years who affected so many people with her love.

Words were spoken about the meaning of the pine tree, words given to us by Grandma Twylah Nitsch. The tree was planted on a small rise overlooking the Sweat Lodge grounds where Grandma, Grandpa, and I had conducted that gathering two years before. This day, we were a much smaller group: my halfside Jeff White Horse Hubbell, representatives from the Ecological Center, a few students who were on the road with me, and some of the participants from that previous gathering.

With the tree, a piece of my heart was being buried.

The Pipe was loaded. A beautiful white pine tree, just as tall as Grandma, stood waiting as we prepared the earth in the traditional way of burial. We included parts of ourselves, food for the Spirits, and things that Grandma might need on her journey. There also were tokens of the things we wanted the world to let go of, like guns, bombs, nuclear weapons, hatred, and jealousy. All were put under the tree, as the Iroquois Confederacy had done so many generations ago. After the ground was prepared, each person picked up the Pipe and reflected about Grandma.There were many wonderful stories, and prayers were made for Grandpa, for the planet, for harmony, and for all the things that Grandma had spoken about. Prayers were made that the technological mind might be used for the betterment of humankind, and not for its destruction. Thoughts and prayers went to Bear Heart, J.C. Eaglesmith, and Sun Bear, all teachers who had recently been at the Center teaching earth harmony.

The ceremony was exactly as Grandma Grace wanted it. I was instructed not to tell others about her passing for at least four days. She didn't want a big hoopla, or fancy-smancy words, or anything like that.

Grandma did want me to say how she loved all her children all over the world and thanked these children for being so nice to her and Grandpa. She asked me to be sure to watch over Grandpa and help him out, because he is so very, very special. It is important for people to listen to Grandpa and the Elders while they are still here and able to take the time to talk to us. She said to be grateful for every day that the sun comes up and for all that Tunkashila gives us.

Our memorial ceremony was completed by the children, Aaron Brocker and Mikey McCauley. They put symbols under the tree for all my children, Richard, Beth, and John Grimes, who love Grandma and Grandpa so much; and also for my two grandchildren, Joshua, Pearl Boy, named by Grandpa, and Heather, Wambli Gleska, named by Grandma. My daughter Beth gave birth to Wambli Gleska barely a month before Sundance. Grandma had been so very proud that there would be a grandchild to carry her name.

Lois Metcalf of Houston had given me a beautiful ceramic Indian doll to give to Grandma. This I had done, after the Sundance, and she had hugged it to her and then given it back to me to pass on to Wambli Gleska. The doll looks just like Grandma Grace. Today it sits in my office on an altar dedicated to her. As soon as Wambli Gleska is old enough, she can have it on her altar.

I looked up as the tree was placed in the ground. An Eagle flew high above and then disappeared. I laughed, because it was not like Grandma was really gone. As I stood there reflecting and starting to get senti-mental, I heard her voice, clear as a bell, saying "Talk about the Pipe now, Thunder. I love you." As we left the Ecological Center, I looked back at the white pine tree covered with prayer ties in the sacred colors. Late sunset light came through the clouds, and there was a feeling of great peace. I knew then that Grandma would always be with me, talking away, right inside my heart.

Check you out later, Grandma.

Our love transcends time and space.

EPILOGUE

On March 13, 1995 I was sitting in the Das Kraut Haus in LaGrange, Texas, where I had just made a 1-800-Collect call to Station Hill Press. (This call had to be collect for our telephone had been turned off due to an indigenous person who ran up my phone bill up several thousand dollars.) On this day of my last conversation with Susan Quasha and Vicki Hickman about the very last questions regarding the book before it went to press, I hung up and started to reflect. I sure did pick a good publisher, for they have been very kind to me and I was very kind to them. They were just great to work with. Then my mind drifted to Grandpa. It had been a long seven-year journey and the only thing that I had not done was get Grandpa Wallace's feelings about the book. Now, I had sent him a copy of the book, but as Grandma Grace had always said, "Grandpa don't read or write so good so you read and write for him!" It just did not seem right for the book not to have some words from Grandpa.

I looked up to see the sister at the counter, saying, "You have a Fax." Tears welled up in my eyes as I read a Fax from sister/student/roadie Sparky Shooting Star, it was about Grandpa. Another Coincidence . . . I don't think so! Thank you Grandpa. Thank you Sparky.

Love, Thunder

To my Dear Sister Thunder:

Call Station Hill immediately . . . I just talked with Grandpa and he felt that this should go into the book. I told him that you loved him. I told him the book Grace asked you to write is ready to be printed. He smiled and said that he felt that Grandma was happy that the book was done and so was he, he is glad the book is finished for Grace.

So, put this into an Epilogue:

Just before we went to press with this book, we were able to speak to Grandpa Wallace Black Elk, a Spiritual leader of the Lakota people and Grace's half-side. He graciously shared with us his last experience with her which happened in the hospital as her spirit was crossing over.

"I was in the hospital with Grace as she was crossing over. There were three medical people in the room with us. Her robe (her physical body) lay on the bed. It was still and unmoving. Then I saw her spirit leave from her body and then saw her spirit standing next to the bed. At the same time that I was also seeing her robe (Her body) was still on the bed. She sang to me the song she wrote a long time ago.

She created this song, the lyrics and the tone. Spirit sang the song in a strong clear voice so that even the medical people could hear. 'Nation look at me. The Chanupa (Pipe) is sacred and I pray with it. For Nation, you shall live.'"

By seeing her spirit . . . I knew she was feeling good and happy. I said to her: 'Let me go and get a tape recorder and tape this.' She said jokingly, 'Why do you want to tape it? You know that song.'"

To be given a song by Spirit is a great honor. *The Pipe Nation Song* is a great gift to all people for the Pipe is for the People and all things with Life. This song is a promise from the Spirit that through the Pipe we all will live. *The Pipe Nation Song* promises everlasting life for the People. This is a prophecy and a prayer.

The story he told was so amazing. It's Amazing because her spirit sang to him as she was crossing over. It's Amazing because the song she sang was *The Pipe Nation Song*. It's Amazing because Grace wrote that song. No one ever told me that. It's Amazing because it's Grace!

When I hear this song when I am dancing at Sun Dance, I know I am alive. I know I will always live. I know I will always be with my Relatives like you, Horsey, Richie, Johnny, Bonnie and all the gang. I know that All the People will Live. I know that life will recreate life and we will be happy and always together and free.

Sparky Shooting Star
March 13, 1995

APPENDIX

INTERNATIONAL OFFICE OF THE
LEONARD PELTIER DEFENSE COMMITTEE
PO Box 583 Lawrence, KS 66044   913-842-5774

Leonard Peltier could be you, could be anyone who stands up for his family, friends, community, and beliefs. Leonard is an American Indian who is serving two consecutive life sentences in Leavenworth Federal Penitentiary, and there is NO CREDIBLE EVIDENCE that he is guilty of the crime for which he was convicted.

In the three years after the siege of Wounded Knee in 1973, three hundred American Indian Movement members and supporters were killed on the Pine Ridge Reservation in South Dakota. Many more were targets of violence at the hands of the FBI, BIA, and the private police force of the corrupt tribal chairman, known as the "goon squad." The traditional people, living in fear for their lives, invited AIM to come up to the reservation to protect them. A spiritual camp of AIM men, women and children was set up on the Jumping Bull compound in Oglala.

On June 26, 1975, two FBI agents drove onto the land, unannounced, following an Indian boy they said had "stolen a pair of cowboy boots." A shootout erupted, which resulted in the death of the agents and an Indian, Joe Stuntz Killsright. Within hours of the shootout, according to the U.S. Civil Rights Commission, hundreds of paramilitary-equipped, combat-clad FBI agents and U.S. marshals in a fever of revenge staged a dragnet through the reservation in which families were searched and terrified, property and houses ransacked. There was no investigation into the death of Killsright.

Leonard had been previously identified as an American Indian Movement leader by the FBI and targeted by their notorious COINTELPRO program which "neutralized" such people by dirty tricks and arrest. Fearing no possibility of a fair trial and perhaps immediate execution, Leonard fled to Canada, where he was arrested and extradited under eye-witness affidavits manufactured by the FBI that the government has admitted are false.

Three other men were initially accused of the murders. Two—Bob Robideau and Dino Butler—were acquitted on grounds of self-defense, and the government dropped all charges against the third to concentrate the full prosecutive weight of the government against Leonard Peltier. He was convicted of the deaths of the agents and sentenced to two consecutive life terms. The government has subsequently changed its theory on who killed the agents and today admits they have NO IDEA who did kill them.

According to the final decision of the Eighth Circuit Court of Appeals (which astoundingly upheld Leonard's conviction), Leonard's trial and previous appeals were riddled with FBI misconduct and judicial impropriety, including: coercion of witnesses, the knowing use of perjury, the fabrication of evidence and suppression of evidence which would have proven his innocence.

The Eighth Circuit Court agreed FBI misconduct in the case had been a "clear abuse of the investigative process." No one deserves treatment like this. That is why 55 MEMBERS OF CONGRESS, the NATIONAL ASSOCIATION OF CRIMINAL DEFENSE ATTORNEYS, CALIFORNIA ATTORNEYS FOR CRIMINAL JUSTICE, and 78 WORLD RELIGIOUS LEADERS, including the ARCHBISHOP OF CANTERBURY, BISHOP DESMOND TUTU, and REV. JESSE JACKSON have filed "Friends of the Court" briefs urging a new trial for Leonard Peltier. That is why AMNESTY INTERNATIONAL has called for a Commission of Inquiry into the role of the FBI in political trials, citing the Peltier case as an example. That is why 30 TRIBAL COUNCILS have passed resolutions in support of Leonard Peltier.

Leonard Peltier is spending his fifteenth year in prison for a crime he did NOT commit. On October 5, 1987 the United States Supreme Court denied Leonard's appeal. The Supreme Court temporarily closed the door on Leonard's chances for a new trial. In July 1989 the Canadian High Court dismissed Leonard's claims regarding his illegal extradition in violation of the Canadian-U.S. treaty. In the process, however, the government admitted to having taken fraudulent action to secure extradition. This admission has prompted a joint effort to set the stage for a meeting between Canadian and U.S. Government officials, with the hope that this disclosure will lead to Leonard's release. Meanwhile, a campaign has been launched to obtain Leonard's freedom by executive clemency. Senator Inouye, chairman of the Senate Select Committee on Indian Affairs, has expressed interest in following up the extradition violation and clemency campaign, and seeking immediate sentencing that would expedite Leonard's eligibility for parole. Hopefully, the door is not closed on justice for Leonard Peltier.

The Leonard Peltier Defense Committee urgently needs your donations and your letters of support to Senator Inouye, Senator John McCain, Congressman Don Edwards, the congress people in your district, and the President asking for their intervention in the name of justice for Leonard Peltier.

Donations may be sent directly to the Leonard Peltier Defense Committee. Checks for tax-deductible contributions may be made out to the Dean's Discretionary Fund, The Cathedral Church of St. John of the Divine, New York, N.Y.

FACT SHEET ON YELLOW THUNDER CAMP

On April 4, 1981, the Dakota American Indian Movement established Yellow Thunder Camp on U.S. Forest Land in the Black Hills outside of Rapid City, South Dakota. A claim was filed for the 800 acres with the Pennington County Registrar of Deeds. On April 22 the Camp filed a Special Use Application for the construction of 83 permanent structures to be used for religious, educational and residential purposes, with a Report submitted on May 29. They have cited the 1986 Fort Laramie Treaty, Article VI of the U.S. Constitution, the 1897 federal statute which allows those living in the vicinity of National Forest lands to establish and maintain schools and churches, and the 1978 Indian Freedom of Religion Act which guarantees Native People access to sites, burial grounds, and the use of their sacred objects used to carry out traditional ceremonies.

An April 11 meeting held at Yellow Thunder Camp drew over 300 supporters, representing all of the Indian Nations within the Treaty area. Two resolutions were passed: one calling for the U.S. Congress to review the Black Hills Claim, particularly Article XII of the Treaty which clearly shows that tribal governments, set up by the

U.S. in 1934, have no right to negotiate claims related to the Treaty; the second calling for a halt to litigation by tribal governments and their representatives.

On August 13, 1981, Yellow Thunder Camp made a formal request to Secretary of the Interior James Watt and Secretary of Agriculture John Block that the 800-acre claim area be withdrawn from the public domain. The request was made under the federal Land Policy and Management Act of 1976, which gives the federal government the authority to withdraw land from the public domain under certain provisions. The Forest Service has sold the timber within the 800-acre area, and logging operations and road building are scheduled to begin in the spring. Also, a cattle grazing permit for some of the area has been issued to a Texas rancher.

Yellow Thunder Camp has the support of many individuals and organizations in the Rapid City area, across the nation, and in many foreign countries. This summer, 38 members of the U.S. House of Representatives endorsed a letter requesting that the U.S. Forest Service approve the Special Use Application for Yellow Thunder Camp. Some of the other supporters are: the Black Hills Sioux Nation Council, American Friends Service Committee, Pennington Co. Democratic Forum, South Dakota Board of Church and Society of the South Dakota United Methodist Church, Black Hills Alliance, the Acting Director of the National Catholic Rural Life Conference, the Vice President of Rosebud Sioux Tribe, and many more religious and social service organizations. On July 8, 1981, the Black Hills National Forest Service held a public meeting to hear comments on the Camp's application. Those expressing opinions were overwhelmingly in favor of the application.

Throughout the spring and summer, the people of Yellow Thunder Camp have complied with laws and Forest Service regulations. People living in the Camp have set up a kitchen, tipis, tents, a solar shower, a solar food dehydrator, and have planted a garden. Meat and wild berries have been dried for the winter. Plans are underway for constructing an earth oven and a geodesic dome to be used as a school and community meeting area, and for winterizing the tipis.

The goal of Yellow Thunder Camp is to build a permanent spiritual and educational community in harmony with the environment, utilizing solar energy and other non-fossil fuels, and constructed primarily from local natural materials. The centrality of the Black Hills to Lakota spirituality is well-documented and is also in evidence within the text of the Fort Laramie Treaty of 1868, the last formal and legally-binding agreement reached between the sovereign Lakota Nation and the United States.

On August 24, 1981, District Supervisor James Mathers of the U.S. Forest Service rejected the Camp's Special Use Application to construct permanent buildings, and ordered that the people leave the site by September 8, 1981. The denial of the Special Use Application can be appealed through the regional office of the Forest Service in Denver, but Camp residents were informed that the order to leave by September 8, was final, regardless of the status of the appeal process.

The people of Yellow Thunder Camp have stated that they will not leave, and will defend their homeland. They are presently faced with the threat of removal. Removal of Yellow Thunder Camp residents by the U.S. government would be a direct violation of the Constitution of the United States, of the 1868 Fort Laramie Treaty, and Public Law 95-341 (Indian Freedom of Religion Act).

ABOUT THE ARTIST CATHERINE WHITE SWAN

Since childhood, Catherine White-Swan has been on a spiritual path with the vision of one day becoming a spiritual artist. This vision is joined with a strong desire to work to bring healing to others and express the vastness of one's being.

Over the past 10 years, White-Swan has shared ceremonies and friendship with Thunder. She met Thunder at a sweat lodge in which Grace Spotted Eagle was the water pourer. Through Thunder she has met a number of Elders who have helped her growth.

Most of White-Swan's current work is in the form of Spiritual portraits. Her development of the image honors the physical appearance while not being bound to it. Something deeper streams forth from the canvas. White-Swan states simply, "I just follow what Spirit guides me to do. It's as if the image were already in the canvas waiting for me."

PHOTO CREDITS

p. ii, Helen Adams; p. vi, 50, Mary E. Thunder; p. xxi, 69, Shirley Starnes; p. xxvi, 23, Sandy Collins; p. 38, 156 Steve Schoff; p. 43, 44, Sparky Shooting Star; p. 54, 167 Martin "Gentle Bear" Rastall; p. 65, 107 Courtesy, City of Indianapolis; p. 81 Terry Gregston; p. 87, 91 Michele Feray; p. 144 Catherine Adelstine; p. 184, 188, John Eric Grimes III; p. 222 Jeffrey "White Horse" Hubbell; p. 233 Mike Hull; p. 234, Wade Batterton; p. 242, Charla Tarwater.

ART CREDITS

p. 1, *Life Forces*, Bonnie Biggs; p. iii, 15, 18, 21, 25, 29, 32, 39, 55, 82, 109, 123, 154, 169, 186, 199, 202, 207, 216, 241, 246, 253 Catherine White Swan; p. 256, Jude Tolley

ABOUT THUNDER HORSE RANCH
AND THEIR SCHEDULE OF ACTIVITIES

At Thunder Horse Ranch, where Mary Thunder lives and teaches at the Spiritual University, there is the Blue Star Store which features Native American arts, crafts, and teachings. Included among these items are: *Emotions: Our Greatest Addiction,* Mary Thunder, an audio tape on expressing, choosing and clearing our emotions ($13); *Journey to the Spirit World,* Buddy Red Bow, audio tape of Buddy Red Bow singing of his love for the Lakota ($15), and *The Legend of the Thunderbird* about Mary Thunder and Buddy Red Bow's friendship, remembrances of his grandfather and the Legend of the Thunderbird ($25). For further information or to order, please write: Mary Elizabeth Thunder, Thunder Horse Ranch, 1700 Makinson Rd., West Point TX, 78963. (Please add $1.50 shipping per order.)